630 MILES

BRAVER

630 MILES BRAVER

Midlifing on the South West Coast Path

ZOE LANGLEY-WATHEN

HeadWriteOut Press

630 Miles Braver – Midlifing on the South West Coast Path

First published in 2025 in the United Kingdom

British Library Cataloguing in Publication Data

A catalogue record for this book is available from the British Library

ISBN: 978-1-0684111-1-3

Published by HeadWriteOut Press

Cover design, interior design and illustrations by Zoe Langley-Wathen

For Mary

Who showed me that adventure has no age limit,
whose spirit soars with every skylark's song.

Contents

SOUTH WEST COAST PATH

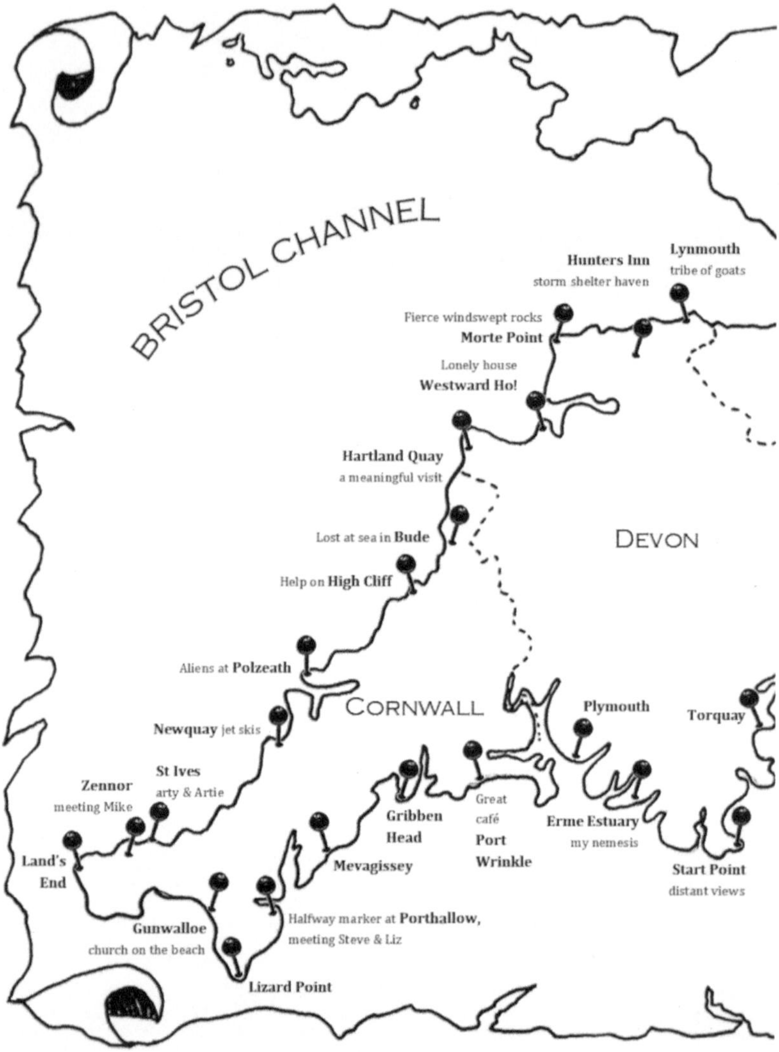

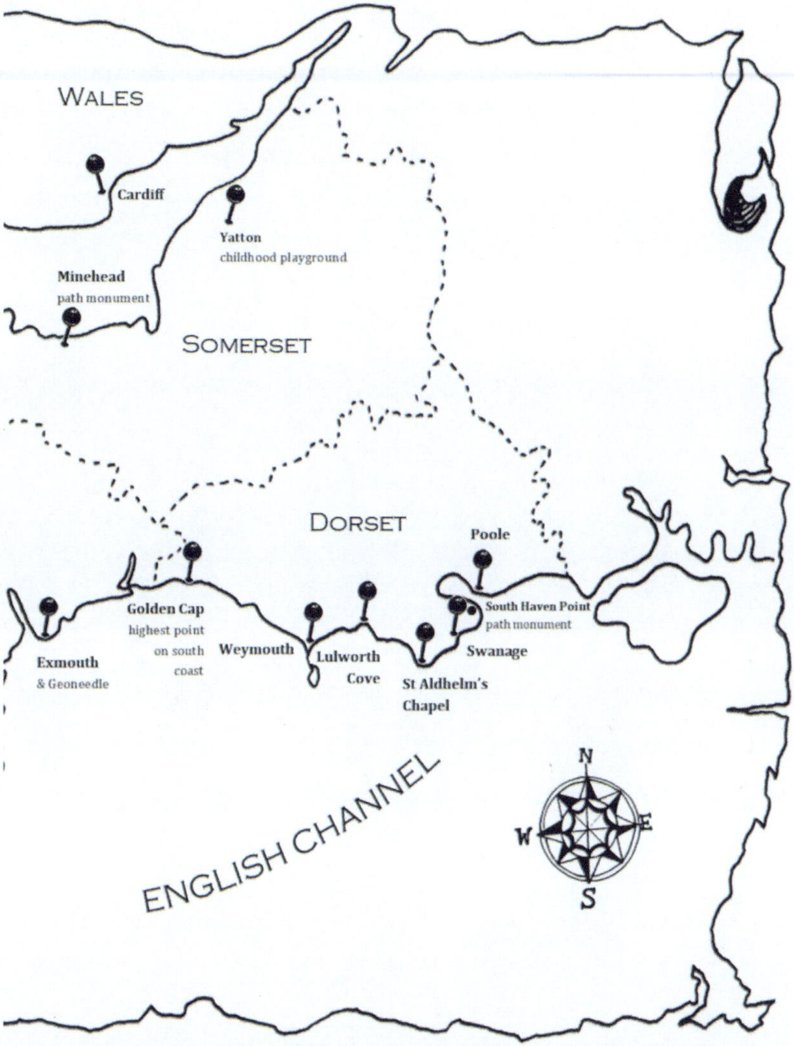

REPRESENTATIONAL MAP - NOT TO SCALE

Prologue

As I lie awake, in the foggy haze of broken images and unsettled mind, I step into the water, intending to cross. In too far to retreat to safety, I watch in panic as a six-foot tidal wave rolls through, lifting me off my feet and carrying me out to sea. I scream from the depths of my belly, clutching at any threads of reality that might release me. Momentarily, I know I'm in another world, but then I slip back underwater for another grim episode.

This time, the surface of the estuary bed is soft, like sludge. I search with my feet, desperate for the terrain to give me more stability as I wade across. The going is tough and as each heavy step moves me forward and into the deepest section of the river, I find myself barely able to move. The expanse of sea to my right beckons with cruel temptation. Frozen by the hand of fear on my shoulder and the grip of mud around my ankles, I am stuck. It beckons once more, calling to end my torment and to relinquish me to its waters.

Not ready to succumb, in a frenzy, I shake my head, screwing up my face in distorted determination. Afraid of what lies ahead, and unable to sleep, these moments of overthinking boil my imagination into a deadly concoction. I know it's unhelpful, but I can't stop myself with all the what-ifs. Relieved it's time to get up, I clamber into the shower to wash away the repeated horrors of my imaginary adventure. As if my overdramatic river scenarios were not enough, the River Erme refuses to stay hidden for long; it's been living inside the back of my mind for months. It pervades my dreams. It eats into every part of my brain like a subconscious worm of terror, burrowing its way into my head, creating epic nightmares of cinematic quality. *What have you let yourself in for, Wath?*

Months before my South West Coast Path adventure had even begun, my waking life felt much the same as my nocturnal one. The anxiety, scarily palpable, had woven itself into my daily thoughts and language. While standing at the staffroom tea trolley, fellow teachers would ask me if my planning for the big walk was going well. With a nod and a smile, I'd always say yes, but somehow the sneaky fear that lurked in the back of my head crept up from behind and tagged itself on the end.

"Everything is going great, but I'm not sure about the river crossing," I announced to one. "There's this estuary that I have to wade, knee-deep." The teacher's eyes opened wider with interest and a raised expression of concern as I joked, "I'll probably get washed out to sea." With my carefully perfected chuckle that lightens the tone of any serious situation, she laughed along with me.

"You're braver than me," she said, smiling in awe.

Clutching our mugs of steaming hot tea, we wandered over to our respective corners of the staffroom, and the comfort of our little social groups. That day, I found myself alone. It wasn't a joke. It was real. True dread. When I talked about it, it compounded further into my mind, where it has now permanently taken up residence. The fear has set down roots, mutated out of control, like an unwanted weed growing aggressively, intimidating and suffocating every other plant within reach.

I understood the reactions I received from staff, so began using this as a tool to gain interest from the students. I peppered my assemblies with fear, excitement, and the possibility of failure – 630 miles, after all, is a very long way, and not recognised in everyday conversations. I planned to take them all on a journey, the rollercoaster of the story arc. Hook them with an unusual beginning, climb through a series of problems, and then throw in a corker ... a potential issue that no one could bear to imagine themselves in. There were plenty of those on the announcement of this adventure to around 1,300 students. Walking 630 miles for starters, because who in their right mind does that? It's not an average Sunday afternoon stroll.

The drama of climbing the equivalent ascent of Mount Everest, four times. The decision to walk and camp, solo. In there, amid the storytelling, sits the Erme. The estuary that fuelled my nightmares and latched onto my quiet daytime moments. It's rich with assembly material and I stepped away proud of my talks on stage, often more performance than talk. Delivered like poetry, not fact. The aerial shot of the river was a definite bonus, as it highlighted just how wide this stretch of water was at the mouth. Once again, "Who knows, perhaps the river will wash me out to sea?" I suggested with humour to the audience. Like a passport, that indelible stamp of fear would never disappear. They all thought I was brave, but I was plain terrified. Acknowledge the problem and then make the worst scenario the focus of every conversation about the journey; it's perhaps the weirdest coping mechanism for managing fear. I may not have realised it back then, but now I see it's my strategy. Somehow it works.

A few weeks before I left, I had my sketchbook out, playing with some ideas for designing my own Christmas card. The caption: "*Christmas came and went, and Wath couldn't work out why it was taking so long to get around the coast ... She had done as everyone suggested and kept the sea on her right.*" It featured me, floating on my side in the water, complete with an enormous rucksack, and a foreground of steeply stepped cliffs.

The idea of being trapped in the water lingered.

Wells's Divine Bookshop

1

When you have been searching for months for a thing, an idea or even a word, when you are consciously looking it never appears. It's only in those moments when you least expect anything to happen that it presents itself.

With my fortieth birthday hurtling towards me, I wanted to find a challenge to help me mark this special life event. It was to be my rite of passage into middle age. To not observe it would seem like a wasted opportunity and dismissive of my life so far, so full of its pitfalls and achievements. Knowing it needed to be a challenge was one thing, yet I didn't know what type of challenge I wanted it to be. I had exhausted all the ideas I could think of. All those adventures I'd once heard about and fancied myself doing. One day.

Scrawled on my bucket list was climbing Kilimanjaro. Definitely one to do, but somehow it didn't sit right with me for my fortieth. Or I could hike the Inca Trail. Years ago, I had inhaled images of the spectacular Machu Picchu from a magazine. I knew that one day, I'd walk there, to quench my creative thirst for natural, historical and architectural beauty. But as with Kili, although both are grand adventures, it echoed as just another commercial tourist destination. It wasn't the meaningful trip I had been waiting to uncover.

Perhaps I should have asked my older brother, Chris, for ideas. He has always had a keen sense of adventure. As a teenager, he would regularly jump on a train and travel for hundreds of miles to a place never explored. Along with his friends, they would often catch an overnighter back home again, using the luggage racks as beds.

I remember one Sunday afternoon, Chris suggested we should go exploring to find the mouth of our local river, the Yeo (pronounced Yo). He was five years older, and I entrusted my enjoyment of the experience to him. I was probably about thirteen. I had a memorable time, for sure, and faced some uncomfortable moments in doing so. Our walk began from the house and passed over a disused railway line, still lined with ballast then, but nowadays maintained as a National Cycle Network route. This brought us into the bushy and sometimes overgrown avenue we used to call The Jungalow, which led to the river. Packed with prickly blackthorn hedgerows, trees and wildlife, in reality it was a high bank built as a flood defence. Either side, deep, Somerset ditches looked thicker than a mousse with the mass of floating green weed resting on the surface. Water like this gave me the heebie-jeebies and I always kept well away from the edge.

You can imagine my dilemma then, when after following the river through miles of fields, we reached the M5 motorway blocking our way. By moving across a couple of fields, we found a smaller tributary of the Yeo and a possible way through. "We have two choices, l'il sis," Chris said. "We either go over the top, or we go under." The thought of going back never even entered our heads.

"We can't go over the motorway, Chris. There's six lanes of traffic!" This was the early 1980s, and although traffic wasn't as busy in those days as it is now, it would have still been a dangerous attempt by a pair of teenagers.

"So it's under then," he said, looking at me with a grin.

I raised my eyebrows and clenched my teeth with a fractured smile. I didn't like what I saw. Little Yeo funnelled water that appeared blacker than coal underneath the motorway via a low, narrow concrete tunnel. The rough bank we had followed stopped and in its place was a water pipe, about wide enough for our feet to shimmy along sideways. We clambered around fans of spiky wire, no doubt fixed there to stop kids or animals from teetering along this pipe. But teeter we did ... the full width of the motorway, to the other side. My mouth dried and my heart banged with fear all the way through the tunnel, but the achievement of reaching the end gave me a buzz I'll not forget.

On reaching the mouth of the river, at the furthest point we could safely get to, we stood looking out to the far side. With the tide out, the river made a good mud bath and feeding ground for the birds. "See those posts?" Chris pointed to a series of raised pillars in the mud. "That's where the railway used to cross the Yeo."

"The railway? Really?" This amazed me, as our dad, a railwayman through and through, had never told me about this old stretch of railway before.

"Yep. And that there is the old wharf where they'd bring the coal in from Wales." He pointed to a dilapidated wooden platform.

"I can't imagine trains going across here, but I'd love to see photos of it one day."

"Well, we reached the mouth of the Yeo, Zo. Better get back." We turned and left. The fragments of history left behind fascinated me. I still carry that awe and wonder for signs of the past in our present day. I also carried the same fear of crossing the water pipe under the motorway, as I had done earlier, but knew I had to do it again in order to get home. The adrenalin was as spiky as the wire fans blocking our way. But it fuelled me and we did it.

It was probably my first adventure memory.

The adventure to top all adventures simply hadn't presented itself to me yet. When it did, I realised that it was a trail I already knew about and had wanted to walk for around fifteen years. It's sad, but when I first heard about the South West Coast Path, all those years before, despite it catching my attention and my imagination, I never thought myself to be capable enough, athletic enough or strong enough to complete it. In short, I wasn't enough. How common that sense of doubt in one's ability is, I've since discovered.

On an impromptu trip into Wells, Somerset, I wandered into a bookshop with my daughter. The markers of adventure were on my mind as, twenty minutes before, we had visited the Wells Cathedral office to offer sponsorship to an old family friend and former archdeacon of Wells. The Venerable Dick Acworth, then seventy-two, had embarked on a "bus pass pilgrimage". He planned a journey to each of England's forty-two cathedrals using his free bus pass over three weeks. In doing so, he would raise money for the Girls' Chorister Trust at Wells Cathedral. It was the first time I had really considered the imaginative aspects of tailoring an adventure. It held creativity enough to capture the hearts of the public, was bold and unusual enough to be classed as a "challenge", and yet still manageable for Dick to undertake. His adventure had inspired me.

With that first step into the bookshop, I may have been unconsciously seeking further inspiration for my fortieth-year challenge, but I hadn't expected to find it directly in front of me as I walked through the doors. It was like a moment of divine intervention. A shaft of light appeared to be shining down upon a single book on the shelf ahead of me. *The South West Coast Path Handbook*. Wow!

This was the trail I had held so much awe and respect for and yet had no faith in my personal ability to take it on. At 630 miles, the South West Coast Path follows as close to the coast as possible from the shores of Minehead in Somerset, into North Devon, along the northern coastline of Cornwall in all its ruggedness and around the toe of Land's End. It then turns to travel through the southern areas of Cornwall and the honeypot tourist spots of South Devon, finally slipping into Dorset, taking in the beauty of the Jurassic Coast and finishing at Poole Harbour.

Here it was, in a moment not unlike that of the church scene in *The Blues Brothers* film. You know, the one where there's a glorious shaft of miracle-performing light shining through the church window. Jake and Elwood do their crazy dance and somersault down the aisle believing they have received a message from God ... it was just like that. Well, perhaps without the somersaulting bit. Yep, it was a moment of divine intervention. Or maybe it was simply an excellent example of great product placement. Either way, I had found my adventure; or rather, it had found me. At last, after fifteen years of wanting to walk the South West Coast Path, for reasons that perhaps I'll never know, I now sensed that I was brave enough to try.

With a grin from ear to ear, and filled with an immediate, empowered drive and determination, I skipped to the cashier to pay for the book. As we left, I talked animatedly to my fourteen-year-old daughter, Laura, about how I had always wanted to walk this 630-mile path. I gushed about its notoriety as England's longest National Trail, how much training I'd need to do, and the kit I would need to buy. Goodness knows what she thought about her mother's sudden enthusiasm. I suspect my excitement carried her along, or perhaps she found it intensely annoying and just humoured me. Maybe she even ignored me. She was a fourteen-year-old, after all. Who knows what she was thinking?

Here you see the beginning of an extended love affair with long-distance walking, a relationship with the outdoors that would bring about changes and developments across all areas of my life. I could never have imagined the way it would affect my well-being, both physical and mental. And it all began with that first step into a bookshop, and an open mind.

Two years passed between that divine bookshop moment to the day I began walking the South West Coast Path. During that time, I planned lots. It was important to figure out how long I would be away as I only had six weeks of summer holiday available. I looked up how long others take to walk the path and then added a week. I called the SWCP Association office to chat with them about my safety concerns and I ordered maps. But the research about the kit I'd need took the longest. I spent a lot of time browsing the shelves and rails in many outdoor shops. As a result, I filled my new rucksack to the brim with a range of gadgets designed to make my backpacking journey easier and my bank balance lighter. My plastic egg box, for two eggs, and a titanium frying pan filled me with eagerness. Of course I'd stop at farmhouses regularly and buy fresh eggs. I bought a little, hexagonal flat-packed steel stove that slotted together, with room for a meths burner, or sticks if I fancied foraging for wood. I even found a lightweight folding seat kit, designed to turn my inflatable mattress into a comfy camp chair. I had all the gear – but no idea, as the saying goes.

Assemblies delivered to students and staff at the school where I'm a teacher meant I couldn't back out of my challenge. I began fundraising for three causes with a hardy and spirited group of grammar school students. I chose Julia's House, a children's hospice charity; Woofability, an assistance dog charity, and our Design and Technology department, as I wanted to start a fundraiser for us to purchase a laser cutter. The chief fundraiser would be the Glitz and Grammar Ball – a glamorous event at a prestigious waterfront hotel with an auction and live band. A massive challenge in itself, with months of organisation and the rallying of willing helpers.

Besides the coordination of the ball and the planning of my challenge hike, regular training walks filled my diary. I set about a new regime of walking the three miles and back to school every day, with longer walks at the weekends and carrying a heavier load each week. Pump, Pilates, spinning and even ballet took my fitness to another level. I was on fire. Somehow, I still made time for my family, though perhaps in hindsight, hardly for friends.

Three months prior to my planned departure, my health took a tumble. My chest hurt, my lungs felt caged by barbed wire, and I coughed until I threw up. Looking at the photograph of me, my partner, Ross, and our daughters at my fortieth birthday meal, the struggle in my eyes is tangible. I'm smiling at the camera, but underneath the façade, I just want to be in bed. Family, school staff and even students suggested I postpone my walk until next year. They almost convinced me, but I could not comprehend the fear of failing before I'd started.

With luck, the hotel allowed a postponement of the Glitz and Grammar Ball until the autumn – the term after I would return from my walk – and this filled me with immense relief. My GP saw me multiple times between April and June. He never quite pinpointed what was wrong with me. I had antibiotics, tests and X-rays. Two weeks before I left, I convinced myself the doctor would advise me to pull the plug on the whole challenge. Instead, I returned from the surgery with an inhaler, instructions to use it when needed, and to listen to my body.

Someone believed in me.

2

A Tough Decision

What a predicament I find myself in. A few weeks ago, my ninety-two-year-old nan had had a second stroke. She had a mild heart attack eighteen months before, so the doctors kept her in the hospital. Although she was frail, the family were not told to expect end-of-life care. But I need to make a choice. Nan has always been a fighter. Do I visit her prior to heading off for seven weeks of walking? Or do I hope beyond all hope that she makes it through to when I return and can tell her all about my adventure? I want to avoid passing my persistent chesty cough on to her. But I don't know if she will be strong enough to make it through until the end of August.

Nan has such an adventurous spirit and I love this about her. She's always been one to make the most of her single life. At seventy-five, she embarked on a solo trip to China and climbed a part of the Great Wall. She was in the Land Army during the Second World War and had six children. After my grandfather left the family home, she brought up the four youngest children single-handedly. The eldest, born during the war, arrived prior to her meeting my grandfather. Nan completed her time serving her country as a Land Girl, while an establishment cared for her baby elsewhere. On returning to the home to collect her baby son after the war had ended, to her horror, she discovered an empty building. There was nothing left, no child and no love affair with a Canadian officer. Nothing.

To my knowledge, Nan's years of bringing up the children were tough, though she drew on her resourcefulness and resilience countless times. There were periods where the four children needed to spend time in foster care. She later lost the battle to keep her home when her husband made her leave with the children so he could put the house up for sale – a shocking situation that wouldn't be tolerated nowadays. Any work opportunities she found helped her to make ends meet. She always worked hard but spoke fondly of her time trained in silver service and as a loyal housekeeper.

Nan never drove a car, but found her way around on a Honda 50 cc motorbike. Family holidays with the children were few. When they happened, it was not unusual for her to hitchhike with all four kids to reach their holiday destination. Like I said, she's always had an adventurous spirit and found creative solutions to her problems.

Lorraine, the eldest of Nan's three daughters, gave birth just shy of twenty years old. She lived away from home for the first five months of her baby daughter's life. After her relationship unexpectedly ended, not knowing where to turn, she applied to travel to Israel, intending to live on a kibbutz. The idea of a fresh start with her baby in a new, supportive, community-minded environment felt like a positive move. Even with an accepted application, however, Lorraine could not raise enough funds to undertake the journey. With no Plan B, somebody suggested she should consider having her baby adopted. She was so young, and without the provision of adequate social support she couldn't give her daughter the life she needed. She agreed, knowing she had a year in which to change her mind.

With no baby, life became challenging for Lorraine, resulting in fear-stricken nights and a heavy cloud of depression clutching at her. She was admitted to a local hospital following episodes of dark thoughts, but back in the 1970s poor mental health, particularly for new mothers, remained misunderstood. Postnatal depression was yet to be a recognised diagnosis.

Lorraine's depression worsened and all the doctors ever seemed to offer were more drugs, which appeared to be the only therapy known to the medical world back then. Counselling never entered the treatment plan. Medicine may have numbed the pain of losing her child but didn't tackle the deeper psychological trauma; ironic when you consider the drugs exacerbated Lorraine's low state of mind. At the advice of a friend, she stopped taking them and boldly asked to speak to a psychiatrist. She received the response that if she wanted the couch treatment, she'd have to pay for it. Angered and at a loss for her own future, Lorraine could bear it no more and discharged herself, retrieving her baby with a positive determination to make things work.

On returning to her flat with her baby, now about eight or nine months old, Lorraine received the hardest news yet. After inappropriate advances from her landlord, which she rebuffed, he evicted her, armed with the blunt reason that he would not rent to an unmarried mother. A temporary move to a friend's place didn't work out either, so Nan's life took on another change as Lorraine and I moved back into the family home.

After lengthy months of searching for an alternative solution, including housing, when I was around a year old, Lorraine was counselled by a social worker who suggested that perhaps the best chance of a better life for her baby would be to allow her to be offered for adoption, again. She battled with the decision but eventually, knowing that she had no social provisions to help support baby Zoe, I went into care to be offered for adoption for the second time. The formal verification of my adoption took place in November 1972. Viv and Linda became my new parents and seven-year-old Chris happily gained himself a little sister, now eighteen months old.

As a cheerful child, I settled well into my new life. I always knew I'd like to find out who my biological parents were. Mum and Dad had remained open about my adoption, sharing little snippets here and there. It felt good to hear "I was special because they chose me". Dad sometimes teased me when we walked past the magistrates' courts in the local town. "You've been in there," he'd say. Naturally, I thought he meant I'd been up to no good ... until he let on they'd formalised my adoption in this building.

At eighteen years old, it happened. I had a boyfriend whose father had a shock discovery of his adoption following the death of his own father. It nudged me to start the ball rolling. Both his parents guided me with much useful advice. I remember wondering if my biological parents were still alive, what they were like, and how many brothers and sisters I might have.

This part of my story had a happy conclusion, with me tracing my youngest auntie, Jane. We hit it off straight away and marvelled at our many resemblances – even down to the shape of our feet! Jane contacted Lorraine, now living in the United States. After marrying an American in London, she had emigrated with him and a new life began for her, about six years after my birth.

Our first communication took place via a long-distance telephone call. Within a matter of weeks, Lorraine flew over to meet me for an emotional reunion. I loved the introductions to the wider maternal family. After a couple of calls, I was lucky enough to be introduced to my biological father, Lyndon, his wife Terry, and two younger half-siblings, Sara and Neil.

As with Lorraine and Lyndon, the very first meeting with my nan was as if we had always known one another. There was no awkwardness. Nothing to hide and only a need to catch up on the years missed, which we did with enthusiasm. Lorraine continued to travel back to the UK for a month's visit every summer.

Every six weeks, I would visit with Nan, coinciding with school holidays and half-term breaks. Mary became the grandmother I never had. With my parents, Linda and Viv, there had only been one grandparent alive at the time of my adoption: my maternal grandfather, Jim, with whom I shared the same birthday. I loved Grandad Jim, and his pet name for me, "Snowy". He died when I was almost five years old, and the joy of sharing experiences with a grandparent while I was growing up was gone.

Nan gave me a second chance, my lost opportunity at being a granddaughter. We wrote cards and letters to one another, and we spoke on the telephone. When I gave birth to Laura, Nan knitted and cross-stitched for us, clearly delighted to become a great-grandmother. Whatever the circumstances of my adoption all those years back, it was a good relationship, just as it was for me with Lorraine and Lyndon.

This decision isn't easy, but I have to make a call. I can't ignore the nasty cough I've carried since early April. It wouldn't be wise to visit Nan in the hospital while there's a possibility I have an infection. I take the ultimate gamble and decide I'd have to visit her on my return at the end of August.

Decision made, I tuck both inhalers into the top of the rucksack, and grin at myself. Nan would laugh at the size of my pack if I were to visit her right now. In her healthier days, she would have wanted to try it on, although I think she'd have buckled under the weight of this one. *I'll come and see you soon, Nan. Stick with it. You'll love the stories I'll have to tell you.*

3 An Imposter

This is it. My first introduction to Minehead's monumental metal sculpture; and depending on your direction of travel, the start or end marker of the trail. Stood in front of this extraordinary work of art, I touch the colossal hands clutching a semi-open map. "God, it's incredible," I say to Ross, half-whispering, in awe of its presence. He nods, smiling.

The map bears a cut-through grid, with a view of the sea through its leaves, the folds of curiosity tempting the viewer to step forward. As I succumb to its beckoning, I find myself lost within and yet embraced by the enormity of the work.

"Let's get some pics," Ross says, lifting his camera. He takes the obligatory starter photo, with my backdrop of metal map and hands. He's careful to line up the words "South West Coast Path" impressed on the map, ensuring they are clearly within the frame. Beyond the sculpture, the white pinnacles of Butlin's holiday park tower into the sky, about half a mile east. The sea and the strand stretch away behind me. To the west, the steep flanks of North Hill overshadow the town. North Hill, standing dominant as a stark warning to all the newbie walkers of what to expect in the coming miles. *Oh, that's me.*

"It doesn't feel real, Ross."

"What do you mean?"

"Well, it's hard to be excited because until now, I'd not really believed I'd get here. I only ever saw myself in the state of planning the walk. Perhaps I was too scared to imagine any further ahead than that." Ross nods in sympathy.

"That's normal, I expect. I'm here for a couple of weeks. You'll be fine." He smiles. "Anyway, you have Piggie to keep you company." He taps my little companion strapped into the side of my rucksack. "Don't lose him. He's one of the family!"

I'm pleased I have Piggie with me. While it might sound childish, he's a familiar face and a token mascot from home, which I think I'll find comforting. Laura gave him to me when she was about eight years old. As a stretchy mobile phone cover, he has a weird-looking pocket on his back. Laura didn't like that, so passed him on to me. Since then, Piggie has travelled to many places with us, including school trips like ice-skating in Central Park, scaling the heights of the Empire State Building in New York, and countryside hikes, and he has even attended art exhibitions, complete with a miniature pig-sized dickie bow. This well-travelled, inanimate toy has somehow taken on a character of his own and, as a family, we're fond of Piggie.

My heady mix of nerves and excitement about beginning my adventure is overwhelming. I'm relieved Ross is here as my support and confidence boost. "Go there." He gestures for me to move to the tarmac path. With his camera poised, he looks up at me, fiddles with the lens for a second and then clicks. This photo, the most poignant of all. I'm standing on the white line officially marking the start of the National Trail, with a bold white arrow heading out behind me. This is it. Ross's camera screen shows a telling image. A veil of trepidation blurs the expression that should shine with excitement.

If I consider that I've been waiting to walk this path for fifteen years, why am I not jumping up and down like a jelly bean? The cold hard truth is that I'm petrified. The demons of imposter syndrome are masterfully weaving, knotting and tying their threads of doubt ever tighter. It feels wrong. How can I possibly be standing here? Carrying this heavy pack? Little me, not athletic enough, not strong enough, not fast enough, and no exceptional ability in anything. I'm simply not enough in any capacity. *How did I ever think I could do this? Everyone will laugh at me. When I don't finish, people will sneer, "I'm not surprised. Who did she think she was, anyway?"*

This should be the perfect start, marking my dream adventure. With my head playing so many cruel games, all I can do is attempt to pull the blind down on the damaging self-talk, kiss Ross goodbye, turn, take a deep breath, and walk away. *I am going to do this. Forward march.* With my heart as heavy as my pack, everything pulls at me, attempting to drag me backwards.

Ross is meeting me later, yet I've squeezed everything into my rucksack. I've decided I need to carry my kit as if I am properly going it alone. Otherwise, I won't have a fair assessment of how I am managing as time progresses. My chest wheezes with the chugging and popping of an old engine. My legs feel as though they won't carry me further than a couple of miles. And my head. My head continues to taunt me.

For the first few minutes, it's an easy tarmac path along the harbour and beside the beach wall where Ross and I cooked up breakfast this morning, using my swanky new ultra lightweight frying pan. Suddenly, one of my rugged non-slip boots glides without warning across an iron manhole cover. I break out a range of interesting shapes, like a cross between a drunken partygoer dancing to "Night Fever", and Bambi, slip-sliding on ice. Desperate not to perform the splits, I pull myself back up, thankful not to face plant the pavement. Less than five minutes into my journey, and already I feel incapable and vulnerable.

After the fourth time of turning around and waving, Ross finally disappears from my view. I hold my breath as I watch the grey roof and red stripe of my black van ease away into a side road, and, just like that, it's gone.

Although I had expected to do this walk solo, at some point Ross said he'd come and support me for a couple of weeks. He'd take it as a holiday from work, drive the campervan and meet me at an agreed spot each evening. It seemed like a great transition for me into the full challenge. We've been together for ten years, and he knows me better than anyone. He loves to walk, has an eclectic taste in music, appreciates art and literature, and is passionate about photography. Oh, and he enjoys a pint or two and a cake (or two) ... but not together.

It had been a difficult few months leading to my separation from Laura's father, and so a mutual friend introduced me and Ross, knowing full well that we had similar interests. In the early days of MSN, we chatted online for many weeks before finally agreeing to meet up. The day came, and we hugged like two old friends reacquainted after years of absence. I felt like I had come home.

This is it.

Those three words keep resounding in my head. This. Is. It. What was I expecting, and more to the point, whatever was I thinking? One foot in front of the other, step by step by step by step. There's an open space of green to my left once I'm beyond the fishermen's car park. Many trees line those steep banks of North Hill above the green. I remember the strip map and, with a quick glance, I spot the closely packed contour lines. I hope I don't have to climb that. What a baptism of fire that would be.

Like starting school with a brand-new uniform that's too crisp and lacking in the telltale signs of mud, wear or tear, I flounder like an amateur. Despite my training walks, nothing feels natural. The kit hasn't grown on me, or more to the point, I haven't grown into it. The sky is flat, and I ascend at a slow but steady pace, where the path changes from tarmac to something more like a coast path. A few stones and dusty ground edged with tufts of grass and mounds of rock.

I spy people coming towards me. *Shit*. This is the first time I've experienced walking past others wearing all this garb. *They'll know I'm not a real long-distance walker.* Frightened to be revealed for the fraud that I really am, I alter my posture ever so slightly, puff out my chest, and set about with a more purposeful, confident stride. "Morning!" I pretend a jovial tone as I stride past them with a pack on my back the size of a builder's hod.

"Morning!" They smile at me, but I'm sure I spy intrigued glances towards my Amazonian-looking adventurer's hat. My large rucksack forces the brim of my hat upwards because it's stuffed so full. They must have spotted the shape of my knees surrendering to the weight, and they're bound to have sensed my fear. I'm carrying it all, and that's a lot to deal with. It's possible they may have wanted to stop to talk to me, but I don't wait around to find out. I keep walking, with that intent manner set in my face and body language. When I'm sure they're out of view, I heave a sigh of relief and I relax a bit. I can't do this every time someone walks past me. *What is going on in my head? Whatever was I thinking? I shouldn't be here.*

The landscape changes dramatically as I climb towards Selworthy Beacon. A blanket of purple-pink hues signals the eruption of the summer heather. The bright sunshine yellow of the gorse complements it perfectly. Despite the drab day, the views across the waters of the Bristol Channel are fair, and I can just make out the coastline of Wales. That looks a long way off. I look along the distant path and realise I could probably walk to Wales far quicker than I'll be able to walk the full length of the South West Coast Path. *This is insanity.*

I descend from the hill into the small hamlet of Bossington. There's a guy, probably in his fifties, wearing a mop of shoulder-length blond curly hair, his face decorated with a neat little goatee. He's sitting in a wheelchair that looks much like a scooter. It's a pretty cool, Heath Robinson affair with a pair of batteries strapped to the front fork of a motorbike with gaffer tape. The motorbike portion connects to the seat and the big back wheels of a wheelchair. *Ingenious!* This is a transportation invention at its best. Sat patiently next to this wheelchair's answer to Chitty Chitty Bang Bang is a dog. It's shaggy and blond and sports a similar styling in terms of fur as the man, though bearded and not goateed. I am interested in the man's venture out on this resourceful contraption, and we strike up a conversation. He's keen to hear about my adventure, too.

Frankie tells me he's had Achilles' surgery but still has to take his friend's dog out for walks as he's dog-sitting. Nonny looks up at Frankie, his furry brows twitching, knowing full well that his guardian is talking about him. It's clear they have a great relationship. Frankie is wearing nothing but the smallest suggestion of shorts and the hospital-issue plastic boot on his right foot that sits almost up to his knee. When positioned with the front fork and batteries in front of him, on first glance you'd be forgiven for thinking he was out on a ride from the local naturist camp. His tanned skin shows me a man who is out in all weathers. Even his hair shows signs of surf-blond highlights, caught by the sun ... I'm sure they weren't streaks of grey.

After I share the story of my intended challenge with Frankie, he reaches into those tiny shorts, somehow extracting a note. "Here you go. Stick this in your sponsorship fund." He humbly hands me twenty pounds.

"Wow, thanks, Frankie. That's kind of you. Let me add you to my list." There's a sponsorship form in my rucksack for recording any donations. *Ask him if you can take his photograph ... But I'll feel silly ... He might think I'm trying to chat him up ... Ask him ... You'll regret it if you don't.* In those few seconds of head battles, I muster up the courage to ask Frankie if I can take his photo.

"Of course," he replies, and for a split second I catch a fleeting expression of shyness as Frankie's eyes glance downwards. "Well, I'll be on my way now. Good luck!" With that, this hairy goatee-guy motions to Nonny and sets off across the nearby field footpath on his motorbikeywheelychair. His shaggy hair blows freely in the wind as he takes the stance of a Hell's Angel on a Harley-Davidson. Nonny lollops alongside his companion, his doggy fur mirroring that of his shaggy human.

Seriously, wow. Frankie will never know just how much impact this has had on me. A fresh spring in my step, I skip along the field paths from Bossington to Porlock Weir, across the footbridges that cross the many drainage ditches. My first on-trip sponsor and it's only Day One! This guy, with all his life experience behind him, had a belief in me. He believed in me enough to give me twenty quid. If he didn't think I could reach Poole, then he wouldn't have donated anything, right? The little voice of destruction begins whispering. *Perhaps he felt sorry for you—* I shut it out. I will not waste this first moment of confidence.

With my spirits soaring, in contrast I wobble and totter my way across the boulders of Porlock beach to a nearby pub. It's another lift for me as I spot Ross at a beer table out front, enjoying a pint and live music at the pub's annual music festival. Result.

4

The Man in the Woods

It’s difficult waking up for Day Two. I’m tired and my cough is still productive in the mornings. I organise myself in the tiny space of the van and Ross drives me back down the hill to my starting point at Porlock Weir. Almost immediately, the path sets off between two buildings and rises high to follow a road on the hill above Porlock.

Today is all about the woods. That’s how it is. No coast. No sky, no view. Just woods. For eight heavy miles. These woods are part of a large estate, from what I can see on the map. The impressive, enormous thatched tollhouse curves to fit well into its surroundings. An integral archway straddles the road to allow cars, or in a bygone era, carriages to pass through.

A moment sitting here to grab a drink is just what I need to get myself back into a positive mindset for the day. As I take in the tranquil beauty of the cottage, I notice there’s a small lump behind my knee ... then I find another. Horrified, I pick away at the multiple ticks that have made table reservations to feast on me. To avoid a teddy bear's ticknic, I quickly stand up and brush myself down in readiness to leave again. On another examination of the map, I look up at the dense woods ahead of me. Once I’ve entered this leafy labyrinth, I’m not expecting to see daylight for many hours.

For a while my route follows an ancient, towering brick wall, aged with years of dampness and dressed with the fairy-tale touches of moss and fern. The wall leads me on through a series of short tunnels. How exciting this would be for children! I think back to the wonderful time I visited Stourhead, adorned with its meandering pathways, bridges and grottoes, with Ross and each of our daughters. Laura, and Ross's daughter, Lara, had enjoyed a fabulous day out. So many opportunities for imaginative play and memory-making.

With the brick tunnels behind me, every few steps the light flickers as it peeps in and out between the thick canopies of leaves above. I'm thankful for the shade, and the effect is enchanting. I marvel at the glorious backlighting of the variegated shades of green along these woody hollows, wishing I could capture it on my camera. It never looks the same, though.

The woods are atmospheric and seem impossible. As I continue through the leafy underpass, the trees astonish me. I wonder how any of them have survived their fifty, or one hundred and fifty years of being rooted to the steepest hillside I've ever seen. It reminds me of a photograph I once saw of a row of trees being shifted by a tremendous landslide, yet every tree remained upright and filed together like soldiers in rank on parade.

Ahead, a solitary deer lazily grazes between the trees, and only at the last minute my footfall disturbs its meal. It glances up at me, vegetation still hanging from its mouth, just long enough for me to catch a photo before it bounds away.

Culbone is my first proper place of interest. My arm caught by an invisible lasso, I'm drawn deep into its magic. Culbone hides a secret that few would realise existed unless they too ventured into the woods. Inaccessible to most four-wheeled transport and tucked into the depths of a tree-lined valley, the track opens up slightly. Between the gaps, the sparsely planted trees are no longer fighting for their quota of daylight. There are no views across the twinkling water and craggy coastline as of the day before. Instead, a glut of oversized rhododendron bushes and tall, delicate fingers of fern replace the trees. Gunnera patches spread with extravagance. Their tightly packed army of wide, umbrella-like leaves guides me down to Culbone's legacy: the remote church of St Beuno.

The church's super-petite, semi-truncated spire catches my attention straight away. The information leaflet states Culbone served a small village parish. It also points out a tiny window at the rear of the church where the priest would administer prayers and communion to individuals from a local leper colony. I wander behind the church to look at the window and wonder what it must have been like. How might it feel to live in the days when distrust of contact with others, for genuine fear of contagion and death, reigned?

The charm of this church and its weathered graveyard captures me. The few time-worn headstones are so old they bear only the flaky remnants of an inscription. Most of these are now indecipherable. Moss, ivy and ancient lichens creep over the stone, conjuring up wild stories of legend and mystery in my head. The early cross guarding the main door is Grade One listed, with the Grade Two listed church purported to be the smallest in England. It's hard to leave the magic behind, but the spirit and ambience of these surroundings will stay with me for a long time.

I pull myself away from the valley of Culbone, and a cottage with exquisite spiralled-brick chimney stacks almost waves at me. *Okay, one last photo ...* then I must go. I wonder how I will ever finish the walk in time if I keep stopping to absorb, take photos and enjoy the sights I see around every corner.

This morning fills me with the need to pinch myself to ensure I am indeed walking my dream path. I've also come to a realisation. Although I'm following a coast path, it's not a case of keeping the sea on my right all the way to Poole. I laugh, thinking of all the people who expertly claimed that at least I wouldn't need a map. "There's not much chance of you getting lost," they said. In my naïvety, I had agreed with them. Here I am, however, on the second day of my coast path adventure, realising how wrong they were and how daft I was for believing them.

There are many occasions where I refer to the map and the guidebook, though for reassurance more than actual navigation. With no buddy to discuss route decisions with, it's all down to me and me alone. The South West Coast Path benefits from small metal tags, known as waymarkers, indicating you're on a National Trail. It's reassuring to see the white acorn on a black background, whether on a fence, gate post, tree or wall. It means I've not veered off the path. Of course, I want to make sure I stay on the right track, and this fear of making a mistake is ever-present in my head.

The lofty slopes continue to dominate these dense, almost sinister woods. Unable to control my overactive imagination, strange thoughts grip me as I experience my first moment of genuine fear.

Ahead, I see the estate management has cordoned off an area of trees with red-and-white tape. My storyteller's mind questions why, though it doesn't occur to me it's most likely a proposed cutting-back or tree-felling area. Instead, I continue my silent narrative to imagine a crime scene, a grisly murder perhaps. Who was the victim? Who was the perpetrator? Perhaps they've taken refuge within the eight miles sanctuary of these woods. They could remain hidden for an indefinite period of time.

They might still be here.

Beyond the fringes of my visualisation, a prickling rasps up the back of my neck and I sense I'm not alone. In this wood where it had been just me, the trees and my thoughts for miles and hours, I turn and see a man, only a few minutes behind me. As I had caught the deer out at the last minute, I too am experiencing the feeling of being trapped.

I am not sure why I feel so uncomfortable, as there's nothing suspicious about the man from what I can see, but I don't want to turn around again and look a second time. That would make me look anxious. I consider my situation. Being enclosed within a wood, miles from open space and not a soul around me, except this guy, unnerves me. That and the indelible effects of my earlier overactive imagination. Like a learner driver, I am still in training on this solo walking malarkey and so, striding onwards, I aim to keep ahead of the man at all costs.

The mission to pick up a pace when you're carrying an unnaturally heavy weight on your back is no simple task. It's not long before I reach a placard stating the path is now closed because of a landslide. My heartbeat quickens as the alarm of being lost rushes through me. The added panic about a male stranger who would soon reach me, as I had now slowed down to examine the diversion route, floods me with anxious adrenalin.

After much internal debate about how to handle the situation, I tell myself to slow down and stop racing towards the end of the wood. Underneath eighteen kilograms I am slower than my usual walking pace; slower than any two-legged being I meet on the path, in fact. While ascending one of the many steep hills, I time how long I take to walk a mile. I'm shocked to learn that I spend a good hour walking that one mile alone. Based on this, the whole path will take me months. Options float around my head until I reach the conclusion that I would let the man catch up. I'd say hello and let him pass.

Incredible as it may seem, he is not wielding an axe and turns out to be a normal, friendly man who shows a genuine interest in my adventure. After a few minutes of discussing the diversion and then strolling together, I think my snail's pace is too much for him. He bids me farewell, and I heave an inner sigh of relief while scolding myself for being so fearful.

Four hours later, I emerge into open space and the welcome expanse of common land, sea and views. Starved by the lack of views in the woods, I am now hungry for coastline, rocks, waves and sky. I hadn't grasped how much I had missed the sky. I've escaped the shadow of the trees and discover that the day is putting on a real summer act. The heat tingling across my skin feels like a luxury denied to me for years.

Despite that initial welcome of the landscape, the area surrounding Countisbury Common soon demands great care. The path narrows and descends the steep cliffs, and fear grips me once again. That uninvited rush of adrenalin running through my legs while attempting to negotiate the narrow path is not welcome. The weight of my bag contributes to the feeling of unsteadiness on my feet, and my shoulders burn under the load. I try not to look at the severity of the cliff as it shelves away, down to the water.

My phone buzzes in my hip belt pocket. I find a spot where I feel safer to stop and check it:

Having a pint at The Rising Sun pub. It's right on the path. See you when you get here.

It's from Ross, and I'm happy to know that I'll soon be reaching Lynmouth. I'm feeling overwhelmed and out of my depth with some of these high paths. I hope I'll get used to that. If I can't, I'm not sure what I'll do. I guess I'll have to just get on with it.

Inside my head I give a little cheer to see a familiar figure sitting on a bench with his back to the white wall of the historic thatched pub. The Rising Sun is such a blessing after today's struggle, so I stop for a cooling lemonade and lime. Ross has been waiting a short time and I'm happier knowing that at least he's struck up a conversation with nearby punters, also holidaymakers in the town. It's much harder for me to not feel guilty when I think he's been on his own all day. In some ways, it's an added pressure, which is the opposite of what I thought it would be, the comfort and security of familiarity.

While chatting with Ross and his new drinking companions, I fill them in on the features of today's walk. The beauty, the woods, the church, and the fear. I announce that despite walking for nearly nine hours today, my day is not yet done. "I need to walk to Lynton – just under another mile to the top of the cliff railway." The couple lay down valid arguments about why I should call it a day here at Lynmouth. Ross, however, understands.

And so, with a plan, I say goodbye once again and leave for another forty-five minutes of walking. Ross, in the meantime, drives into Lynton and walks down to meet me at the foot of the cliff railway. Together we walk the steep zigzag path. We stop at each of its two little bridges that cross the railway, joining the higher town of Lynton with Lynmouth, to admire the town, sea and hills beyond.

Destination for tonight's dinner and entertainment? An old spit and sawdusty-type pub advertising an open-mic night. We enjoy traditional pub grub, having a few drinks and laughing lots. It's good to relax again, but it's not long before the landlord hears about my challenge. "Do you play an instrument?" he asks me.

"Not really, only a harmonica. Badly."

"If you pipe a few notes on a harmonica, I'll send a hat around. How about that?"

"Ummm, okay then!" I reply, a little nervous but already feeling braver than I would have yesterday. A chap sitting at the front playing a guitar offers to stay put for support and to add some background chords if I need it. A few sucks and blows later on a borrowed harmonica, I painfully squeeze out a couple of tunes from my limited repertoire. With my heart still banging like a broken washing machine, I race back to my seat, having kept my part of the bargain. The landlord brings over the hat of change and I'm delighted to discover that my racket has somehow generated nearly ten pounds' worth of coins. I write the pub name on my sponsor form and hand over the change to Ross to take home. Carrying so many coins will only add to the already hefty pack I'm lugging around with me.

It's been an eventful day. By 9.30 p.m. I am a hundred per cent ready to head back to the van to work on some much-needed sleep. We leave the pub, and walking hand in hand, I feel a pang of guilt again for Ross. This is his holiday. Is he enjoying it? He's been walking, exploring, and taking photos, and there have been some good pub discoveries, which of course always means a pint of the local brew. "Are you having fun, Ross?" And in the way I have come to expect from him, my man of few words, he just smiles gently, and nods.

5

An Old Face

Ordained into the ways of long-distance walking over the first couple of days, I better understand how I need to start my day. I could use reminders of the importance of following intuition and when not to let my imagination run away with me. Expectations of the path are clearer now, improved by more regular checks of my map. I've taken to carrying it draped over my rucksack hip belt, like some kind of holster worn by Indiana Jones or Lara Croft. Of course, all this is fine, until the weather unleashes its best performance yet.

Lynton has held me back for just a little longer than perhaps it should have done, for a multitude of reasons. I am feeling tired after two days of walking with more weight in my pack than I had carried on any training walks. It's taking its toll. Also, I'm sure I will walk myself fit, but this cough hasn't helped. When in full swing, it's louder than a foghorn and I'm sure I've already scared off a few seagulls.

Sleeping in my basic campervan hasn't been the most restful either. There's a part of me that is really looking forward to setting off, fully solo, as trying to get organised and away early from the van is hard and, well ... disorganised. There is a mixture of sleepy-headedness, faffing, and a repeated daily reluctance to leave the familiarity of my van and Ross. He's also not the most organised of individuals, so having a routine is near impossible. This said, I'm so appreciative that he's taken the time to come with me for the first two weeks, to ease me into being totally solo.

Then there's the weather. Today, the sky is launching rods that bear no resemblance to the pretty, well-formed raindrop of my childhood storybooks. These are more akin to the rains of biblical stories. Rather than take off onto a sodden and seriously windy coast path, Ross and I retreat to a small café in Lynton.

For those who, like me, always forget which is Lynton and which is Lynmouth, I have found the perfect way to remember. Lyn-mouth sits at the mouth of the River Lyn, at the point where it escapes out to sea. Lyn-ton is Up-Town and therefore high above the river. Fed up with forgetting which is which (like all the time), at last this is something that works.

We've chosen a window table inside the café. Hot chocolate, coffee and toasted teacakes beckon, so we succumb as the weather continues its tiresome onslaught. I spend a few moments reflecting on the previous day's walking from Porlock Weir to Lynton by skimming through the photographs on my camera. It helps me to remember the experiences and the views. Already I see that it's so easy to forget from one day to the next, which considering I'm only on Day Three means there won't be much chance of me remembering anything from the forty-seven days I've planned to be away at this rate.

A photo pops up in the camera gallery from our stop in the pub last night. Ross's eyes twinkle with amusement at my harmonica efforts. While I was grateful that the landlord had suggested they would send a hat round the bar, they had inducted me into the world of public performance. "I'm not sure I want to do that again in a hurry – I wish I could have practised beforehand, if I'm honest."

While sipping from my mug, I watch the rain hammering on the windows. A slight, solitary figure slopes past the café, with his collar turned up, dark-rimmed glasses looking misty and his few wisps of hair damp and slightly askew. There is an asymmetry about his mouth. I sit bolt upright, eyes wide. The figure had passed in less than two seconds, but that was all it had taken to recognise him. I'm catapulted in an instant thirty years back to my junior school days. Darren Kellow! No way – I thought he was gone. Seriously. After the momentary shock of seeing the ghost of a boy, I blurt the news out to Ross across the table. "Shit, I'm sure I've just seen Darren go past the café and I've not seen him since I was ten years old!"

"Who's Darren?"

"Darren Kellow, oh my, I can't believe it was Darren Kellow! He was a lad at our school who had leukaemia," I explain. "He had a film crew follow him for a while as they made a documentary about childhood cancer. I remember him losing his hair and wearing a beanie hat, and all the kids wanted to rub his bald head. To be honest, he was always so frail-looking, and as I hadn't seen him after leaving junior school, I assumed he'd not survived." I pause for a breath. Ross looks as shell-shocked as me, probably for different reasons. *Lesson One, Wath. Assume nothing, okay? This could get you into trouble.*

"Are you sure it was him?" For a moment, Ross sows a seed of doubt into my head. Before it can take root, I shake the uncertainty away and trust myself.

"Ninety-nine per cent – he hasn't changed a bit. Except that being an adult now, he's taller," I say. "And he's even wearing the same style of glasses." Back when we were children in the seventies, there was the grand choice of black, pale blue or tortoiseshell National Health glasses. If my memory serves me right, Darren used to wear the black specs.

You should've gone out to say hello ... I know, but I didn't want to look stupid ... You've missed an opportunity ... I know, but it might not have been him ... You know darn well it was him. You're a coward ... Okay, okay, I felt shy. Leave me alone. I glance upwards at Ross just as he's scooping the final dregs of froth from his cappuccino, and he looks back at me. "You should've gone out to say hello," he presses gently. I sigh in defeat.

"I know. I'm not sure why I didn't. It all happened so quickly, I didn't have time to think." That was at least partly true. "I wish I had now."

Moping in a puddle of regret would not help me. Never thought I'd hear myself say this, but it would be better to be drenched outside than allow myself to sit around any longer. I needed to move on, for both the mental benefits while learning from the experience, and the physical. With miles to achieve today, ruminating in a café is no help.

With grit on my face and hot chocolate in my belly, I waddle-walk my way back down through the town to the top of the cliff railway. I'm relieved to be back on the South West Coast Path again, rain or no rain. Until I begin each day's walk, it never seems real. The desperation to feel like I have started on the *real* journey weighs almost as heavy as my pack. I love coming back to Ross each evening, but I'm not yet feeling the challenge. I need the adventure of pushing myself beyond my perceived capabilities, experiencing all the path has to give me, and that means going alone. Solo.

The path contours around the foot of Hollerday Hill. *How apt*, I chuckle to myself, though I can see now this walk is going to be no holiday. The hill ascends to my left, which, at this point of the path, is southwards of me. Over the three days, I have engaged more with the map. Updates for myself about the walking direction and the distant landmarks I can make out around me help keep my mind focused. I enjoy comparing my location with points in South Wales, across the Bristol Channel. I'm now in Exmoor National Park. If the weather was kinder and the cloud higher, looking north I would see a point directly between Port Talbot and Swansea. I deliberate my lack of travels into Wales, and reach the conclusion that I am now further into dragon country than I've ever been. Bizarre, considering I'm not even "in" Wales.

More and more, the surrounding terrain transforms into an object of rugged fascination. As I wander down into the Valley of the Rocks,

I spot the largest, beardiest goat I've ever set eyes on. I would say horniest too, but will avoid it for fear of misinterpretation. Based on the assumed stance, high on a splintered rock, above anything else within striking distance, I'm judging that I've just clapped eyes on Chief Posing Billy of Lynton's resident tribe of feral goats. He waits for me to take a photograph, as if that's what he expected me to do. Then, with beard blowing in slo-mo, he makes a lithe mix of hobble and leap to spring down from his parapet, off towards a group of nannies further away.

With my brain full of goat and camera, and my attention caught like a fly in the sticky web of a house spider, I've not spotted the lone figure. He wanders across the turning circle between the landmarks of Rugged Jack and Castle Rock. The wisps of hair are smoothed over his head and the collar of his coat is turned down now, as the rain has at last taken its marching orders. As I look up, the black-rimmed glasses and offset mouth are all I need. I'm being given a second chance and this time, I'll snatch it. Before he has time to reach the far side of the turning circle, I pad over to him under the weight of my rucksack. With an outwardly confident voice, despite still feeling that little demon of doubt at my back, at last I open my mouth to speak: "It's Darren, isn't it? Darren Kellow?"

"Yeah, that's right." He squints a little at me from behind his glasses. The lenses are still as thick as I remember. His mouth shows signs of the beginnings of a smile, as if there is a semblance of recognition.

Before any opportunity to fire a "Who are you?" at me, I pipe up: "I'm Zoe – Zoe Wathen." A broad, slopy grin breaks across his face.

"I remember you," he says, nodding slightly. "We were at junior school together, weren't we?"

"Yes! You were in my year, but I think you were a year older than me?"

"Yeah, I had all that stuff going on where I missed months of school. They brought me down into your year. It was alright."

"Over the years, I've often wondered what happened to you after we left to go to comp."

I'm so happy at this point. A familiar face from my childhood and a wonderful surprise to learn he fought his cancer successfully. "Where did you go, anyway?"

"I went to a different school, and only kept in touch with a couple of friends from the juniors."

I nod. "So what brings you down here in this rain, then?"

"Oh, I like to come out to Lynton most years. Something great about this place, even in the rain. I don't drive but there's a little coach company I use. I like it and it's familiar." That sideways smile peels across his face again. "And I like the goats."

"I was just admiring the goats too!" I tap my camera to acknowledge I'd just snapped a few photos of them.

"What are you doing with that big bag on your back? You look like you're walking a long way?"

"Yep, I'm on Day Three of about seven weeks of walking the South West Coast Path. I'm doing it for charity, but also to mark my big birthday. Of course, you've already had yours last year!" We both laugh at this.

"Blimey. Well good luck with that, then. Can't imagine walking all those miles. Think I'll stick to what I know."

We catch up on the missed years in the space of about ten minutes. I glance at my watch and know I have to get a shifty on if I'm to make any progress at all today.

"Well, I've gotta go, but it's been great to catch up. Say hi to North Somerset for me, and let's hope it's not another thirty years before we bump into each other again!"

Pleased with the unlikely yet coincidental outcome of being given another chance to step out and speak up, I set off westwards. Who knew I'd bump into Ross and the excuse to stop for yet another hot chocolate at Lee Abbey Tea Cottage? I'll be lucky to make five miles today at this rate ... But when the rains fall and the stars collide, sometimes good things happen.

6

The Phone Call

As seems to be our way, we sit in the Tea Cottage at Lee Abbey for way too long. At less than two miles into my day's walking, I know I should get moving and stomp out some more miles today. Although I'm grateful the rain's stopped, for now, I can see a bank of dark, foreboding cloud in the distance, and it doesn't look friendly. I wish with everything I can muster that it'll hang around out there, out of the way, until tonight.

The cottage garden table is nothing more than a lightweight aluminium bistro-style affair. The many birds flitting and foraging for crumbs left by previous customers absorb my attention. Bird feeders hanging around the gardens are a magnet to all the sparrows, blue tits and finches, adding to the feeding frenzy. Such a vast company of feathers, with many so tame. A sparrow lands on the back of a nearby chair, with head cocked to one side. He gives me a look that pushes me to reach for my camera. Whatever the bird was willing me to do, in my mind, he was saying "C'mon, take my photo. Is this my best side?" Dutifully, I snap away, zooming in to capture multiple pictures and feeling very smug about the outcome. I look intently at my little feathered friend, sending him a thank you. He appears to bob his beak in appreciation and takes off to perch on the roof of the tearoom as quickly as he had arrived.

Although I should be on a mission to crack out more distance, somehow this seems like a little portion of heaven that I'm reluctant to leave. I am surrounded by nature, the tamest garden birds I've ever witnessed, incredible views, hot chocolate, and cake. What more could a woman wish for, other than to share the moment with her favourite man? My love and my world. I gaze over the top of my mug at his deep brown eyes, the line of his jaw, and his long fingers wrapped around the steaming mug. Those sculpted fingers that know so much, especially how to touch and trace the shape of my body in our intimate moments. This wash of intense devotion and joy fills me, from my muddy, wet boots upwards. He's so willing to support me on this crazy adventure, and I feel lucky to have lost my heart to this man all those years ago. Ten years on, he still grips my heart with his, and in this moment of reverie, I have never felt more secure.

There is a little shop within the tearoom. An outside canopy protects a display of colourful rag rugs, which catches Ross's eye. He's left the van parked up elsewhere and knows that if he buys a rug, he'll have to carry it back. This idea doesn't seem to faze him. He's so taken with the colours of one in particular that he impulsively makes a purchase. With the rug draped over his shoulder like Clint Eastwood, Ross arrives back at the table, looking thoroughly pleased with himself. I wait while he threads the rug underneath the top flap of his rucksack, the bulk of rolled rags and fraying fibres draped heavily on either side. He walks with me awhile, knowing that once we reach Heddon's Mouth we can walk together up to where he has parked the van for us to sleep for the night.

The foreboding cloud that I'd spotted earlier doesn't take long to put in an appearance. We walk westerly around the sweep of Woody Bay and the foot of The Beacon, which I believe is the remains of a Roman hill fort. The heavens that were so appealing to me earlier suddenly open up, dumping rain over us, bucket after bucket after bloody bucket. There's no warning, no time to pull out and climb into our wet-weather gear. The irony is that despite packing waterproofs, we are now utterly wet through. I grapple myself into my waterproof trousers and smock with the awkwardness of a toddler straight out of a swimming pool. As body and fabric sticks, we walk into the prevailing wind, steps now super slow. I concentrate on watching my footfall to ensure I don't slip on the steep cliffs under the weight of my pack. I've zippered my waterproof up to my nose, and I keep my head facing downwards, away from the wind-driven rain. The smock is doing its job well, despite my body being wet underneath. Within the drudge of all this, I laugh to myself that I might start steaming in a while.

It's only Day Three, but the effort and challenge during this storm is intense. The humidity feels high and my chest bubbles and wheezes as I ascend and descend every hill and valley. *What am I doing?* At least Ross is with me on these few miles. I can't imagine doing it on my own. *Gah, it'll be a nightmare.* There's a sudden flip of nerves in the pit of my belly as I realise this will happen soon when Ross needs to drive home. He returns in a week and a half. Then it'll just be me and me, walking with me.

Heddon's Mouth gives us some brief respite. It's still raining hard, but the slight protection we gain from being in the valley means it's no longer driving straight into our faces. With no way to cross this gorge, we walk south, inland for half a mile. Further down, it's easy to cross over the stream and climb the bank up the other side. At the point where I'd cross and carry on and Ross would go back to the van, we stop and look at one another. We're both dripping with the knowledge that the weather dealt us an unfair card. "It's at least six miles back to the van," Ross estimates. "What do you wanna do?" He searches my face for clues for a plan. It's usually my schemes that we follow.

"There's a hotel a little further up this track. How about we treat ourselves to a room for tonight? We can dry ourselves out and have a lovely evening together, instead of being cramped up in the Bongo. What do you think?"

Ross smiles and nods. Though he says little, I recognise his look of approval. He's always willing to rough it when necessary, but where home comforts, tea or cake are involved, he's easily won over.

The rain still beats down with gusto as we reach the Hunters Inn. It's around 6.30 p.m. and the carrot of a warm bed, bath and hot food has propelled me up the track towards the pub. There's a peacock, sat on the veranda balustrade with its long, blue-green tail sweeping away behind it. His feathers are stuck tightly to his wet body, and I sense he's looking and feeling as forlorn as us.

What a relief to step in through that doorway. We wait as the lady behind the bar serves a customer, though it seems quiet in here for an early July evening. It's midweek and not yet the official summer holiday, which I keep forgetting as I've already left my school for the summer. Lucky me! The lady behind the bar turns to us with a kind smile. We must look so pathetic.

"Hello." She glances at our dripping clothing and bags. "How can I help you?"

"Hi, do you have any rooms for the night, please?" I ask.

"We do indeed." Turning to her computer screen, she gives us a breakdown of the tariff. My heart sinks at the prices. It's too expensive.

"I'm sorry. That's not affordable for us." I lower my head in disappointment as my hair releases another drip. It trickles its way down my neck and into a puddle that collects at the small of my back. "I'm doing a charity walk along the South West Coast Path, and I'm supposed to be camping ... but the weather tonight ..." I pause and look outside. The landlady's eyes follow my gaze, to the storm beyond the window, and without another word, her expression alters.

"Let me see what I can do," she says, leaving the bar area for a moment.

An older chap propping up the bar nearby had overheard our conversation.

"You wanna get yerselves on laterooms-dot-com," he suggests. "Book on there and you'll get a room here for little more than peanuts." Ashamed that a man twice my age is guiding me in the ways of internet hotel booking, I thank him graciously. I'd heard of people booking hotels online, but it's not something I'm familiar with. There's no access to the internet on my phone, but I had brought my new Kindle keyboard so I could write my blogs en route. It's still a faff, though. Nothing seems to allow me to get through to the sites easily, and the connection is always so slow.

It's not long before the woman returns.

"You can have a room – we're quiet tonight. We'll give you a fifty per cent discount. How does that sound?" I acknowledge my delight with multiple thanks, and we follow her up the stairs to our room. It seems decadent to be paying for accommodation on the third day, but I can see I'm going to have to ease my way into the absurdity of wet-weather walking. Still carrying my productive cough is another good reason to be in a warm bed and to enjoy the luxury of a bath. My chest will thank me. So will my feet.

A little later, downstairs in the bar, I'm working on writing up my day's blog, having connected to the pub's Wi-Fi. My phone buzzes on the table beside me and I see on the screen it's a text from my daughter:

Trying to ring you, Muvvy. Can't get through.

I look at how many bars are displayed and sigh. As suspected, it teeters between one and nothing. Signal down here in this combe is diabolical, and I wonder if Laura is managing okay without me.

At sixteen, Laura is sensible. She's not prone to wild parties and can cook. In her early years, I ensured I taught her how to keep herself fed with valuable cooking skills. I wanted her to fend for herself, to be self-sufficient if she headed off to university. The plan had always been that Ross would come to spend the first two weeks with me on the South West Coast Path. That would mean two weeks for Laura to undertake a rehearsal; a home-version test-run of what it might be like to live independently.

Since the initial organisation of this walk, there has been a slight change of plan. Lorraine, my biological mother, has lived in the United States since 1976. She is moving back to the UK this summer. With her, she is bringing her beloved Australian Cattle Dog, Rosie, and her three-legged ginger fluff cat, Rudy. Her date of arrival is the eleventh of July. With me travelling to Minehead on Saturday the second, this now leaves just nine full days for Laura to be on her own. We have some super neighbours who are quietly looking out for her well-being. She also knows she can go to them if she needs anything at all. I have faith that she can do this. It's almost like an adventure for Laura, and a safe one too.

Lorraine needs some time to search for somewhere to live, so she's going to stay with us for a while. Well, not with me exactly, as I'll be walking until the third week of August. But she'll be with Laura in the beginning and then with Ross too, when he arrives back from leaving me at whatever part of the coast I've reached by that point. Hopefully, everyone will have settled into their new routine by the time I return.

I set the Kindle back down on the table, and leave Ross to enjoy his pint, and wander over to the bar. "Would it be possible to use your landline, please? My daughter's been trying to call me on my mobile and I don't have enough signal." The lady smiles at my plight and lifts over a large telephone, pushing it towards me across the bar. As I hear myself saying the words to her, I can't help thinking it sounds like a feeble, First World problem.

"Of course. Take as long as you need." I thank her and dial home, looking forward to my catch-up with Laura, making sure that her post-GCSE days of free time are going well.

The phone rings multiple times, and just as I think I'm going to have to leave a voicemail for her, Laura picks up. "Hello?" It's so good to hear her voice.

"Laura, hi! It's Mum. How are you getting on, my love?"

"Hi Muvvy, I'm fine. I've been trying to call you. It's a bit quiet here, but I made myself eggs Florentine today for tea, and there'll be some left for tomorrow too." She sounds chuffed with herself, although there seems to be a "but" follow-up that isn't quite forming for her.

Eggs Florentine is my signature dish at home and Laura's absolute favourite – next to avocados. I have a theory: if I keep dishing up regular variety with the favourites thrown in for added excitement, then we have a contented teenager. Mostly. If only food was the straightforward answer to balancing and navigating those formative years! I think I've been fortunate, to be honest. Laura doesn't smoke, has tried alcohol to excess once (I don't think she'll be doing that again in a hurry) and has strong opinions about drug use. There are times I have wished she would go out more and let her hair down – obviously not with drugs – but I can't push her to go out with friends if she's not ready. She'll branch out soon enough, I'm sure, and will find her own way, in her own time. I'm happy for her to go at her own pace.

"Are you sure you're okay, Laura? You sound a little on edge?"

"Muvvy, I tried to call you today." There's a pause.

"Sorry, yeah. I saw that in your text. The signal is bad here and I can't make any calls at all. Oh, and the weather's been awful today too, so I had to keep my phone stashed away in a dry bag. What did you want to talk to me about? Is everything alright?"

"Yeah, I'm okay. I'm managing fine. Mum ..." She takes a breath. I'm not sure what's coming next.

"Great-Nan died last night."

It takes a second for Laura to utter those five words, those monstrous, ugly yet heartfelt words. My heart drops like a glass elevator, shattering into a pit sixty floors below me. Stunned, I try to say something, but no words come out.

"Mum, are you okay? I'm so sorry, Mum ... Mum?" She sounds pretty together about it all.

It's difficult but I try to remain quiet as I whimper into the phone, "No, no. Nan ..." I heave out a small sob but stifle it, as I'm sitting at the bar, with the pub landline still clutched to my ear. This isn't a private space. I urgently need somewhere I can go. A space where I can cry in whatever way feels natural.

It's a while before I can whisper a reply. "I just wanted Nan to hang on." More tears fall. "No. I willed her to wait." I shake my head and my voice trembles. "I wanted to see her before I left."

"Great-Nan would have known that, Mum. She knows." Laura gives me the time to cry quietly into the phone. She is so good with me, calming and comforting. Within that moment alone, my teenage daughter grew up. She had taken control of a situation that no teenager should ever have to do. Being the recipient of bad news is one thing. To be the deliverer of bad news is on another level, way above anything I'd ever had to deal with at Laura's age.

Ross notices the wipe of my eyes and the sleeve across my nose and knows something is wrong. He picks up a box of tissues and brings them over, placing them in front of me without a word. "How did she die?" I finally bring myself to ask. As I wait for Laura's response, I see Ross's eyebrow raise in concern and then a wave of realisation draws across his face.

"She had another stroke."

"Oh ..." My eyes stream long and steady now. I snivel some more before managing a coherent reply.

"We were expecting it could happen, but without a crystal ball, no one knew when it would be. I should have gone to see her. I should have gone ..."

"Mum, you didn't go but you haven't been well, and Nan would have understood that."

"Thanks, my love. I know."

"I'll let you know if I hear anything about the funeral."

"Please. I'd appreciate that." There's a still moment between us. "Laura ..."

"Yes?"

"I love you."

"Love you too."

Proud of my daughter but still wracked with intense guilt for not visiting Nan, I say goodbye to Laura and promise to call when I have a better signal. Retreating to our room, Ross runs me a bath filled with bubbles from the complimentary toiletries supplied by the inn. I lie there, looking in disbelief at my tired feet. I wiggle my toes. They hurt, yet they still move me. Lifting my knees, I notice the reddening from the hot water. The hot water that would usually soak away all my aches and pains, but today, as much as I wish, it can't soak away my emotional pain. It sears, it hurts, and it stings. But I deserve it. I should have visited.

Ross wraps a fluffy bath sheet around me, scoops me out of the bath, dries me down, and leads me back into the bedroom. He pulls his T-shirt off and slips it over my head to wear as a nightie, and silently we clamber into bed. As he holds me, I allow the tears to fall. Without warning, the weight of exhaustion takes over, and the night pulls its comforting veil temporarily over my grief.

A Hangman Farewell

7

The valley track at Heddon's Mouth soon leads to a steep climb, back up to the coast path. I am sorry to leave the Hunters Inn this morning, the warmth of the bed and a dry refuge away from the rain, which still falls heavily. Not dissimilar to how my heart feels today. Ross and I part company where I will head upwards and westwards, with my destination aim today around Ilfracombe. He's going to walk uphill from the valley, with the plan to head east, back to where he parked the van yesterday. The severity of our climbs will be the same, just in opposite directions.

On higher ground, it's strange to look back and see my six foot two inches of man reduced to a tiny dot in the distance. Just large enough for us both to raise a hand at each other and wave a fleeting farewell, for now. Although it's not a last goodbye, it sets my emotions off for another session. Nan is gone. I allow the tears to fall again as I heave myself up the steps in this unkind weather. It's all so fitting, given the circumstances. Even the weather is punishing me for not visiting.

As I weep and walk, I push my poles hard into the path around the steep steps to avoid slipping. A shape on the ground catches my eye – it's a rose-coloured rock with flecks of creamy quartz shimmering through its curves and dips. I stop and bend down to pick up the stone and am surprised to see that it is a perfectly formed heart shape. With a rush of spontaneity, I call up into the sky. "Nan, today this walk is for you!"

The terrain means I must concentrate hard on my footwork, but a few paces onwards I can hardly believe my eyes. There on the ground in front of me is another stone, this time more tan in colour than the previous find. Astonished that here, at my feet, is a second perfectly formed heart-shape rock. What serendipity. "Thank you, Nan!" The tears keep coming in waves and I allow them to. Sometimes they flow as nothing more than a trickle, yet in the next moment, my face is awash with a spring tide. This is medicine. This is what I need. I cry for my Nan, who had loved life, loved people, and loved the opportunity to make people smile with her chatter, her warmth and her incredible handicraft skills. I cry for me, for my inability to see Mary one last time, and the guilt that, although I know will eventually fade, still at this moment is a tough pill to swallow. And I cry for Lorraine, for her mother's untimely death.

Lorraine's decision to move back to the UK after thirty years spent in the US came about for a variety of reasons. She wanted to be closer to me and Laura, as the annual visits for a month every year were becoming more difficult for her as the years progressed. She also wanted to be closer to her mother, to help her sisters with her care and for the chance to say goodbye in person when the time came. Tomorrow is Lorraine's birthday and in just four days' time, she will have at last arrived after a long flight to resettle in the UK permanently.

Despite wishing *if only Nan could have hung on for a few more weeks*, of course I know this was unrealistic. From Lorraine's point of view, however, I deeply wanted Nan to have lived for just a few more days. It's been a year since Lorraine held her in her arms and hugged her. With an extra four days, Lorraine could have shared that closeness with her mum once again. But life doesn't work like that. It wasn't to be and so I cry some more.

After much ascent, and a little more cloud lift, I reach a junction in the path. The stormy sky offers a superb backdrop to a dry-stone wall and weather-beaten fingerpost, dripping with lichen. It begs for a photograph. Now I'm up on the high ground, I'm no longer struggling to clamber up that muddy path, over the slippery stones. I'm grateful the weather has eased up a little too.

The staggering synchronicity of nearly five miles of walking, coming to terms with Nan's death on the fifth of July, and accomplishing 555 metres of ascent, brings me to the hill known as Great Hangman. Near to the summit, at just 318 metres above sea level, there is an enormous cairn: a conical pile of stones and rocks, hurled one on top of the other by hundreds, maybe thousands, of walkers over the years. Instinct kicks in and I know what I must do. I unzip my hip belt and pull out the rose-coloured heart rock that I'd found while spilling tears on the way up. I throw it into the air towards the cairn. "Here you go, Nan. This one's for you!" The rock lands a little off-centre of the cairn but tumbles its way to rest neatly in a gap that appears perfectly reserved for my heart-shaped stone. As it lands, a skylark soars, twittering and calling with its shrill, undulating notes. On and on it continues its song as I walk. It hovers and follows high above me, offering me a sense of consolation and support. The skylark will always remain with me, serving as a reminder of my Nan's spirit and her absolution of my guilt for not visiting her before her death. With a deep sigh, I make peace with myself and promise never to allow that weight of regret over not visiting Nan to haunt me. Instead, I vow to celebrate her life with my adventure.

Although I'm feeling more uplifted now, my eyes are smeary and wet. My nose is soggy too, so I retrieve my cotton hankie from my waterproof smock to mop myself up. With the hankie in my hand, I acknowledge the good advice once given to me. Tissues would have disintegrated by this point with the extent of the rain I'd encountered so far. I'm grateful I listened.

At the summit of the hill, I come to a crossroads on the path. It sits in a wide-open space, and there's a couple standing at the point where the tracks meet. They're eager to talk with me. I gauge they're in their late fifties, perhaps early sixties.

"Hello, you look like you're going a long way?" says the woman.

"I guess I am," I say, finding my first smile of the day. "I'm walking the South West Coast Path."

"The *whole* thing?" The man looks incredulous.

"Yes, but I'm very slow."

"Oh, but that's admirable. How long do you think it will it take you?"

"I've given myself eight weeks as I've done nothing like this before. I hope it'll only be seven, though."

"We've walked sections of it, but never managed the whole path, though we'd love to, wouldn't we, Peter?" the woman says.

"Yes, most definitely, one day," he replies with enthusiasm.

"So why are you walking, and why this path?" asks the woman.

"Several reasons, really. It's my big birthday walk – I turned forty a couple of months ago and I wanted to find a challenge to mark it. It's an opportunity to raise some money for charity, and it's a path I've wanted to do for years. I never thought I'd do it, but here I am."

"That can't be easy," she replies. "I mean, fundraising, mainly. The walking is difficult when the weather is like it has been, but the money side of things is even tougher."

"Oh gosh, yes, I'm with you on that!" I say, nodding vehemently. I share about the organisation of the auction and ball and my relief of postponing until November.

After a few more minutes of chatting, the woman says, "I'm Jenny, by the way."

"Hi, I'm Zoe, and I think I caught earlier you're Peter?" I ask her companion.

"I am," he replies. "And you are an inspiration to us, young lady."

"Thank you." I grin softly, tipping my head down with a shyness of the compliment I'm not sure how to handle. *That's something to work on, Wath.*

They spend a good ten minutes with me, wanting to know more about my charities, my family, and my fitness. They ask all their questions with a genuine interest. I say nothing about Nan's death, the skylark, or my tears, but perhaps they can read an expression in my face or my body language that needs no words. I leave them with a lightness in my step and continue onwards to the smaller sibling of Great Hangman.

Little Hangman rises above Combe Martin. As I walk, breathing in the view and the fresh air, I scold myself for not sharing more with Peter and Jenny.

Ready to descend back into civilisation again, I make a beeline for the public loos in the car park at the bottom of the hill. I've not quite reached the toilet block when I recognise the blue fleece, blonde hair and proper walking trousers of Jenny, and the tall security of Peter. How could this be? What are the chances? Without doubt, fate has stepped in. I skip my way over to them with a broad grin, calling out "Hellooo!" Their smiles tell me how delighted they are to see me again too, and we spend at least another fifteen minutes chatting. Once again, I have a second chance, and I know what I must do. "I didn't tell you something back there, but I wanted to thank you for taking the time to talk to me earlier."

"Oh, that's no problem," Jenny said, sensing there was more.

"I learnt about my grandmother's death yesterday." My head drifts downward again, and my eyes well up. I feel that sharp sting of emotion spreading through my chest. *Come on, Zoe, you've got this.* "Just before we started talking, I'd had a skylark following me and calling overhead. I found it comforting, you know, in the way people do after someone has died, with other birds. Robins and whatnot."

Jenny reaches out and squeezes my arm before taking my hand in hers. "Sometimes, Zoe, you'll find yourself in the right place at the right time, for reasons you'll maybe never understand."

"And you don't have to, that's the beauty of it," Peter chips in, a kind expression on his face.

"Thank you. Thank you both. All the time I walked down that hill, I wished I'd told you about how much you lifted my spirits and had helped me. I was so cross with myself for not being brave enough." Looking at them both directly, eye to eye, I say, "This was meant to be. Thank you."

Sharing a warm, meaningful hug with a pair of strangers who I may never meet again is such a healing and poignant experience. It's so powerful that I almost forget I need the loo. By the time I return, their car has gone, and I know that's the last time I'll see them. The way they made me feel, however, will stay with me for many years to come. Kindness, care, consideration and empathy. The value of these gifts is priceless, and I feel richly rewarded this morning as I continue my journey back up and out of Combe Martin.

Westwards out of the village, it's not long before I reach Watermouth Castle, a place I've visited twice before; once at around seventeen years old, with my school friend Jude. We spent a long weekend down in North Devon and Jude had just passed her driving test. I still had my L-plates. She drove her mother's Vauxhall Chevette, in an early shade of duck-egg blue, down to Devon from North Somerset. We had so much fun, being independent and sharing stories together. A test of our ability to handle difficulties came when the car's exhaust pipe broke on the way down. On arriving in Barnstaple, we had to find a mechanic (and some money) to get it fixed. At Watermouth Castle, we both indulged in some immaturity, with the skill and flair that only a late teen can pull off. I visited the second time with Laura's father, my then new fiancée, soon after our engagement. I'd love to revisit the place and maybe recapture some of that spirit of fun. At twenty, when I was first engaged, it had only been three years since visiting this place with Jude ... but now, at forty, it seems a lifetime ago. It's a momentary treasure to lose myself in these castle memories.

The coastline around Ilfracombe is not disappointing. The shapes of the rocks, the headlands and the inlets are spectacular. Dramatic folds, the tumbling and chaotic nature of the edges, sharp at intervals and frozen for an eternity. Ledges, filled with seabirds, frothy waves spitting at the foot of each cliff face or cove. The rain has subsided, and the cloud has lifted, and so I enjoy taking many photographs along the prom. I can't help but laugh at the funny way Dad pronounces it "Ill-frack-com-beee", and whenever I spot a sign bearing the town's name, I repeat it in my head. If the "coast" is clear, I might even say it out loud. "Ill-frack-com-beee!" I shout out ... usually in my best West Country accent.

The Victorian buildings of Ilfracombe remind me of other seaside towns I know well. Grey stone houses with large bay windows and colourful doors. I remember other coastal towns where I've lived, worked and played, in North Somerset, Bristol and Dorset. These places are also a haven for such elegant buildings. Often split into flats, the multiple-occupancy or flat-life telltale signs are consistent, as I see here in Ilfracombe. Victorian elegance discarded alongside the excessive abundance of rubbish bins; swathes of odd fabric remnants, or even better, an old duvet cover hung at a greasy window; a box of empty beer cans dumped outside. In fairness, it's not all like this. Just an observation that I've unconsciously made over the years, while summing up my enjoyment of architecture.

This theme of architectural appreciation continues as I head towards the local theatre. I find The Landmark's conical twin roofs impressive, even if the modernist styling is heavy in its use of concrete. Visible from a distance and aptly named, it is a landmark indeed. A new walking game, experimenting with the shapes in my imagination, I reach the conclusion that the roofs remind me of Bill and Ben, the Flower Pot Men. I wonder if their redecoration could become a new, giant installation artwork for a future promotion of the theatre and the town. Ilfracombe. "Ill-frack-com— Ross!" He appears from around the side of the theatre. It's so good to see him. I sink into the familiarity and reassurance of his long arms that I'm sure could wrap themselves around me twice over. He's parked the van just the other side of the theatre and suggests we should find somewhere to eat. We can scout out a place to park the van to sleep for the night later.

In a nearby pub, with a beer and a plate of hot food, we talk about our experiences of the day. "Didn't you see me trying to wave at you to get your attention?" I'm puzzled but have to wait for the follow-up as Ross finishes a long, drawn-out chew of his food. "A buzzard attacked me today."

Setting my fork down for a moment, I look at him in astonishment. "What do you mean?" I know it's a bird of prey, but I'd not heard of a buzzard attacking a human before.

"Bloody lucky I had my Beverly Emu on." He touches the top of the brown leather bush hat, placed on the seat beside him. "It just came out of nowhere. It swooped twice, and I shouted at it. Thankfully, it flew away. Excellent protection, that hat."

"Blimey, you were lucky you didn't overbalance up there," I say, thinking of how steep and narrow that path had been approaching Heddon's Mouth. I'm partly relieved I hadn't been with him when it happened. I'm not sure how I would have reacted, although I'll admit to being a little disappointed to have missed out on the action.

With my belly full and rehydration levels topped up, I sit there, content that my miles for today are done. Despite only banking twelve miles, I reckon all things considered I've not done bad. I'm still coughing, and it was a rough start, mentally and emotionally. Doing twelve miles had to be okay, and I know I need to learn to be kind to myself. If nothing else, Nan, the skylark, Jenny and Peter had all taught me that much. Tomorrow will be another day and I hope to start with a lighter heart and better weather than I did this morning.

8

Caught in the Act

The path continues its theme of breathtaking, rugged and rocky coastline. Turning a corner, I gasp at the peachy-cream-coloured jaggedness of Morte Point rocks. This sharp headland, rising from the sea like a beast, blocks the intensity of the wind. It soon hits me head-on the moment I clamber around the rocks to the other side. The winds bluster around me, and I'm sent into a panic. It's a fear of being blown off the ledge and into the sea below. I know deep down that I should capture this moment, otherwise I have nothing to share but the same old pretty land and seascapes. As I'm collecting sponsorship, people need to see the daring extent of the challenge and the tough stuff I'm facing. I must at least take a photograph of Morte Point. The severity of the rock formations above my head is out of this world, but it would mean some careful, one-handed tactics with my camera bag and walking poles. These rocks look slippery, meaning I can't dig the poles in to anchor myself, either.

With great care, I pull out the camera and turn my body. My movements are slow and considered, nothing sudden. All the while, I hold on so tightly to a rock on my left, my knuckles turn white. If I turn to look right, I'll see the sea. In fact, it's behind me, to my right and ahead of me. But I don't want to look out there for too long; I'm already feeling vulnerable now. As if sensing my fear, the wind continues to push me around, teasing me with boisterous playfulness.

Just as I line up the frame, a child of about seven or eight years old hurtles around the rocks towards me. She steps forward as if to climb the rocks below me. "Don't go that way," I squeak, trying not to show the fear in my voice. Inside, I'm freaking out.

"Walk above. Here," the mother calls out as she also turns the corner, holding the hand of a much smaller child. She points to an area of rocks above where I stand, while I'm feeling pathetic, holding on for dear life against the wind. The child is so petite, she looks like she might take off like a kite. That deadly cocktail of mother's instinct, fear and self-preservation torments me. I battle with it as I watch the family carry on to safety around the rocks and back to a proper path, so I look away. The sick feeling of knowing I am out of my comfort zone rapidly changes to euphoria, but only once I too am back on the terrain that I've now grown accustomed to. At last, I can look back and realise it wasn't so dangerous. If that family could do it, so could I. At some point I must teach my brain to understand this.

The appropriately named Windy Cove soon leads me beyond the excitement of Morte Point and into Woolacombe. I could have easily carried on from here, but trying to find suitable spots for Ross to park the campervan and meet me is a daily conundrum. I also don't want to keep him hanging around anywhere for too long, as this doesn't seem fair either. So after a little over seven and a half miles today, I stop, with a greater piece of me hoping and hankering for more miles tomorrow.

With a windy night, I didn't sleep so well in the van. We probably could have found a more sheltered spot, but this lay-by is closer to the coast road where Ross will drop me off in a while. I fumble around for my belongings, trying to organise my life and ensure I'm wearing or at least carrying everything I need for the day. It's a mammoth task. If I had a little more space and I didn't need to worry about waking my Sleeping Beauty, then it wouldn't be so hard. Finally, after bootfuls of faffing and a decision to find breakfast somewhere, by 9.30 a.m., I am ready to go. Ross, a little bleary-eyed and more quiet than usual, pours himself off the Bongo bed, straight outside and back around the van into the driver's seat. The configuration of the central console means there's no way to step from bed to front seat without having to go outside first.

With my Day Six breakfast consumed, I'm fuelled and feeling more able to meet the day head-on. Ross drops me back down at the public loos on the beach where I'd finished walking yesterday. The set-off from Woolacombe is easier on the body today as I follow above a long stretch of beach. This high track overlooking the sands is easy and gives me plenty of space and thinking time, though not about anything in particular. It's simply that I no longer need to focus on every step. With uneven terrain, I'm always looking for slip hazards, like roots and rocks. Even navigating my way around a town is hard work. Right now, I can focus wholly on my inner self, listening to the external sounds of wind, waves, and the occasional car in the distance. I guess this is what they call mindfulness.

The two and a half miles of glistening, picture-perfect beaches of Woolacombe and Putsborough Sands below me are just the medicine I need today. I had started, just as I'd wished for, with a lighter heart this morning. Six days in, however, and I have learnt such a lot already. So much so, I now sense that something isn't right about the way I handle each day. I crave and yet lack a routine. I know I need to pay attention to this, but with Ross around, it's difficult to adapt.

The headland of Baggy Point feels like I've reached an invisible milestone. I smile to myself, noting another minor accomplishment.

The tall post set in the grass on the top of the cliff looks weathered and battered, a bit like me. I'm not sure of its purpose, to be honest. I walk around the mast to inspect it close up and decide it must be some kind of shipping marker. Yet another turning point to tuck into my bag of miles walked. This one, higher than Morte Point but easier, sends me inland towards Croyde.

My phone rings as I approach the village. "I've booked us into the Old Chapel B&B for tonight," Ross says. "Fancy finishing a bit earlier?" My heart does a little skip but sinks at the same time. Of course I want to spend this time with my love, but I also feel like my days are dwindling away too. Like unmonitored money in a bank account, before long, it's gone. Time is a concern for me as I worry it will run out and I won't finish the walk. I know I have extra time as I'd had that gift of being able to start earlier. With eight weeks available to walk the path, in the planning stages it seemed plenty. At this rate, after six days and only covering fifty-five miles, there's a real risk I might struggle to complete the full 630 miles. To complete the path in eight weeks, I need to cover just over eleven miles per day. My past six days have given me an average of only nine miles per day. It may not sound much, but that's an enormous difference when you add it up at the end of the week.

"Of course, thank you!" I push those worries about not making the end of the path to one side. I'd figure that out and make up the miles lost later.

Ross is waiting for me at the dunes where the burrows meet the beach, and we walk back into Croyde village together. It's close to 3 p.m. so we have time to spare. We can check in at our accommodation and if there's a bath, I can soak my body and my sore feet. I wish above everything else that if I have lost miles today, it would be to spend quality time with Ross. And to have a bath. It would be worth it if I could have these two things.

Sure enough, the bed and breakfast is exactly the tonic we need. Time to spend together after a week of me walking and Ross following along in the van. Although we'd had that unplanned stay in the Hunters Inn a couple of nights ago, it wasn't quality time for us. The news of Nan's death had hung heavy over us both. Although the tears of grief filled every corner of the room, finding ourselves in "proper" accommodation that dismal night had been a blessing. There's no doubt about that. This quaint little place will soothe our souls and bring us closer together. A springboard for me to take off again tomorrow morning, knowing that both of us will leave refreshed, relaxed, and loved just a little more.

The morning arrives, and as hoped, Ross and I have enjoyed a close connection again. Contented, and having consumed a full English and all the works, I feel less inclined to head off for a day of walking. It's an odd place to find myself in, but I'm stuck both ways. If I sleep in the van, I can't get off early because there's no routine and I don't want to wake my partner. If we stay in a B&B, we have to wait for breakfast to be served. Once we're finished up and ready to go, it's often 9.30 a.m. or later. I can't have it all, I know that. Last night was lovely. Sleeping in a comfy bed, spending time together and enjoying a bath has soothed all my aching muscles, not to mention quelling our need for intimacy.

Destination Braunton today. With a quick scout at the map, I see the terrain will be less tiresome on the legs, with much more flat work to do. It's only the small climb out of Croyde that will give my legs any hills to conquer. It'll be level between here and Westward Ho! As the crow flies, there are few miles for me to cover. On closer inspection of the route though, I can see there are multiple reasons for the long, drawn-out distance over the next couple of days. I'll have to navigate all the wiggles of the two rivers, Taw and Torridge, and then I spot there's an RAF base at Chivenor to walk around. The marshes have also created an obstacle that the South West Coast Path couldn't bulldoze through, nor, I'm sure, would the planners have wanted to.

As I walk, I realise how lucky I am. My feet may be sore right now, but this walk touches me on so many other levels. The physicality of being outside, observing the landscape and meeting the people. It's a powerful thought to know that in adding to my life story, I have become a part of its history. I love that it meanders with care through such a diverse range of terrain and environments, too. I know those who maintain the path give much consideration to ensure minimum impact on habitats and the places in which we walk. The opportunity to experience all these different places first-hand is an utter gift, however brutal it feels in the moment.

In the way I find I'm learning about this long-distance walking thing, in a sniff, I swing from mellowed acceptance and appreciation into a desperate longing for it all to be over. The old military road, known as the American Road, is hard on my feet. Although wide and endlessly straight, small rocks litter the ground ahead. If I don't pay close attention to where I'm walking, I could twist an ankle, or worse. It never seems to end, but at last, after almost two miles, the terrain changes and I'm off the tedious "road to nowhere". Instead, I move up onto a breakwater that edges the bank of the River Taw. I look down to the water. With the tide out, it's as though someone has pulled a plug at the other end. The steep-sided river has drained to mostly mud, with nothing more than a shallow trickle left in the bottom for a river. It makes for an interesting walk, high above the boats precariously balanced in the Taw sludge.

A left turn now sends me wandering up yet another tributary river: the Caen. Sounds French if you ask me ... I reach Velator Quay, where I see many boats moored, some tipped at strange, acute angles, resting in the mud. It brings me out onto the road and where I can now text Ross to let him know he'll be able to meet me. Thankfully, that's more miles than yesterday with nine bagged, but to be honest, I'm happy to finish after the tedium of those long, flat tracks.

The South West Coast Path has shared its route with the Tarka Trail since Lynmouth. From Braunton, I'll share my path with a cycle track, taking me through Barnstaple, Instow, Bideford, Northam and Appledore, primarily on a disused railway line. It's then on to Westward Ho! This will be a super-wiggly route and could really mess with my head. The map shows me multiple points where the opposite banks across the rivers Taw and Torridge are only whistling distance apart. Yet, it's going to take me two, maybe three days to navigate this tangle of footpaths, towns and rivers. I'll have to pull out every trick in my bag to avoid any internal tantrums. *Don't think about it, Wath. Enjoy the surroundings.*

The Tarka cycle-track-cum-footpath is sometimes narrow in places and with vegetation growing up either side, I'm aware of the need to keep an eye and ear out for cyclists. I follow the razor-wire fencing of RAF Chivenor while humming various tunes to myself, and then pop out beside the River Taw, on my way to Barnstaple. The boats rest awkwardly in the mud, awaiting their next floating on the incoming tide. Although it's a tarmac trail and not great for sole comfort, I'll admit to enjoying the ease of the terrain and watching out for the whispers of railway history. Stone bridges now wrapped thick with ivy, spanning what would have been the track in its heyday. Signals, old gradient signs, crossing gates. It keeps my mind busy.

At Barnstaple, it's a good time to stop and pick up some snacks. Inside the shop, I unclip my hip and chest belts and carefully swing off the pack, using one knee to ease it down to the floor. There's a pack-sized cubby hole beside the ice cream freezer which is a perfect place to stash it. I slide my poles behind, making sure they can't slip to the back of the freezer. That would be just my luck! Food bought and stuffed into my bag, I heave my pack back on, then note the raised eyebrows of the shop assistant and grin. "Just out for a stroll!" I nudge myself to pick up my poles and breathe in as I squeeze myself through the doorway, like that's going to make any difference.

The road becomes a bridge and I cross the river and continue up the other side. I've turned to walk in the opposite direction now – pretty much walking back along the route I'd just travelled, but now from the other side of the Taw. This Tarka version of the South West Coast Path maintains the narrow tarmac, although this time, I'm on a raised strip of bank between farmland and marsh. Beyond the marsh, to my right, the river continues to carve its deep shapes through the mud.

A predicament presents itself. I need the loo. I mean I *really* need to use the loo, big-style. I walk a bit, hoping I can encourage it to pass. I think of Ross's daughter, Lara. This is what she would call "baking it". I smile at the thought, but it's so uncomfortable I'm unable to distract myself for long. This bank, like a sea wall set out in the middle of nowhere with open landscape and water laid out ahead of me, features no bushes, trees or walls to hide behind. I might as well be on a stage. The best I can do when I realise I can hold on no longer is to clamber down off the raised path and head for a corner of a nearby marsh field. I'm grateful it's not too boggy and that no one is around. I prep my trowel and bag to carry out the paper. Mid-job, I hear an enormous whooshing sound and a deep, rumbling drone of an engine that fills my whole body. There's no escape. The sound comes closer, and yet glancing around me, trying to maintain my balance and a little dignity, I can't see where the noise is coming from.

In that last moment of a push towards feeling as free as a bird and ready to take on the day again, the wall of sound hits me head-on. It's now too late to react or hide, not that I could have found a hiding spot. If I stand to pull up my shorts, I'd bare all anyway. So I stay put, cowering on my haunches, looking like the metaphorical rabbit caught in the headlights. The RAF helicopter passes directly above me, so low I can hear the voices on board. The dread of my dilemma rushes through my legs and into my chest. Without the option of becoming invisible, I wish for the ground to swallow me, though preferably not into the hole I'm still hovering over! I'm sure that one day, I'll appreciate the hilarity of my timing. Right now, I shrink away with painful embarrassment. Without a doubt, I'll be the talk of the mess at Chivenor tonight.

Back in my stride again, I'm able to focus on noticing more. The trail is greener as the path keeps a greater distance from the mud-lined edges of the river. A repurposed building, from signal box into cycle-trail café, makes perfect sense, though it's not open for me today. I pass under a number of railway bridges and then through a short tunnel. I have a childlike wonder for tunnels, caves and cellars. I'm not sure what's so fascinating, but the variation in sights makes for an interesting walk along an otherwise flat and unremarkable terrain.

Someone has maintained the old signal box at Instow. The shiplap is spruced up with a lick of creamy apricot paint, while the building corners, which seemingly hold everything together, along with the windowsills, door and Instow sign, look smart in a shade close to British racing green. The broad brick chimney stack once kept the duty signalman warm, especially during night shifts. He might have made a hot mug of tea on the stove and dried his wet clothes after walking the track. To see it intact gives me a warm glow and a sense of familiarity. The Wathen family, steeped in railway ancestry, has blessed me with a profound fondness for all things relating to trains and old railways. This signal box, which sits beside the road, next to a traditional gated level crossing, is no longer in use, yet the wooden steps leading up to the door pull at me, making me wish I could enter and stop a while.

As signal boxes go, this one is small, not much bigger than a large garden shed. It's low, with only nine or so steps leading up to the door. Many boxes are built high, to give the signalmen a good vantage point of the trains and tracks. As I notice the elaborate pattern of extending bricks at the top of the chimney stack, it leads me back to a story Dad once told me. Aside from being a porter and a bellboy, my father used to be a signalman back in his early railway days. He took a nap while on a nightshift, waking to the sound of an explosion. He scrambled to his feet thinking a train had derailed outside, only to discover the remnants of his stoneware hot water bottle, shattered over the top of the stove and the surrounding floor. Over the years, Dad's shared many great stories like these.

Malcolm, Dad's brother, and also a signalman, had a keen interest in photography. Back in the fifties and sixties, photography would have been unusual for a signalman as it proved to be an expensive hobby. As a result, his unwavering passion and keen eye has preserved images of life inside a signal box, as well as visiting steam engines and station activity, for future generations to appreciate. Uncle Malc's photos are now on permanent display in the waiting room of a local heritage station in North Somerset. I take a photo of the signal box so I can show Dad on my return. He'll love this.

I leave the level crossing, where it feels like I should nearly be back on the coast again, yet my route takes me on another detour; this time, along the banks of the River Torridge. Beyond the assembly of small boat masts in the boatyard, I can see Appledore across the river, but I know with my slow pace it's still over three hours away on foot, at least. I follow the Tarka Trail and the river under the imposing concrete Torridge Bridge, towering high above me, carrying busy traffic on the Bideford bypass. I'm pleased to reach the historic Bideford Bridge. Long Bridge has twenty-four irregular arches, and an information leaflet tells me that it's one of the oldest medieval bridges in England. I remember Jude's mother, Meg, telling me why each of the arches is different. They acknowledge a different nobleman or family who had helped to fund the bridge. I appreciate little snippets like this. More photos taken, I move on as I must reach Westward Ho! today, which I think I've calculated right at eleven miles.

It's a slap-me-in-the-face-with-a-wet-fish moment. I have just under four miles of today's walking left before I reach Westward Ho!, but as I stand on the water's edge at Appledore, I'm shocked at the story the map tells me. Broadsands to Braunton, according to the map, is only one mile across the water. The route from Instow to Appledore, via the ferry, is less than half a mile, and Instow to Broadsands is only just over half a mile. It has taken me two days to walk a stretch of paths navigating three rivers that could have been twenty minutes with a pair of flippers. But I'm a purist and I'm here to walk the South West Coast Path. Nothing else. If I detour off the path or take a shortcut, then I'm not experiencing the path as I intended. So stick to the path I will, with no grumbles ... whether I walk river, forest, country park or coast. It's outdoors, and I know I'm one lucky lady to be here. That's what I keep reminding myself, even on the most painful of days.

I leave Appledore and immediately find myself on open, bumpy land, rather like a common. This is Northam Burrows Country Park, and I walk it reliving and laughing out loud at some special memories. It's where Jude allowed me an unofficial driving lesson in her mum's little blue Vauxhall Chevette. I'm not entirely sure if Meg would have appreciated knowing I was behind the wheel, as a learner driver. We were on private land and I'd already had a few lessons back home, so we thought it was okay. If I remember, though, it wasn't long before Jude insisted she took the helm again. Many years later, when I'd driven us both somewhere as adults, she ribbed me, saying, "Well, at least you're a better driver than you were at Northam Burrows ..." Over thirty years on, it's funny it still stirs up the same amusement.

My wanderings along memory lane drift into the background naturally as my thoughts turn to Lorraine. I skirt the edge of the country park across low dunes, well-nibbled grass and around small, water-smoothed boulders. The landscape has changed dramatically today, and I appreciate this view across the bay while considering the enormity of Lorraine's international move. The waves gently roll themselves to the shore with a steady rhythm. No more mud or river. No more industry or barracks. It's not a hot afternoon, but the sun is warm on my face, and I can tell this place would be a perfect spot for people to watch the sun set over the water.

After thirty-five years living in the United States, today is the day Lorraine lands back in the UK. I know how tired she must be and wonder how her animals have coped with the journey. My attention is caught momentarily by a man and a child skimming stones into the water. The child cheers as the man's stone dances over the swash of surf, and my heart gives a little cheer along with them. Ross gets on well with Lorraine, so I feel assured that her transition to resettling in the UK, temporarily via our home, will be a smooth process. Once I'm finished for the day, hopefully I can find somewhere with signal or at least a phone box, so I can check in with her and Laura this evening.

My thoughts cycle through the possibilities of getting back home so I can attend Nan's funeral. I still don't see how I can make it work. If it was within a day or two of Ross returning, I could ride back with him, but it's not likely to be. I can't afford to lose too many days of walking, in case I run out of time. People have sponsored me to walk the South West Coast Path, so I feel an obligation to ensure I achieve my goal. A momentary tightening of my gut lets me know I've acknowledged the pressure is on. I'm nine days into a 630-mile challenge and by the end of today, I'll have ticked off only eighty-five miles. Something is going to have to change. Even if I speed up, how can I lose whole days to say goodbye to Nan *and* still make it round to Poole before I go back to school in September?

I shake the problem out of my head for the time being as I focus on the approach to Westward Ho! With my day almost done at eleven miles, I amble past a gift shop, ice cream stand and modern seaside dwellings. The beach huts strive to look colourful in front of an unattractive holiday park. Northam Burrows painted a scene of natural beauty, but I'm not feeling the charm of Westward Ho! I find the last stretch of road that's suitable for our van to access and wait on the prom for Ross to collect me. Despite pushing the thoughts of Nan's funeral to the background, I think my head has closed the blinds to any urban aesthetic of interest around me. I can't help but go over the options again, even though it leaves me feeling discontented with the likely outcome, and unusually disconnected with my surroundings.

You'll work something out, Wath.

9

Imagination and Reverie

My dismal mood from the day before has lifted and my thoughts about Westward Ho! lacking interest are reset as soon as I see the red-brick derelict house. It dominates the clifftop, capturing my imagination in an instant. Ross drops me off on the prom for my tenth day. As I approach the building, situated right on the coast path, it sends an eerie shiver down my spine. The shape, location and condition are the epitome of a haunted house in a horror film. Yet there's something else about it. Its high wall bordering part of the garden features a wooden double door, sat underneath a mock pitched roof. It spells fairy tale, curiosity and a secret garden in my mind. Boards nailed up at all the lower-floor windows with the words "KEEP OUT!" daubed in blood-red paint make their bold message perfectly clear. A ladder set beside the western upper-floor window shows signs of unauthorised occupancy: a wine bottle on the sill and the sash window slightly open. I see a curtain twitching delicately in the morning sea breeze, and it makes me wonder if anyone is standing behind it.

This house, whatever its backstory, piques my interest. I want to go inside. I want to see for myself and imagine how the previous owners had once lived here. What was its purpose? Was it a grand residence for someone of notable fame? Or was it the setting of an infamous crime? Perhaps it had just been a hotel. Its double-fronted Victorian appearance with square bays, mock Tudor façade and a spooky attic dormer adds charm and character. So does the sponging in dirty engine oil, or that's what it looks like.

Render or tiles have fallen away to one side of the second-floor feature window, revealing the lath construction of the wall behind. There are at least eight or nine upstairs front windows. The feature window looks as though it may contain stained glass, or it's a vast amount of small, square leaded lights. I imagine a grand old staircase set behind. A further seven or eight tall, thin windows would have allowed light to flood the downstairs rooms, if not for the unwelcoming boards. Roof tiles have slipped or are missing altogether. The tall chimney stacks show no signs of emitting any smoke in recent times. In fact, the chimney pots are more like flowerpots with the allotment that now prospers well up there.

This derelict mansion, while on top of the charts in owning the cliffs, looks solemnly out to sea, as though it needs a friend. I hope it gets a new lease of life one day. I take a few more photographs to add to my rapidly increasing collection and then head up the hill. To begin with, it gently weaves me away from Westward Ho! but soon I am back into the land of steep cliffs and mini rollercoasters.

Hills like this are still tough for me. Fitness-wise, my legs are okay, but my chest holds me back. I've not needed to use my inhalers much, but I continue to rattle and cough occasionally, particularly in the mornings. I'm seeing signs of improvement, though, so I may send them home with Ross if I don't use them in the next few days.

This stretch of North Devon is not unfamiliar to me. I am filled with the anticipation of reaching Buck's Mills, the seaside hamlet in which Jude lived for a while, some years ago. She rented a clifftop cottage from the National Trust, with the beach and the sea as her back garden, accessed via a long slope down from the cottage.

As with my reminiscences of Watermouth Castle a few days ago, I guess I'm keen to relive my memories of coming to stay here with

Jude. We grew up together from the age of eleven, shared holidays and sleepovers, and have remained best of friends since.

I remember walking along what we called "Jude's beach", being excited by the waterfall cascading a constant stream of water from the cliff edge, at least twenty metres above us. It had carved a gully between the pebbles and rocks on the beach and found its way out to sea. Photo opportunities always pushed to their max, I remember clicking my Pentax S1a at pretty much every Kodak moment I spotted. Taking photos before they released digital cameras proved expensive for every thirty-six-exposure roll of film to be developed.

These memories of exploring my longest friend's beautiful beach and staying at her dreamy cottage warms my heart. Despite the gradients of the walk today, after just six and a half miles from Westward Ho! I realised with surprise that I have reached Buck's Mills already. Occupying my mind makes the time fly.

My heart sinks and memories shatter when I see how different Buck's Mills looks twenty years on. The shop is gone and almost every house is now a holiday let. The previous, visible character of the place has died, with each cottage looking clinical, like a show home. There's no sign of anywhere that's lived in, no pots or trays of flowers outside to be tended daily. Despite a few houses occupied with holidaymakers, it no longer feels welcoming.

It's a wake-up call for sure. For a moment I dither about whether I should take a photo of St John's Cottage, Jude's old place, so I could send it and show her where I'd been. She might be upset by how dead the place looks now. I decide that she probably already knows this anyway, with friends and old neighbours still living in the area, if not in the hamlet itself. I take a few pictures, tuck my camera back into its little bag on my hip belt and pause in front of the cottages just for the briefest time, to afford me the memories without having a camera held out in front of me.

My last memory of this place was of standing in the front garden of the cottage next door to Jude's. I look out over the steep cliff to the bouldery beach below and the expanse of sea beyond. The shed I'd stood next to all those years ago, while marvelling at the view and the proximity to this other world of sea and open adventures, is no longer there. In fact, it isn't so much that the shed had been taken down ... more to the point, that entire plot of garden no longer exists. I realise in horror that the shed, the garden and anything else that had once grown there or been placed there had in fact fallen away. It had succumbed to the dangerous power of the elements and the inevitable demise of the shrinking coastal fringes, because of erosion. I shudder, wondering how long it would be before these cottages of around a couple of hundred years in age could stand the test of time no more, lost at sea. Literally.

It's time to shift my head away from this reverie and concentrate once again on the path for today, where I know I'm still only averaging nine and a half miles per day. I spot a sign directing me out of Buck's Mills. It leads me up a sharp hillside track, with a thick bank of woods blanketing the cliff face, dropping away to my right.

I plant my focus firmly on getting myself to Clovelly, which I'm also looking forward to. The next four miles are predominantly through managed woodland, known as Hobby Drive. Created in the early 1800s, it gave employment for local soldiers returning from the Napoleonic wars while celebrating the artistic beauty of nature. Trees open up to tease me with occasional picturesque views of Clovelly Quay, but mostly I find myself preoccupied again with thoughts of Nan, Lorraine and Laura. How has Laura coped on her own? Lorraine will have arrived at our house by now, so Laura has company from here on. How is Lorraine feeling with the emotional weight of her mother's death and the overseas move tangled around her?

While I'm still sad, I don't have the urge to cry now, but I still feel the scrapings of concern reaching out for me. There is the guilt of not being there for Lorraine or for Laura. Should I have returned home immediately when Nan died? When would Nan's funeral happen? How would I get there? Until I know when the funeral is, I can't possibly make a plan so, as I keep doing, I push the heavy barrage of thoughts to the back of my mind but know that I must call Lorraine this evening as I hadn't managed to yesterday.

Walk. Absorb. Breathe. At last, Hobby Drive soothes my over-active brain. There's something about being outdoors that gives me a refreshing dose of thinking space that allows me room for alternative perspectives.

On reaching the top of the village, I find a shop and barrier where tickets are now purchased. I'd visited Clovelly many years ago. I don't remember it being such a vast tourist attraction, although there was a largish car park, even back then. I'm told by staff in the shop that as a coast path walker, I won't have to pay to continue through tomorrow. I have an ice cream craving needing attention, so after achieving over ten and a half miles today, I reckon I deserve to treat myself. With the chest infection and lack of experience, I've realised the importance of walking myself into it gently over these ten days.

Ross is waiting for me in the van, up in the village car park. "Hello you!" I hobble over and we greet with a big hug. "What have you been up to?" I dump my rucksack inside the side door of the van.

"I spent most of my day in Clovelly, people-watching on the beach and getting some great pics."

Ross has a posh digital SLR camera. God, I love that camera but wouldn't be able to carry anything like that while walking and hauling around the rest of my gear. The pack's heavy enough as it is. "I had the village cat come down to meet me. It took up residence in my camera bag. I didn't have the heart to shoo it away."

"Hah, that's funny. I'll bet it recognised Charlie's smell." Charlie was our gorgeous grey cat, but sadly, we had to have him put to sleep a few weeks back. It's the first time in nearly twenty years I haven't had a moggy around the house. I miss Charlie Barley, and I know Ross does too. I had never seen him cry until the day we said goodbye to that velvety fluffball of love and attitude.

"Any news on Lorraine?" I ask him.

"Yes, she's busy settling herself in at the house. She's pretty jet-lagged but trying not to sleep much during the day."

"That's good. I'll call her this evening if I've got enough signal."

Despite just devouring an ice cream, after all these miles I've been developing even more of an appetite than usual. I'll admit to owning a pretty good appetite as it is. The front passenger seat beckons me, so I tip myself into the van and look over at Ross with a beaming grin. "I'm famished. Let's find somewhere to eat, my love."

"Yep." He smiles and nods. "And I can show you my pics over grub, too." He turns on the ignition and as we drive, with him concentrating on the road, I steal a few glances his way, losing myself in his presence. I love that we both share a keen interest in photography. I love that he enjoys walking. I love his bony wrists that connect to his large hands that have full control of that steering wheel. I love the flecks of grey that pepper his short, dark cut. I love his quiet temperament that requires only a nod or a smile for me to know what his intention is, and I love that he is so supportive of me doing this walking challenge. How lucky and loved I feel.

In this personal moment of quiet adoration, a wave of emotion kicks back at me. In just two and a half days, he'll be gone, and I'll be doing this walking thing on my own for another month. With a deep breath, I stifle the tears and stroke the back of his head. I try my hardest to ignore the pounding pain radiating through my feet. Ross turns to me briefly and a small glimmer of upturned lips stretches around his mouth before he turns back to focus on the road ahead.

10 Satish and June

The rain falls and once again the walk claws at me more like a chore to be dealt with than a delight. The departure from Clovelly this morning exacerbates this even further. I encounter a large herd of cattle blocking the path, assembled like an army sheltering under the trees. Some look like a rare breed, with scary, long, sweeping horns. After taking photos from a distance and swearing a few times under my breath, I decide to take the easier option. I walk up a slope into the cows' field, where these bloody bovine blighters should have been. Fingers crossed there will still be a way back down to my route from up here. I'm certain I'm not the only walker who's had this problem. It looks like these animals are especially familiar with using this part of the National Trail as their regular drying room.

As the rain lessens, I reach an unusual wooden shelter with a wide roof. It boasts exquisitely carved supports and centre post, not unlike a carved totem. The pavilion is a perfect place for me to stop and strip off my waterproofs – I'm overheating. As I repack my bag, a man, out on a day walk, heads past me and I waste no time in asking him to take my photo. He's happy to oblige. It's occurred to me I have so many photographs of pretty landscapes, the sea, cliffs, and even this shelter. Except for a handful of photos that Ross has, there are few pictures of me from this trip. I'll need images about the walk for the school assemblies ready for my return.

I chatted to Lorraine and Laura last night. They're both doing fine, though as Ross said, Lorraine is super tired. I think she's on overdrive, organising her space in the family room, which will be her bedroom for the coming weeks, and working on creating a routine for the animals. She also confirmed the date for Nan's funeral. I'll give the logistics some thought, but I still can't get my head around leaving the path and finishing in time.

The coastline takes my breath away now, in every sense of the term. I'm coughing less, but these hills take the definition of "steep" to the extreme and make me wheeze. Despite this, while the route is demanding, the view is equally spectacular. I want to keep taking pictures, to capture a permanent record of every detail I see. Sometimes I just can't stop myself. I'm mesmerised by the rock formations and the ruggedness of this part of North Devon.

I reach a hill where I need to descend. My head fills with uncertainty. *Damn, that's impossible!* In a slight panic, I scour the area around Mouth Mill and the mess that was once the coast path steps, now given way to the elements. I see no alternative route down. *Shit, you think you can do that? Well, here goes.* With my walking poles gripped firmly and pressed solid into the ground, I descend slowly, making sure of every single footfall. With deep breaths, I concentrate hard while trying to ignore the pulsing adrenalin ramped up to its highest level.

In my favour, the terrain is now more damp earth than gritty. If dry, it's the stuff I know my boots would slide across, but with the morning's rain, it's holding well. In the usual way, I'd never have attempted this on my own, but here I am, with no choice. I can't head back, and I'd have so much to lose, including my pride, if I did. I feel the quiver of exertion and fear in my thighs, but once I reach the foot of the hill, I turn and look back up at the severity of the path. Yessss! *Bloody hell, Wath, look at that.* I gawp in amazement ... at it and at myself. *You did it. Carrying a heavy pack, you did it. Why the hell didn't you take a photo coming down?* I heave a sigh of relief and take the photograph from the bottom instead to evidence my success.

Something about that struggle and the subsequent feeling of achievement injects a lightness into my head. This walk conceals an unexpected healing magic. The concerns of the previous day and the grief of losing Nan fade as my focus is finely tuned into survival mode, looking after my body, and the appreciation of each new stretch of path ahead. It's not that I don't care. It's more that I can't look after myself if I'm not in the moment. In doing so, my head readjusts.

More of my squeals and buzzing with all the joy of a child comes when a short distance on, at Windbury Point, I have my first sighting of a dolphin. *Woweeee!* Then I see another and another. They leap from the water as I count forty, perhaps fifty. It's hard to tell. *Is this what they call a pod?* I stand and watch in awe and respect, and as a couple climb the steps towards me, I jump up and down animatedly. "Have you seen the dolphins? Look!" They turn and watch with me, sharing the dolphin love, and I feel warm and fuzzy when they tell me it's their first dolphin sighting too. I'm happy to be on my own in these moments, but sharing it with someone else feels deliciously special.

After the hiccup of facing the cows earlier today, watching the dolphins go about their watery travels fills my metaphorical boots with a renewed spring. My physical boots, however, are another matter. Filled with painful blisters and sore feet, I'm learning that this walk is not so much about the physical ability and demands on the body as much as it is a mental game. I do my best to harness the power of my mind to adapt to the pain, pretending it's not there. With more of this, I could overcome all the hurting in my body. *You've got this, Wath.* With a fresh determination, a vision of those dolphins, and the stunning views surrounding me, I keep going. Up and down, I tackle yet more rollercoaster coastline to Hartland Quay, and the end of my day's walk of nine and a half miles.

With plans made to meet with a couple at their house nearby, Ross is waiting for me at the Hartland Quay Hotel. We drive back up the hill into Hartland village for my eagerly awaited visit with Satish and June. Many years ago, while my daughter was just a toddler, I'd had the pleasure of accompanying Lorraine on a visit with them at their picturesque home. Satish Kumar is a former Jain monk, a founder of Schumacher College, author, ecologist, past editor of *Resurgence* magazine and a peace activist. In the 1970s, he embarked on a Peace Walk, a monumental walk of 8,000 miles. It carried him and a friend to the four corners of the globe, to the capitals of some of the earliest nuclear-armed countries.

A powerful memory of this first visit with Satish and June is of a little Laura exploring their extensive garden. The beehives fascinated her, as did the many flowers, typical of a cottage garden. I admired such organised vegetable plots. The care, the ethos and the results inspired me, and I learnt a new term that back in my early twenties I had not come across before: permaculture.

It had always been my intention to revisit Satish and June while walking the South West Coast Path as the route passes within just three miles of their home. After arrangements made prior to setting off, June sent me a postcard, letting me know the best days and how to contact them once I was on the trail. I called to let them know I was on my way and Ross said he'd meet me in the van, down at Hartland Point. It's a fair distance up the road to their home. Luckily, taxi driver

Ross collects me, and we reach Satish and June's home feeling fresher than if I'd opted to walk there.

June greets us at the door. "Hello, Zoe, it's good to see you again. Do come in."

"Thank you, June. This is my partner, Ross." They shake hands and our conversation is instantly easy.

"Satish is meditating but will be down shortly. How far into your walk are you now?" she asks me.

"A little over a hundred miles. My walk has been slow. This is my eleventh day." June nods as she listens. "I've not been well, though, so it's probably best that I'm taking it easier for a few days."

"Oh dear, what's been the problem?"

"A chest infection and cough, probably picked up at school. It's hung around for about three months, although I think it's petering out now. I'd prefer not to use the inhalers the doctor gave me."

"If you can avoid that, it would be best," June agrees. She beckons us through the kitchen. "And are you walking the path too, Ross?"

"I'm doing small sections of it, but Zoe wants to do her walk solo. There's plenty of things to occupy myself with. I'm taking photos and enjoying exploring."

Satish, now seventy-five, treads down the stairs, and I feel as if he's just floated into the room. His presence is calm and full of a tangible, positive energy. It's as though he radiates light, warmth and kindness from every pore. "Hello, Zoe, and Ross, is it? It's good to meet you again." He takes both my hands in his and conveys a smile that pours over me. I relax fully into their company as June invites us out into the garden, where our reacquainting continues over tea and cake.

"So, tell me, Zoe, how long is it since we last saw you?"

"It must be at least twelve years. I'm surprised you even remember me." He and June both laugh warmly.

"Oh, we remember you. We were so fascinated by your adoption story. Lorraine's story, in fact, which became yours. It was a gift," Satish says.

"We chatted about it after you left," June adds. "You had the gift of life experiences because Lorraine made a terribly painful choice." I nod and continue to listen. "Without those choices, you may not be who you are today."

"Or you may be," says Satish, grinning. "What is wonderful is that you bear no ill will towards your mother for her choice. You hold her, and all your family, in your arms, as one. Quite remarkable."

"Thank you," I reply. "Lorraine just moved back to the UK a couple of days ago. She's staying with us until she can find herself somewhere to live." Both Satish and June nod. They never seem to hurry a conversation along. I love this way of talking. After a pause, I decide to share more. "Lorraine's mother, my grandmother, died just over a week ago. I was only three days into the walk. It was hard news to receive, but even harder knowing that Lorraine missed seeing her by just a few days, and she had her birthday last week, too."

Satish bows his head and his eyes close for a moment. He looks up at me. "These times are sad, but you will both find strength. Will you have to leave the path for the funeral?"

"Yes, but I'm not sure how that will work out. Ross goes home in two days, but I can't leave with him then as it won't give me enough time to finish the walk. I'll figure something out." Ross lifts his teacup and sips quietly, usually preferring to listen to a conversation than contribute. "You wouldn't have known this," I say, "but our visit with you the last time we were here had a profound effect on Laura, my daughter."

"Oh yes, she was just a toddler, wasn't she? I remember watching how she explored our garden with such curiosity. Do you remember that, Satish?"

"Yes, how joyful to watch her curiosity instinctively guide her around the plants," he says. "It was a garden adventure unfolding, and look, now here *you* are on an adventure!"

"I wanted to thank you both. Laura must have been three or four years old, but the experience of your garden had such an impact on her. For many years afterwards, she would enthuse over and over about 'Satish's garden'."

"Now that's so good to hear. Thank you. We work hard on our garden," says Satish. "But you are on a long walk, yes? You know we are both used to long distances on foot. Tell us more, please. Why are you walking, and how are you faring?"

"Yes, it's going alright. Better than I thought. I'm walking the path as a challenge to mark my fortieth birthday, which was a few months ago. I'm easing in slowly because of a chest infection. The pain in my feet, and blisters, has been a struggle. Ross is probably not aware of this, but they're keeping me awake at night. It makes it hard to get going in the morning. The landscape, though ... it's demanding, but spectacular. It's totally blown me away!"

I speak honestly about my journey, and we discuss massaging my feet as a tonic for the pain. June offers me an interesting take on managing the blisters, and for once, it doesn't involve using Compeed or even walking boots. "The Romans had to walk many hundreds of miles and did so in crudely made sandals," she says. "I've embarked on many hikes of my own, wearing just that – sandals. It's all about a greater connection between the land and our feet; an experience that is lost for most of us."

"But what about these blisters?" I ask.

"Sheep's fleece," she says, matter-of-factly. I am surprised at this, but it makes sense. "It has perfect padding properties, and the natural lanolin within the fleece keeps the skin soft. If it can work for the Romans, hopefully it'll work for you."

I know there are different attitudes towards how to avoid blisters, but I'm suffering so much I'll try anything.

One of our closing chats is about Satish's love of wild places. He tells us that his favourite place to go is Dartmoor, so wild and untamed. I haven't explored Dartmoor, and he expresses an urge for us to go soon. "Dartmoor is a perfect place to clear the mind and spend time with nature," he says. The way Satish pronounces "Dart ... mooor," echoes in my mind and I'm sure will stay with me a lifetime. It's like poetry in two syllables.

After an engaging hour and a half with Satish and June, not wishing to outstay our welcome, we say our farewells and head off to recce a Bongo sleep spot. It's not long before we locate a suitable area, so we retreat down to Hartland Quay again for food and some time to relax together in the seafront hotel.

As I reflect, I look forward to trying out June's wise advice and sense the aura of Satish's serenity will travel with me through any challenging days ahead.

11 An Irresponsible Teenager

It was always going to arrive. My thirteenth day, and Ross's last day in Cornwall supporting me on my South West Coast Path adventure. I'm both relieved, ready to be released into the wild fully solo, and sad. It's not a sadness filled with despair. I just don't want to say goodbye, but know that in order to achieve my goal, I'll have to.

As a treat for us both last night, we stopped outside The Beeches, one of Bude's many bed and breakfasts, and agreed to stay if they had a vacancy. It looked clean and pleasant, and how lovely to spend our last night for many weeks in a comfortable bed together. We didn't plan on leaving early this morning. I would make the most of having my man with me for as long as possible. Such a pity that Mrs Cartel, our landlady for these past few hours, is keen to have us up and out by 10.30 a.m. We enjoyed a delicious curry in town last night and now it has come back to bite me on the bum … literally! I could have used another half an hour in our room while I allowed my curry tummy to decide whether it was going to settle or park. The notes I write in my logbook read "Mrs Cartel – a bit jobsworth …"

There were other moments during our stay, where I sensed Madame Beeches wasn't as accepting of her residents' pursuits as one might have hoped. After all, regardless of your own opinions, if guests are staying, you should be in the business of making them feel welcome. While she might be different on another day, sadly, this wasn't her manner today. She asked about our plans while staying in

Bude, and naturally, I shared the story of my South West Coast Path adventure challenge. Shocked and uninspired by my revelation, she knocked back the idea that *any* woman should undertake a journey of this nature solo. She even stretched to suggest that I was irresponsible and asking for trouble. Despite my age, I suffer the psychological pain of being reduced to an immature, feckless teenager who doesn't have a clue and probably doesn't care.

I've had many people offer their opinions and questions about the walk. It's usually comments like "Wow, you're brave", "I'm assuming Ross is doing it with you, then?" or "Won't you feel scared on your own?" Until now, they have all been valid points or questions. Of all the comments, this is the first time someone has out and out accused me of putting myself in danger unnecessarily.

Yesterday, I was ready for this new chapter of my walk on my own. Today, Mrs Cartel has blown it out of the water. *What the hell am I doing? What if I get into trouble? It'll be all my fault.* My heart is thankfully still in it, but it has sunk lower than it has been in a while. It's going to take some stern self-talk to pick myself up out of this head mess.

Ross and I take a little wander around Bude to find me some lightweight leggings and a long-sleeved top to sleep in. Bude isn't a Mecca for nightwear, so I make a mental note to find somewhere else en route. We detour to a café, where we find something far better with which to salve my emotional wounds: a cup of tea and a strawberry Danish. "I don't know how I'm going to do this, Ross. You know I'm determined to do it, but I'm terrified." I lick the icing from my fingers.

"It's just putting one foot in front of the other. It's nothing you haven't done before. The only difference is you need to find somewhere to camp. You'll be fine."

"I know. It just feels so far from what I'm used to."

"You'll be fine," Ross says again. "You have all the kit you need to make it work."

By 1.30 p.m., it's time for Ross to leave Cornwall to go back home to Dorset. This is the moment I've been eager for and yet dreaded in the pit of my stomach. The emotions could not have been more conflicting. In the car park, I drag my heels, collecting my gear together while unconsciously delaying the inevitable. At last, I heave on my rucksack, having left a couple of items in the van for Ross to take home. I'm sure there will be more stuff winging its way back over the coming weeks.

Well, this is it. How many times have I said those three words on this trip? At least every morning. This is bloody well IT! "Keep me posted how Laura and Lorraine are, please?" Ross nods and climbs into the van, having given me one last hug and kiss. Once again, I see my black van with the grey lid and a red stripe along the top ease around the corner and disappear. What a monumental moment this is. Excitement and fear. The longest I will have been away from my love in ten years. The longest I've ever been away from my daughter has already been and gone. In this moment, I choke back the tears, while standing between the white lines where the Bongo and my Ross stood just a few seconds ago. The tears fall rapidly, stinging hot on my face, but I wipe them back with my sleeve.

Like a swimmer dropped into the sea, I stay put for a few seconds, treading water while I get my bearings. Rooted to the middle of that car park, I look around me to see if there are any signs of a coast path or direction I should follow.

Completely lost at sea in this whirl of emotion, I turn to the sanctuary of the RNLI shop to check the directions to the coast path from here. The ladies are so helpful, and in a turnaround from my experience at The Beeches, the chance to talk to them about my walk injects a positivity back into my stride. They are eager to hear what I'm up to, about my charities and how long it will take me. My mojo is back, and all it needed was a fleeting conversation with two women who understand my motives for wanting to go solo.

12 Guardian Angels

The path is tough beyond Bude. After at least nine or ten physically demanding ascents and descents, I stop at the Coombe Barton Inn at Crackington Haven for half a pint. I'm awkward and self-conscious about being in a pub on my own, especially as I slide the large rucksack off my back now dripping with sweat. Supersensitive that heads have turned and people are watching me, I sit at a table, considering my options. It's time to collect my courage. I conclude that there's no way I can avoid anyone seeing the wet imprint of my sweaty back on my walking shirt. I'll just have to harden up and ignore my worries about what others might think.

While sipping my refreshing beer, tasting like the elixir of a long-distance walker's life right now, I call a nearby campsite in St Gennys. I tell the proprietor, Tina, that I can finish my beer and then walk up. "No, no! It's an hour's walk, at least. I'll come and pick you up." What a gem. In the car, Tina explains they are a club campsite, and they don't normally permit tents, but as I needed somewhere, they're happy to make an exception. I offer Tina payment for the ride, but she refuses. Tina and Graham Bland – such compassionate souls. So kind and welcoming.

For the past two weeks, I've carried a lot of gear around with me that I haven't yet needed. I could have left it in the van, of course, but I wanted to get used to the weight of my pack and find out if it was manageable.

It wasn't. My sore shoulders have constantly complained to me, so I culled the kit and sent a few things back with Ross, including my bright yellow egg box and mini frying pan. I laugh now when I think of the eager anticipation I felt about buying and using them.

One item that's come along for the ride but never yet seen the coast path is Harry, Harry Hilleberg. The Hilleberg Akto is my one-person, four-season, all-singing and all-dancing whizz-kid of a tent. He sits low and green, with only one pole to thread through, and is easy to put up, as the inner stays attached to the fly sheet. I practised a few times at home, so I hope I'll at least look like I know what I'm doing.

I pitch Harry in an area Graham and Tina suggest is likely to be sheltered from the wind. Bad weather is coming in, they inform me, including powerful gusts of wind for the time of year. *Great, just my luck*. I'd do well to stay as sheltered as possible and set off early tomorrow. While deep in tent research, the Hilleberg Akto came up time and again as being able to withstand all the horrendous weather conditions our climate can bombard us with. It's not cheap, but I decided on reassurance and safety as my top priorities, so I sold a monster twelve-person tent we'd nicknamed the Eden Project to help pay for this little one-person. Plus, the lovely staff at Ray Mears gave me a great discount when I approached them with the details about my charity walk plans.

With Harry set up under the comforting shadow of an L-shaped hedge, I begin to organise my belongings. This is new territory. At last, I don't have to leave all my kit in the rucksack in the front seat of the van. Instead, I can spread out. I place each little roll-top dry bag in an area of the tent where I think I may need it, ordered by likelihood of use today, overnight, or in the morning. Every bag is a different colour, to help me remember which one is which. I've already got used to which is my stationery bag – that's orange. I keep a pen, logbook and sponsor forms in that one, though I scold myself for not keeping any detailed notes about the past two weeks. Another fallout from being supported, as I didn't want to ignore Ross the moment we were reunited at the end of my day's walking to write up my logbook. I kept thinking I'd remember to jot things down during the day, but guess what? I didn't.

With my sleeping mat inflated, and mummy bag laid out on top, I'm ready to hit the kitchen. This is a little trickier as I don't yet have the experience or the knack of creating a quick set-up. My choice of cooker is a stainless steel, flat-packed stove. Six sides or four sides slot together into a hexagonal or square shape, depending on how big I want it to be. It provides multiple options for grilling, burning foraged sticks, or using a fuel burner sat in a baseplate underneath. After I've been meddling with the stove for a few minutes, Tina comes over to see how I'm getting on. "I forgot to say, if you want to pop into the common room and use the kettle, please feel free to help yourself." Is she aware of my camping cluelessness? I wouldn't have thought she would know what I'm trying to do, as the stove pieces don't yet look like a stove, but I can't be sure.

"That's amazing, thanks!" With a slight notion of pretence that I'm busying myself with something else, I discreetly slide the stove parts into the vestibule of the tent and grab my titanium pot, long-handled spoon and a packet of Super Noodles, and head for the campsite common room. *Hah, you need a bit more practice with the stove, then, eh, Wath?*

Back at the tent, it's time to relax and take stock of today and what I should expect tomorrow. I have a lightweight nylon contraption with a couple of thin rods that tucks over my inflatable mattress, turning it into a chair. As I lean backwards at an unusual yet strangely comfortable angle, sucking each chicken-flavoured noodle from my spoon, a thought crosses my mind. Among the mess of setting up my pitch, it hadn't occurred to me until now that this is the first time I've camped on my own. Ever. I'm not sure how I feel about tonight, but in the way I've become accustomed to, I push it to the back of my head and know that I'll deal with it later. The voice in my head has figured out the sum of it ... *It's not tonight's sleep you need to be worrying about. It's the weather tomorrow.*

The campsite is quiet, with only a couple of caravans in this evening. They're too far away for me to feel self-conscious about them. I'm relieved to be tucked into a corner and able to keep to myself, if I'm honest. I'm within striking distance of the toilet block, so if I need the loo in the night, I've not far to go. "Right, Piggie, let's do this." I place my little mascot into a mesh pocket beside me. How can I even think I'm alone when I have Harry *and* Piggie to keep me company? My tummy flutters a little, but I'm in the zone and ready for my first night outdoors, alone.

I snuggle down into the sleeping bag and grab the orange stationery bag to make some notes about today. It's hard to believe that a few hours ago Ross had wrapped his arms around me. I write in my log-book: "Ross left at 1.30 p.m. I cried but I coped." I think that's the way I'm going to muddle through all of this. Even when things are hard, I usually find a way to cope. I scribble a note to myself at the end to remember to leave a positive review for Tina and Graham on the Camping and Caravan Club website. It's my way of saying thank you. I hope I remember to do that.

Graham continues to press his point. "There's no pavement. You don't wanna be walking down there. I'm calling you a cab." Tina and Graham are kind people, and I am so grateful for their support and hospitality. They are concerned for my safety on the cliff paths today. Graham tells me about the weather warning. "The reporter says there's a terrible front and high winds closing in on Cornwall in the next few hours."

The taxi arrives and Tony hops out to help haul my enormous pack into the boot of the cab, but I've already swung it in. He's a friendly Cornish guy and interested to hear about my pursuits. "I've walked parts of the coast path," he says. "Couldn't do it all in one go like you, though. That's a big thing you're doing. Where d'ya need to be dropped?" He parks the taxi at the bottom of the hill in Crackington Haven and dives out to do the part of his job where he opens the boot and lifts out the luggage. "My god!" He tries to pull my rucksack out of his car. "How the devil d'ya carry this thing?" With a slight change to his stance, he shifts it with both hands.

"You can leave it on the boot edge if you like. It's easier for me to feed myself back into the straps. How much do I owe you, Tony?"

"Ahhh, no charge," he says, waving his hand dismissively. "It's a free fare for you today, young lady. I admire your courage. Good luck and be careful out there. Weather's comin' in." *Take the hint, Wath. How many times do you need to be told this?*

"Oh, thank you!" I could have hugged him. I'd already spotted the meter said ten pounds, so the fare would have been at least this. He is not the first to caution me about the weather, though, and this bothers me; though how bad could it be in mid-July?

Along the cliff paths, climbing upwards into a dense wall of low cloud, visibility is almost zero. Well kitted up and looking like a coconut-flavour Quality Street wrapper in my blue waterproof get-up, I know I'm as prepared as I could ever be. Everything I wear or carry will get a right proper testing today. Even the hood that zips up my neck, under my chin and beyond struggles to stay in place in the gusts of wind now threatening me. *They said to expect bad weather ...*

It's a long, arduous slog up to High Cliff, the highest point of the Cornish section of the South West Coast Path, at 735 feet. That's

224 metres in new money. The heel impact has trapped my feet in a painful hell. The constant pounding of feet on tracks, rocks and especially tarmac or concrete pavement is hard on them, day in, day out. Added to this, my blisters have re-emerged and are causing me no end of problems. I'm yet to find any sheep's fleece, though I often see it caught on barbed wire, looking like little pixie beards put out to dry. If the wind wasn't driving the rain so hard, I'd stop to readjust my socks and laces, but the weather is so appalling I don't see the point of trying much else except getting up the hill. I carry on trudging, more aware of my concern with every step.

It's the wind. An aggressive behemoth. Bigger than a coastal monster unleashed. I naïvely thought a day of rain and wind would be manageable, but as it worsens, it forcefully pulls at my pack and in a second almost whips me off my feet. My apprehension is palpable as my breaths come rapid and shallow. I'm as vulnerable as the last remaining leaf on a tree when the seasons call time on autumn. The wind spirals around and around me and then, with an almighty blast, pushes then pulls me backwards in a spin. I can hear it knocking at my hood, ripping at my clothing, looking for a way to topple me, and at once I am stricken with panic. With white knuckles, I force my walking poles into the track even deeper, anchoring myself. I'm tense across every muscle and sinew of my body and almost too frightened to lift my foot. The wind abates for a second and then trades me another blow, knocking at me like a punch in the face.

There's no let-up. I'm unable to keep my head up. With my eyes looking down at my feet, I lock horns with the wind and battle forward, inching my way to the top of the hill until I can take it no more. Even in the low cloud and horizontal rain, I can see where the path disappears over a precipice. At least that's what it looks like to me. It's too steep. How have I found myself in this situation?

They warned you.

At the summit of the highest sheer cliff in Cornwall, and only two and a half miles into today's walk, for a moment my soul is black and my spirit close to breaking. I drop to the ground and hunker down. I want to cry, but the onslaught is so intense, I do nothing but cower and concentrate. My walking poles still anchored in front of me, I sit with my knees drawn up to my chest, facing away from the wind. With my rucksack attached to my back, securing me tightly to the terrain, I'm not sure what I am expecting, but all I know is, for now, I cannot continue. This storm is a horrific and angry beast. I'm tired, wet, severely anxious, and to top it all, I'm facing my fear of heights, head-on. A walk along steep cliff paths is one thing. Doing it in a summer storm that is buffeting me from every angle, aiming to tip its opponent out of the ring, is not a game in which I feel fairly matched to compete.

This is stupidity.

My lack of courage fills me with despair. I feel thoroughly out of my depth and so I consider my options. As the wind and rain seek every weak spot where it might penetrate, both clothing and spirit, two large, tan dogs bound up the hill towards me. Tails pert, noses wet and breath warm, they both search eagerly for the seeds of attention, or food, from this strange mass of human sat in a heap in the storm. "There's no picnic here, boys," I whisper. I look up to see their owners striding confidently up the hill, deep in conversation. They seem unaware of the intensity of the wind and rain. How are they able to stand so upright? Perhaps it's just me. As a light switches on in my head, I am ashamed. My inner voice scolds me. *You're not tough enough for this. You should harden up, Wath, or go home.*

Scrabbling to my feet, I make the first move. "Hiya! Isn't it a lovely day for walking up here?" I call out, with a hint of friendly sarcasm in my voice.

"Hello!" they both call back in unison.

"We love a bit of liquid sunshine," says the woman.

Wow, now that's a game changer. I've never heard this before, but "liquid sunshine" has beautifully spun all my thoughts of despondence and failure out of today's mix.

"Would you mind if I walked down the hill with you, please? The weather has caught me off guard, and I'm not sure of the way down."

"Of course! Follow us. It's not too far down." What the man doesn't mention is that once we're down, we'd be going back up again. Several times. Although I now expect this as part and parcel of the coast path terrain. Rob and Katie are absolute medicine and exactly what I need in my moment of panic. They walk with me for a short while and then head off. They were always going to be quicker than me. "Take care coming down Beeny Cliff. It gets steep, but not as much as what you've done now."

"You'll be fine from there, straight into Boscastle," Katie says. They have been splendid company. I thank them and they carry on their way. They'll never realise the full extent of my fear-induced predicament up there on High Cliff. Like guardian angels, they came into my life when I needed them the most and left with nothing more than the knowledge that I was safe.

As Rob told me, Beeny Cliff certainly is tricky, but not for the reasons he'd suggested. The cows are being awkward, with no intention of budging. I'm not sure how to herd them out of the way, either. Just tackling the wind, the rain and the heights is quite enough entertainment for one day. So I climb a fence, detour around the cows and climb back again. Problem solved – until the next time, that is. Mental note: sort out a training course in cow-crowd control when I get home.

It's always been said that out of all the negative things that happen to us, it's good to find the positive. Well, my positive is most definitely the waterfall at Pentargon, which drops just beyond Beeny Cliff. You see it best from the approach, as once you're on top of it, you don't get to appreciate the full experience. With the endless quantity of rain that has fallen in Cornwall today, the waterfall is at its most *Niagara spectaculorum* – or in English, flippin' Niagara magical. When I witness natural beauty such as this, nothing else matters. My feet, the rain, the wind. It's a moment that I won't allow anything to spoil, even if it is only a moment. Then I plod on my way with a brightness that feeds the next few miles.

There's been extensive practical learning over the last few hours. Forced into a face-off with my fears, to re-evaluate my capabilities and address how I should handle difficult situations, not to mention heeding advice. I have lots to reflect on and there is no better way to do that than stop at the first café I reach in Boscastle and order a cream tea, dripping and grateful they're open. This is my first cream tea of the trip, and I don't mind crowing that after today's colossal challenges, I deserve it.

The Harbour Lights serves up the perfect tea for me to cogitate over. After piles of Cornish clotted cream, lashings of sweet strawberry jam, and the loveliest, chunkiest scones I could wish for, with a pool of water surrounding my feet, I reach a decision. While I've only tucked six and a half miles into my rucksack today, it doesn't seem sensible to continue any further. The winds are increasing, and the heavy rain is still falling outside. The forecast isn't great for the next twenty-four hours. I'll finish up here and find myself some accommodation for the night. I don't think even my bombproof Harry tent will stand up to this weather, plus I could do with another serious drying-out session.

The helpful assistant in the tourist information shop makes multiple phone calls on my behalf. She establishes there's no accommodation in any of the small bed and breakfasts in the village. The last remaining room is at The Wellington. I make my way over to the hotel wearing my huge rucksack and muddy clodhoppers. This is the epitome of weirdness. The receptionist talks me through the tariff, and I balk at the expense. The only room available is an executive single for ninety-five pounds. "I'm sorry, it's not within my budget," I admit to the receptionist. "I'm doing a charity walk, and although I'm supposed to be camping, the weather is too wild out there tonight." I must look like a sorry case. She agrees and hits a few keys on the keyboard. "How does seventy pounds sound?"

"That's more manageable, thank you," I reply, smiling gratefully. I still haven't budgeted for this, but what the heck, it's a necessity.

With the key in the lock, I turn the handle and slowly push the door open. *Wow!* Although a single room, it's every bit the luxury I need this evening. My boots are off in a wink, and leaving them near the door, I hobble back to the chair by the window. I slide off my wet overtrousers, my waterproof smock, and finally peel away my two pairs of now soaking socks. I inspect the damage. My feet have caused me so much pain today and looking at them, I can see why. They are a mess. Red, inflamed, massed with blisters. In fact, one foot seems to be covered with just one enormous blister. I don't know what to do, but I know this can't go on. I also know that I can't even muster up the energy or pain threshold to deal with walking downstairs later to get myself dinner. This is a first; I dial down to reception and order room service for an hour's time. Extravagant but needed.

In the meantime, I sink into the hottest of bubble baths to soak my aching feet and contemplate an alternative plan. If the weather is this horrendous tomorrow, without question I do not want to be up on that clifftop heading towards Tintagel. Regardless of my fear of heights, it doesn't speak of safety. Knowing I could be battling gusts up to 50 mph, I'd rather be down here on the low levels. Sometimes taking a risk isn't the best choice. But if I stay down, then I'll have to find somewhere to stay again, and I can't afford a second night in The Welly. Then there's my Nan's funeral ... that's happening on Wednesday. I want to be there, but I'm not sure how I can get back or if it's even realistic for me to try now.

With a quick slide, I sink my body and head down under the bubbles. The hot water tingles as it draws the accumulated tension away from my scalp. If it costs as much to stay in the hotel as it does to get back to Poole, then my decision is simple. The receptionist might help me in the morning to find some bus and train timetables. I'll call Ross later, to let him know I'll be travelling home tomorrow. It'll be a Sunday service on public transport, so I'll have to bear that in mind too. Availability is likely to be limited. It's no more than a decision, but the wave of relief is fierce.

A Sunday morning wake-up in The Welly feels so decadent and not what I'm used to at all. I've slept well, although not fully undisturbed as the horrific weather overnight reached gale force. The gusts sent sound waves moaning, whistling and screaming around every nearby tree or chimney stack. I look out of the window. It's still stormy. I'm happy I've made the right decision not to walk high today, and definitely a sensible decision last night not to camp.

My continental breakfast waits for me on a tray outside the hotel room door. I pull it inside and sit on the bed, looking at the tray in front of me. A thought flashes through my head. I don't remember the last time I had breakfast in bed. Not wanting to wait any longer, I eat with the appetite of an athlete, despite not appreciating myself as one.

Operation Homeward it is, then. I set about packing my bags and wibble my way down to the reception desk to ask for timetable printouts. For once, my soft heart and bonkers head are working in partnership, both in full acceptance of this fresh change of plan.

13 After the Funeral

After a long ten hours travelling home from Boscastle, beginning the entire journey again to return five days later now seems less daunting. Nan's funeral had gone well, and I appreciated making more connections with my extended family. My grief has lightened since the funeral, too. Perhaps I needed to feel like I've said goodbye; and yet, a funeral is just a ceremony. A cultural way of approaching closure. More importantly, I spent time with Lorraine and accompanied her to the Chapel of Rest to say a proper farewell to Nan. I've cried multiple times, but it's been a release and good to have a few days with Laura too. Somehow, I'm returning to the path lighter. That's my head. I'm not so sure about my rucksack.

Not wishing to spend unnecessarily on another B&B, I decide to camp at a nearby site in Tintagel. It's run by the Caravan Club and expensive for non-members at almost thirteen pounds per night, which irritates me. With no other options available that I can see, I pay for my night's outdoor lodgings. While setting up camp, my mind wanders to wishing I had the courage to head out on the path and camp there instead. Somewhere. Anywhere. That's always been my plan, but as I've only camped one night on my own, I haven't yet got my head around it. To put it another way, I'm scared.

At last, in my sleeping bag, I can debrief myself on the day's journey. The trip back down to Cornwall had been uneventful, though I had met some special people again, as regularly seems to happen. One woman in particular, Angie, approached me at Southampton railway station: "Hello, I hope you don't mind me asking, but are you doing a charity walk?"

"I am, yes! I'm know I'm in the wrong place for it, but I'm actually in the middle of walking the South West Coast Path. I went to my grandmother's funeral a couple of days ago, so I had a few days off." I gave her my spiel about why I'm walking to mark my fortieth birthday and the charities of choice. "You know, Angie, I've wanted to walk this path for such a long time, but I never thought I could do it. The first hundred miles have challenged me to my core, but I still believe I've got it in me." As I talked, I'm not sure where the words came from. Whatever and wherever they're from, it was as though I said the words as much for me to hear as for Angie, to convince myself.

Angie took a seat on the bench next to me to hear more. I felt like she heard everything I told her, and she cared. She knew of Satish, appreciating his ethos of walks, words and teaching. As a nurse in end-of-life care, Angie billowed with empathy. Her manner, compassionate and endearing, meant I connected with her immediately. Before we parted company, she tucked a five-pound note into my hand with a warm smile, saying, "This is for your cause. I've loved meeting you. What you're doing is an amazing thing, and I wish you a safe onward journey."

While sat on the train from Poole, it occurred to me I had left my walking poles standing by the front door. As the realisation sank in, my tummy churned with sick frustration that I had neglected to ensure all my kit was present. I gave myself a bloody good telling-off on the train. This is not the first time I've left my walking poles, either. I haven't yet secured a routine that keeps them beside me, no matter what.

My Friday morning wake-up in my tent offers me little invitation to walk today. There's nothing out there but rain and heavy grey skies to see me back to Boscastle. It's as though the Cornish weather bouncers have arrived to escort me off the Caravan Club site. My presence as a lone female in a small tent on a site of plush caravans and couples is about as welcome as a wasp at a family picnic. It's a depressing scene.

Packed up and ready to go, I wait at the nearby bus stop. Bus drivers seem to come in two groups. Either the hellishly grumpy variety or the jolly, keep-my-passengers-happy-at-all-costs variety. This morning, I've landed myself with the latter. Unbeknown to me, it turns out to be the same driver who dropped me off at the campsite the day before.

"Hullo, young 'un," he says, grinning.

"Morning!"

"Didn't I drop you off at Bossiney Bay yesterday?" Gosh, a bus driver with friendliness and a splendid memory for his passengers!

"Yes, you did ..." I pause, not knowing if I should say anything.

"Darn senior brain, I'm sorry. I realised after I'd driven away that I dropped you at the wrong campsite." I brush it off and smile to him reassuringly.

"That's okay. It was only a mile or so up the road. I got here in the end."

"Well, I can only offer you my apologies for being such a dafty. You head on back there now and don't be paying me no fare today." He waves his hand towards the back of his bus.

"Thank you, I appreciate that!" These tiny acts of kindness mean so much, and I beam with joy.

It's a short ride back to Boscastle. The lanes are winding and the little top-heavy bus shoots along at breakneck speed. The narrowness of the roads, the gradients of the hills and the sharp bends make for an interesting ride. I clutch my rucksack in front of me for fear of losing it, or me, back down to the front of the bus. As I hold on tight, I grin to myself, knowing that even if his driving is erratic, this driver's heart is rich in goodness.

I step off the bus at Boscastle feeling awkward. Without my walking poles, I might as well be trundling down the road naked. You know what it's like when you leave the house without a trusty handbag, watch or mobile phone. It's not right with them missing. Anyway, I won't be able to navigate those steep cliff paths safely without them. An urgent call to Lorraine back at my house yesterday means that she will have packed and posted them to the Boscastle Post Office via special delivery. That way, they're guaranteed to arrive before 1.00 p.m. By 12.30 p.m., they have landed and, still standing in the Post Office, I hastily unwrap them, like a child ripping open a birthday gift. With a big thank you to the staff, I turn and stride out of the door, fleeing Boscastle for the second time.

Despite my lightness of heart after Nan's funeral, there's a grumpy undertone to my pace this morning. I had dearly wanted to make Port Isaac by this evening, to watch the group of local men known as the Fisherman's Friends singing down at the harbour. They have become quite the weekly attraction on a Friday night. The telly programme *Doc Martin* uses Port Isaac for outdoor set filming. This has helped catapult both the village and the Fisherman's Friends to national levels of celebrity status.

In fairness, I admit I'm keen to see Martin Clunes too, the lead actor in *Doc Martin*, but I need to time it right. There's every possibility he might be in the crowd, enjoying a drink while listening to the dulcet

Cornish warbles within the sea shanties. I'd love to approach him at some point, to see if he would attend the Glitz and Grammar Ball I'm organising to complement the fundraising for this walk. He's the patron of Julia's House children's hospice, one charity benefitting from my efforts, so it would be a great idea to ask him. If I could meet him first over drinks, that might pave the way a little before making the formal request.

My grumpiness is valid, as it's now 1.10 p.m. and I am only just walking upwards out of Boscastle. With the harbour falling away behind me with every step, I am keen to get a stomp on, to see how far I can make it. Deep down, I know with just under thirteen miles to go before reaching Port Isaac, I can't make the 6.00 p.m. singalong. *How could you be so stupid, Wath? If you'd had those poles, you'd have had no issue getting there in time. Keep an eye on the friggin' poles next time ...* That voice continues to berate me.

Too busy scolding myself, I almost miss the rock that I've had my sights set on for a few days. I've heard a lot about the "Ladies Window", and local legend suggests a woman leapt from the natural arch to escape smugglers. Whatever the reason for its name, I'm pleased to have not passed it by. A few minutes of observing my surroundings is all I need. At last, I realise my focus has shifted from self-punishment to being absorbed in the landscape. I am in awe of the natural beauty here and once again find myself unable to stop taking photos. Is there such a thing as a photograph addiction?

As I pick my way down the steep and well-worn steps towards Arthur's Castle near Tintagel, my boot slips from underneath me. In a split second, my heart has deployed the ejector seat, and my bottom makes a sudden impact on the ground. The weight of my pack acting upon the laws of gravity forces me backwards and pins me against the steps. Shocked to have taken my first tumble of the trip, I'm grateful it's not any more serious – especially coming down steps like these. A slip backwards and ending up on my backside is far less eventful than tripping and falling forwards. The what-if haunts me for a while, however, as I scoop myself up, brush my shorts and legs down and discreetly take stock of my surroundings. In all honesty, I'm looking at how many people may have seen my drama. Only a couple, and they're way behind me. Phew.

Tintagel appears underneath my boots at around 4 p.m. and having only walked just under six miles, I feel bound to staying here now. It's my first day back walking after five days off. It's too late in the day to be heading back out onto the clifftops; the stretch between Tintagel and Port Isaac looks likely to be steep and challenging. With my lack of confidence, I have the tendency to take my time and play it safe. It doesn't sit well with me, but I walk up the road towards the Headland Camping and Caravanning Park. Perhaps with more experience under my belt, I may have made an alternative decision ...

The Headland owners, Max and Sheila, show a keen interest in my exploits and kindly allow me to pitch my tent free of charge. This is an enormous boost, particularly considering I paid almost thirteen pounds for using a loo and sleeping on a flat patch of grass last night. As equal in measure to sponsorship, it enforces the message in my head that people out there believe in me.

I set up Harry and drop Piggie into his little pig-sized pocket inside the tent. I'm finally resigned to the fact that I'm unable to reach Port Isaac today. Today may not have panned out the way I had hoped, but with reluctance, I've allowed myself entry into the acceptance room. I lay my sleeping bag out neatly and begin the process again of tucking each item of kit into a useful place inside the tent. This time I slot the stove together with more finesse, but grapple for a moment with my inflatable mattress and the fold-away seat it slides into. Still proud of my new comfy camp chair, I reach for the lighter. With a click, the burner is lit, my pot of water rests above and I patiently wait for it to boil. I sit, watching the sky melt into the diffused light of early evening, listening to my surroundings. The gulls employ their angst-ridden shrieks high above me. I hear the thud and swoosh of children playing Swingball nearby and the hollow bumping of footfall inside the nearby static caravans.

I sense a cold is brewing, so I gulp back some paracetamol with a swig of water and lose myself in recording the day in my logbook. Placing the pen and book beside me after a few bullets noted, I settle down and let my thoughts wander. It's weird how such a lot seems to have taken place despite covering so little ground. Is the mileage progress so important? Perhaps not. Maybe the experiential progress is of much greater value than even completing the walk. Full-on spectacular scenery, physical demands and emotional challenges, this trip has become so much more than a visual feast. Beyond the pain I put my body through, and even beyond the tears and the head-talk, I sense there's more. Somehow, there is a profound growth propagating in the depths of my subconscious. I can't name it. I don't recognise it. I have no idea what it is ... but I guess it'll surface when it's ready.

It's 7 a.m. and although I'm awake, I'm still lost in my headspace. I'm enjoying the sounds of the birds and the campsite gently unravelling its occupants into the freedom of the day. Until the family from hell arrives, that is. They didn't sleep here last night and are not in tune with the rhythm of the surroundings. Two adults and four young children, with no other method of engagement with one another than screaming and shouting. Playful shrieks are no problem, I could stomach that. But these are aggressive and quick to react. No doubt the parents shout at one another and shout at the children, and it's a cycle they can't jump from. It's a scene I *can* jump from, however. Blasted out of my slow awakening, I pack up promptly while growling inside, and take myself out of the shouty environment.

Despite the ugly start to the morning, it was only a brief stick in my spoke of wonderful experiences. It's a short walk from Tintagel to Trebarwith Strand. The continuation of spectacular views soothes away any sour taste left from witnessing the family edition from the House of Commons (isn't that where all the shouting in the country happens?). Stopping often to take more photos, I am lost in reverence. This coastline truly takes my breath away, and I laugh at myself as I realise the double meaning behind this notion. I stand at the top of the cliff, looking down towards the inlet and beach of Trebarwith Strand. Ahead of me is yet another steep ladder of steps and path heading into the hamlet, and a near-vertical climb winds its way back up the cliff on the other side. As I tentatively work my way down the steps, I count them out of interest, while humming that catchy Berlin song from the eighties – my teen years. By the time I get to the bottom, I've lost count and the breath to sing or hum.

I've made many steep ascents and descents today, and although I don't mind the steps, the scree, shale or loose gravel unnerves me when the terrain is this steep. I'm grateful to have met Monica, a petite German lady wearing glasses and a buff, which holds her short mop of curly hair up and away from her face. She is friendly and we walk together between Tintagel and Port Gaverne, with plenty to chat about, including the hell of loose stones on steep terrain. We are both enthusiastic about the ground today, however. There's something different about it ... it sparkles! Perhaps it's that my childlike enthusiasm is infectious and Monica doesn't feel like she can pooh-pooh my excitement.

Whatever, we both inspect the path with amazed curiosity. I'm guessing that quartz particles from the rock have filtered their way into the soil. It's quite the spectacle and when the sun shines, it is the twinkliest terrain I've ever set foot upon. I'm honoured.

Port Gaverne is Monica's stopping point for today, but I'm keen to cover the extra short distance into Port Isaac itself. I need to buy food for this evening and for breakfast, with a plan to head back to a campsite in Port Gaverne later. I never enjoy having to backtrack, but sometimes there is no option, and a rucksack resupply with food is necessary. Monica invites me to stop for a drink before finishing the rest of my day's walking. It doesn't take much persuasion, but not wanting to get too settled in, I only have half a pint. There's also the consideration of loo stops between here and Port Isaac. Beer always heads south quicker than anything else.

With many friendly souls in the pub, it's not long before we're all chatting. Pat and Trevor become additional on-trip sponsors, donating ten pounds to my charity fundraising. I share with them about some of the other people I've met today. There's Martin and his daughter, Natalie, who helped me through a herd of inquisitive cows this afternoon – though to me the animals looked and behaved as if annoyed; no doubt my fear talking, again.

Then there's Jan and Eggy. I bumped into them earlier when they were looking for a place on the coast path to fill up their water bottles. They'd come out for a walk but hadn't realised it was going to be that far and so ran out of water ... something about the mileposts being weird. They let me know about a great little campsite in Port Gaverne where they were planning to camp their Toyota HiAce. We parted company but, determined to see these signposts for myself, I kept a look out. Sure enough, at the top of the hill it stated "*Port Isaac: 3 miles*". When I reached the bottom of the hill, fifteen minutes later, another sign read "*Port Isaac: 3 miles*". So that's Cornish miles ...

Time catches up with me, nudging me to leave the pub and say goodbye to the chatty crowd. Alone again, I wander down the steep road that leads into Port Isaac. I have a feeling that something is missing, and I raise my hand to my head to find my sunglasses are gone. Oh heck! I'd pottered around with my rucksack on the wall next to the pub. I'll bet they're still there. The walking pole fiasco is still fresh in my memory, and now a similar angst floods through me. I force an injection of speed and determination into my legs to carry me back up the hilly road of pain. I must find my sunnies before someone else does. *Yesss, there they are!* It's lucky, as although they're lying on the road, I can see they are still intact. Relieved, I slow down.

There's a saying somewhere about never taking your eyes off your goal or not celebrating before the race is done. How pertinent, as a car speeds down the hill towards me and pulls in, as if having made a split-second decision to park just beyond the pub. Right over the top of my glasses. *Noooo!* I run towards them, waving my hands frantically, shouting, "Stop! Please stop!" I can't imagine how I must look, but I don't care. I simply want my sunglasses back. Intact. God, I hope they're intact.

Bemused, the driver stops any further back-and-forth to parallel park his car and instead opens his window. Huffing and puffing from my exertion of racing up the hill, I just about manage to spit out, "My sunglasses!" As I point downwards at the road, I also wipe my mouth, just to be sure I'm not spraying him. "My sunglasses are underneath your car." I'm more composed this time.

"Oh crap, I'm sorry!" Without warning, he dives out of his car and scrabbles underneath with his long arms. Fully expecting to retrieve a crumpled mess of plastic, I'm amazed when he resurfaces, grinning. "There you go. Sorry about that. Bloody lucky the wheels missed them." My mouth is wide open in amazement. "Reckon you should buy yourself a lottery ticket tonight!"

"Thank you, thank you!" A quick wipe over and I set them back on top of my head, grateful to be reunited.

Back down the hill again then, mission accomplished. With the wayward sunglasses, poles and all my gear present and correct, I'm off to the nearest Co-op to resupply with food and, of course, to take more photos. I just can't help myself.

14
Familiar Faces and News

I spent my sixteenth night on the path at a small, intimate campsite. It was worth walking the extra mile back to Port Gaverne last night, although with walking back to Port Isaac today, that'll bring my total miles to date to 142 instead of 140. No doubt by the end of this walk, I'll have clocked up way more than the 630 miles of the actual path, because of backtracking like this, or getting myself lost.

I know I need to up my game. There are still 490 miles before reaching Poole and only around thirty-two days in which to achieve that. I would have had longer, but after taking five days out for Nan's funeral, my available time is limited. I'm not yet up to averaging over fifteen miles per day, but I seriously need to pick up my pace.

Brooklands Farm has a basic set-up. Nestled in a tree-lined valley with just a toilet and a shower, there's enough space for a few tents or campervans in a small clearing. Ann, the owner of the farm, gifted me the night's pitch, although to be fair, it would have only cost me five pounds if I had been a paying guest. It must be one of the cheapest and loveliest sites I've visited so far. It's not all about well-stocked games rooms and luxurious facilities. I need little: just a loo, a shower and somewhere to fill my water bottles for the following day's walking.

Jan and Eggy, the waterless walkers I'd met the previous day on the path and in the pub, are on a nearby pitch. Thrilled I'd taken their advice and come back to Brooklands, they invited me over to their camper for drinks and nibbles in the evening. This little campervan that looks so compact somehow turned into a Tardis of goodies. They brought out an extra chair for me, filled a glass with beer and set it on the table in front of us. Jan produced a cream tea – the full works: jam, clotted cream, big chunky scones – followed by a steady stream of nibbles interspersed with a pasty or two. I ended up staying with them, chatting and enjoying their company until the darkness fell around us. Before retiring to our sleeping quarters, besides treating me to a wonderful evening, they insisted I take a five-pound donation towards my fundraising. I feel honoured to have met this beautiful couple.

After packing up my life and saying goodbye to my new friends, I take the walk from the campsite towards the main road. My face lights up as I bump into Monica outside the Port Gaverne Hotel. We stop and chat, although I'm disappointed to hear she's not planning to walk today. The break with Monica leads to conversations about the forecast, and looking at the sky, I decide to put my rain cover onto the rucksack in readiness for eventful weather. I slide my waterproof smock over my head, this time being careful not to lose the sunglasses that sit as a permanent fixture on top of my head regardless of the elements. Back down into Port Isaac, staying observant the whole way, I'm disappointed there's no sighting of Martin Clunes. *Dang.* I realise I'm hot again too. I roll my eyes, swing the pack off my shoulders, remove the smock, and stuff the rain cover into a pouch on the side of the rucksack.

Not far out of Port Isaac, Port Quin is attractive and atmospheric. Shrouded in mist, it looks like a landscape torn from the pages of a Cornish novel, with legends of smugglers and highwaymen woven around the folly, the tip of which peers mysteriously at me from above the low-lying cloud.

There are many old mineshafts in this area. I shine my head torch into one of them and can see a little way down. It stirs my creative mind, conjuring up tales of trolls or sea fairies who live in the darkness of the underground shaft. An older man stops to talk to me as I'm lost in fascination with these remnants of Cornish industry. Bob is perhaps in his seventies, with a big white beard and a mop of curly white hair. He sounds Australian and confirms this as we chat. The mines fascinate him too, though I very much doubt he's even considered my fairy-tale creatures. We're not talking for long, but I hope we'll bump into one another again.

Almost missing Lundy Hole, a naturally formed rock arch, similar to Durdle Door but attached on both sides, of course I stop to take a photo. From a distance, The Rumps double headland looks striking and makes me think of the Lulworth Cove dragon that, as a rocky formation, wraps itself around the shape of the cove. I'm sure there are fables and legends connected to The Rumps that only the locals will know. As I approach it, I think about the vertical plates of rock, set upright and in a row, as if waiting for the next fifty-cents-a-try at a Wild West shooting gallery. I decide their tales would most likely feature a dinosaur. The more I look, the more I see it. The stegosaurus, turned to stone, preserved for eternity as the earth splits, fires rage, the floods rise and the ice forms around it. It keeps me amused while I'm walking.

I meet lots of dogs during my days on the path, and today is no exception. Cherry, a big fluffy creature that looks as though she's just stepped out of a tumble dryer, and Scrappy and Barney, two spaniels with boundless energy. Their owner is hanging over the side of the cliff, calling anxiously at Barney. He bounces towards her, ears flapping wildly, with a bundle of fur secured neatly in his mouth. "Darn dog thinks it's caught us dinner and brought this rabbit up from the side of the cliff," his owner tells me in despair. "But every time I send it over the edge, he scoots down and brings it back to me again."

"Ooops. Do you want me to hold on to him while you deal with the rabbit?" I noticed she wasn't carrying leads for the dogs.

"Yes, please! Here, give him these." She hands me some treats to occupy him while she walks back along the path. She hops over a stile and into the previous section of coast path, where Dead Rabbit receives his first and last flying lesson. Goal achieved, she returns, and I release a bouncy Barney, though not before I'd secured a doggy hug and sloppy kiss for good measure.

Polzeath forces me to scurry through as quickly as possible, as if I'm out of my territory again. The place is teeming with people. Rude people. Families and children keen to get to the beach push past me. Others look away when I walk by, like I'm from another planet. These are not locals, they are holidaymakers. My heart is heavy from the impression they give me of my debut visit to this popular seaside village. The same happens in Lulworth Cove. I know, I lived there. A handful of locals stand no chance against an army of tourists. They have to hope their care and attention to detail leaves a trace of positivity with the visitors. It's sad, but the litter I see suggests not. I harrumph to myself as I remember the words I spotted earlier from my path on the cliff, *"Hello Aliens!"*, scored in the sand below. Indeed, it rings true; I am an alien here.

My first ferry of the adventure takes place at Rock. It carries me across to the even busier harbour village of Padstow, nestled upstream on the western bank of the Camel estuary. It's hard to believe that so many people can fit into one small village. I've planned to meet Ross's friends here. They are on a two-family camping week and have kindly left room for a little tent to be pitched between them for one night. At the sight of familiar faces outside a famous chef's fish and chip restaurant, I could cry. It fills my heart to see friends, and I embrace all four adults and the three children within seconds of meeting up.

With only one child in their car, James and Kerry have just enough room to squeeze me in, to take me back to their campsite at Higher Harlyn, a few miles west of Padstow. Doog suggests I keep my tent pitched for a second night. Between them, they're happy to pick me up at whatever point I walk to and drop me back the following morning. It's a plan.

James gives me a ride back to Padstow. It's a foggy morning and I can imagine what it's going to be like out on the coast path. The views will be invisible today; I'll be like a blindfolded traveller in a foreign land. It is at least mild, but when the sun disappears, it can take me off guard as I get cold easily.

If James hadn't taken a detour to the nearest supermarket, I would have had an empty larder in my rucksack. After thanking him, I walk through the entrance, taking a quick glance at the newspaper headlines, as I'm accustomed to doing when I head into a shop nowadays. While out on the path, it's the only way for me to stay connected with the outside world. I don't buy the paper as I'd have no need for it, aside from perhaps scrunching up the newspaper to dry the inside of my boots if they're wet. It's just a quick scan to update me, and as I skim today's news, I'm devastated by the news of the death of Amy Winehouse. A little flick of the pages and it reveals the horrific Norway tragedy, too. I may just be a walker, minding my own business as I get on with my madcap idea to walk 630 miles, but both news articles leave me reeling in shock.

James is waiting in the car. As I clamber into the front seat, I share with him what I'd read. "I didn't know about the Norway attack, James, and I can't believe that Amy Winehouse has died. I know I came home for a few days for Nan's funeral, but other than that, it's like I've been in this bubble where none of the outside world can reach me."

"It didn't occur to me you wouldn't know," James says. "We were too busy chatting about other stuff last night for us to even think to mention it."

"That's okay." I look out of the window but without really seeing. The car passes through housing estates, winding down towards the harbour. "To be honest, I'm a little ashamed that I didn't know about these things. It makes me wonder what else I've missed." I don't know why I think I should be aware when I'm out walking. It's impossible unless I pass a newsagents. Yet somehow, I feel a sense of inadequacy for not keeping myself informed.

Monica finds me again as I'm taking an early morning, glassy water shot of Padstow harbour. She offers to take a photo of me with the harbour behind. I jump at the chance as I know there are still very few photos of me from these past few weeks. We walk and talk again as far as Merope Islands, where Monica turns inland to head back to her accommodation.

By a huge blowhole at Trevone Bay, I look down, amazed at the depth of this colossal chasm. Not only does it look deep, but it's wide too. Just when I thought I'd seen the biggest possible blowhole in the coast path, I reach another at Dinas Head. Now this one is enormous. To put this in perspective, it's larger than our school car park. The hole is so deep, as I peer down I experience the unsettling sensation of being drawn into it. I step back and shake my head, as if to flick away the fear that catches hold of me, before it tightens its grip any further. Perhaps this is what it's like to be standing on a high ledge and discover yourself falling, despite not having chosen to jump? I consider how many deaths have occurred like that. It's not a sensation I'd experienced before. I picture an evil Cornish imp luring me to my demise ... and that's how legends and folklore begin, I guess.

These feet are giving me such trouble today. I have intense pain in the soles and walking is slow. It's hard work. I'd thought the pain was because of a verruca on my heel, but having stopped for a break, I sit down and remove my boots to give my feet an airing. On inspecting my pads, I can see how soft the heels are and scold myself for not noticing that my boots have been leaking. They're wet inside and I'm heading for a bout of trench foot if I don't sort this out soon. I make a promise to myself to decide what to do with the boots by the end of the day.

Beyond Trevose Head, I notice how the waves have changed. Their size, the pattern they create in the water, and even the sound has altered. It's a stark difference as I watch the height of the waves breaking around the rocks and the enormity of the crashing I can see and hear. I shudder as I imagine what it would be like to be caught in a ship, battered by a storm, sea and rocks. A little further on, I see a stretch of headlands that remind me of fingers – these must be the coves of Pepper, Warren and Fox.

Majestic and picturesque, yet so intimidating. The Cornish mist veils and threads delicately around the sinuous features of this mighty landscape. I know about one of these coves from the stories told to me by Bran and Morwhenna, a couple I'd met yesterday. The legend tells of a drunken captain sailing his ship into Padstow. Clouded by an alcohol-befuddled brain, he'd mistakenly guided the ship into the treacherous Fox Cove, where the sea tore the ship apart and the crew were lost to the waves. No doubt there's a haul of treasure involved, and probably a few ghoulish sightings beyond the swell. I've heard more shipwreck stories on this walk than I have since my childhood. The Cornish are masterful at retelling them too. Regardless of whether they are fact or folklore, I appreciate their artistry.

Arthur

15

It's a teary goodbye with James, Kerry, Doog and Ali. Doog, with his usual smile and jolly nature, helps to keep me buoyant. James kindly drops me back to Porthcothan, my point of finish yesterday. I make the difficult choice to leave my walking boots with him to take home. They're not much use to anyone, with the sole now completely separated from the boot. Ross can collect them from James in a few days. While I'm still in the car, I text Ross and ask him to order me a new pair of boots and have them sent to Redruth, to Lea and Steve's address. They're parents of my childhood friends and I'm looking forward to seeing them again.

The walking is fairly easy. I'm happy about this, as I'm now in my Keen sandals and it's a welcome respite from the tough sections experienced over the last few days. It's quiet and relatively early for a summer holiday morning when a lot of the holidaymakers are still making the most of their beds. A warm, gentle breeze keeps the edge off the light drizzle.

Movement in the grass, about ten metres away, distracts me from my morning thoughts. I stop walking and watch, not sure what I expect to see. To my surprise and delight, a hare bounds out of its hiding place and leaps purposefully across my path and off into the distance. I am so excited by it and know I am blessed to have witnessed this moment. Right place, right time. Another second later and I'd have missed it. Moments like these are precious, and more and more as I get to know the path, I find I'm getting to know me, too. I am learning about a much deeper appreciation I hold for wildlife and natural beauty. It's about understanding the need to be present in the moment, in order to witness it.

While walking, I notice in particular the sounds of the birds. One bird has an unusual call, a clicking sound. It reminds me of my days spent as a child with pieces of flint, knocking them together in fascination to make a spark. At Bedruthan Steps there is an information point, so I go in to ask if they know which bird makes this sound.

"Ah, it sounds like a stonechat," the warden informs me.

"Of course! Why didn't I think of that? Thank you, it's been bugging me for ages that every time I hear this bird, I can't identify it. Now I know, thanks!"

Within twenty minutes of leaving the information centre, I'm stopped by a man. He's looking wistfully out over the clifftops and the mizzly cloud that hangs over the sea, but points out to the bushes on the cliff below. "You look like the right person to ask. Do you know what this bird call is?"

I can hardly believe it. "Yes, that's a stonechat. There's the male, with the more prominent black on his cap."

"Well, thank you for that information. It's been bothering me for some while."

"No problem." I'm grinning sheepishly inside, but decide to leave it at that. Sometimes it's easier that way than getting into another conversation about how I didn't know either and I'd only just found out a few minutes ago. *Wath, you're such a fake!*

Above Beacon Cove, a Yorkshireman carrying a large rucksack catches up with me. He's talkative, and he seems to want to walk and chat with me for a while. It's hard to keep up with him in every meaning of the term. Sometimes his chatter goes off topic and I'm searching for the thread of that conversation as he's scurrying through the next. As I strain through his broad accent and "isms", I pick up the pieces of what he's trying to tell me. I just about knit together sufficient parts of the sentences to share enough back to develop a fruitful conversation.

In a little over a mile and a half, I've learnt a lot about Arthur. He's walked the South West Coast Path fifteen times and lives on his own. He keeps a record of all the wildflowers he spots along the path, and used to work in a joinery before retiring. While I don't feel threatened and I can see what a pleasant chap he is, today is not the day I feel like working at a conversation. Instead, I need time to think. I've been with people for the past couple of days, and my head needs a recharge. I also have to work out how I'm going to get my boots if they don't arrive at Lea and Steve's by tomorrow. These sandals won't be up to covering all the miles for the rest of the South West Coast Path, though I reckon Satish and June would disagree with me on that. Anyway, I know I just need some space.

Watergate Bay exhibits an array of Porsches, BMWs and an Aston Martin parked outside the local hotel. After commenting on how Ross would have liked to drive the Aston, I spy a cue: the beachfront public toilets.

"Oh look, I thought I'd never find a loo. I'm going to have to pay a visit to the ladies. It's been lovely to meet you, Arthur." I smile and hope he senses nothing more than me needing the loo. I like him and I don't want to hurt his feelings, but I also can't muster much more conversation today. With any luck, I'll get to see him another time.

"Yes, of course," he replies. "I'm sure I'll bump into you again at some point. It's been good to chat with you, too." A hearty grin lights his face. As I step into the building, I turn to see nothing but the bulk of his rucksack above a pair of tanned legs, walking across the back of Watergate Bay. I know that when I step outside again, I'll have the quietness I crave ... that is, until I reach Newquay.

16

A Jet Ski Near Miss

The familiarity of the small North Somerset village in which I spent my formative years meant I got to know not just the area well, but the people, too. One such couple was Lea and Steve. They were the parents of Marie and Bobby, sisters with whom I'd become friends following their move back to England from Singapore in the late seventies. Lea became good friends with Mum, and in the latter years of being in the village, they lived in the same street as us. Then came the time when Lea and Steve moved down to Cornwall. Redruth, to be exact.

It was no surprise, then, when I decided I'd walk the South West Coast Path, that I wanted to incorporate a visit with Lea and Steve. It had been many years since seeing them. I hoped I might even stay overnight, to give us the opportunity to catch up, with the bonus of a real-bed break for me, too.

Once in contact with them, and after explaining the situation, Lea was happy for me to call them when I knew a date I'd be arriving. A few days before, I was better placed to give them an estimated arrival. After a little over eleven miles, it's been a mixed bag of both weather and terrain, and I arrive in the notorious surfer's hot spot of Newquay. Lea and I had arranged that she and Steve would meet me near the Gannel and Crantock, on the other side of the town, to take me back to Redruth.

It's the usual thing. Landing at a destination where there are people, I get chatting, despite my earlier need for quiet. I stand at the little wooden hut that serves a small boat cruise company here in Newquay harbour, talking to the woman sat inside. She must be in her late forties, and as I look at her tucked into the booth, it reminds me of a human Punch and Judy show. Just without Mr Punch. Or the mop hat. And there's no gaudy make-up either. Well, it's nothing like a Punch and Judy booth then, but that's how I see these huts. An older lady in her sixties walks over from the local boat club building to join in the conversation. Christine is the mother of the non-lookalike Judy sat inside the booth.

The tide is in, so I ask the women about the best route from here around the harbour and onwards to Crantock, as there would be no cutting across the harbour today. Some water sport enthusiasts are packing up their gear around us. I notice a guy with a large black Jeep hooking up his jet ski trailer. As Christine, her daughter and I continue to chat about the South West Coast Path and the route around town, I keep up with my observation of the bustle going on around us. I have my back to Towan Beach and the harbour is to my right. Directly ahead of me, I watch the Jeep drive up the steep, narrow road that weaves upwards out of the harbour.

Within moments, as the Jeep turns the corner at the top of the road, the trailer suddenly releases from the tow hitch. It all happens so quickly, like a flash of lightning, and yet in a weird, suspended slow motion, too. The trailer rolls backwards down the hill, at first looking sluggish. Then in a split second it gains momentum, increasing speed, rolling down the road towards us. I step backwards sharply, shouting as I do so, but I'm too late. Christine has her back to the road and hasn't seen the alarming developments of the last few seconds. There's only enough time to turn her head, just as the trailer smacks into the side of the booth with her daughter inside.

The booth takes the full brunt of the collision, but the jet ski has also caught the back of Christine's leg. We're all shaken, and as we consider the position of the little hut, we realise the jet ski has shunted it to within mere inches of the edge of the harbour wall. The shock is not just about what had happened, but at how near the miss had been. It could have struck any of us, full-on, knocking us into the harbour with potentially disastrous consequences.

My teacher's emergency head kicks in. While Christine and her daughter are busy exclaiming about the what-ifs and how lucky they were, I grab a photo of the registration plate. I encourage the women to exchange details with the driver, who is much less chirpy chirpy Jeep Jeep. Instead, he's full of apologetic phrases he knows the women would want to hear. I suggest he calls the police, as there had been an incident involving people, but he repeatedly tells me he will call them when he gets back. The women are ready to accept this, but I'm having none of it. He's more likely to just scarper and hope that everyone forgets the whole shebang. I press the point again. Eventually, he calls the police. Names and details exchanged at last, and I am noted as the primary witness.

Time is ticking on, so my next task is to call Lea and Steve to ask if they would mind coming down to Newquay harbour to collect me from there instead. I feel like a naughty schoolgirl asking this. Nothing to do with the way they make me feel; it's more about the guilt of asking them to drive into a town at the end of a summer weekday where it's likely to be super busy. I teeter around with the thought. Whichever way I look at it, there's no way I can get myself around to Crantock now before 6 p.m., which is the time I've agreed to meet up with them.

Lea and Steve's presence at the harbour as I see them walking down the hill makes me skip inside. As we hug for the first time in years, a cloak of instant peace wraps itself around me, keeping me safe from further runaway jet skis.

Lea and Steve

17

It's a wonderful dinner together, during which we share stories of the past, news about our respective families and how my parents are. It had been some years since Lea had dropped in to see them. They serve me a dessert too, which I hadn't expected. I sense a motherly insistence from Lea to ensure that I would eat plenty to have enough body fuel to burn the following day. In my room, I can see that I have a comfortable bed. *Oh my, this'll be heaven!* I set about reorganising my life by emptying the contents of my rucksack there and then, and begin the process of selecting other stuff I could do without.

Steve offers me the use of their computer to write up my blog. After a delicious bath, amazing food and now in a change of clothes, I am ready to write about my day's experiences. I don't have access to the internet on my phone. Many people have been talking about smartphones recently, but they are expensive, so I haven't yet bought one. I still make do with my Nokia 1508. The Kindle keyboard I carry is my best chance of blogging while out and about, as it has basic internet access. Most of the time, I rely on internet cafés or kind people to allow me half an hour to use their computer.

It's hard to keep my eyes open, so with a few words recorded for my blog, I say goodnight. That comfortable bed welcomes me. I'm utterly at home and relaxed, and fall asleep before my head even touches the pillow.

The following morning, we're preparing to leave Lea and Steve's home at around 8 a.m. so they can drop me back in Newquay. Over breakfast, they offer me a proposal.

"Zoe, we talked last night and would like to invite you to stay at our home for the period it would take you to walk to Fowey," Lea says.

"This would be our way of sponsoring you," Steve adds. "We'd pick you up each evening and drop you back at the same point the next morning, so you can continue without breaks in the path."

"And you can leave some of your things here to avoid having to carry everything. It'll give your back and shoulders a break." Their offer extends to feeding me and providing as much support as I need.

Speechless and hugely touched, I say yes to their generous offer.

The first day from Lea and Steve's is my twentieth day on the coast path. Newquay to Perranporth is littered with wonderful wildlife and points to pique my interest. After I navigate my way through the town, that is. The sight of the first acorn sign of the day reassures me I am back on a National Trail. As an inanimate object, it's odd how it has a way of making my heart skip with excitement and relief, though Piggie often has the same effect!

An attractive, white-washed stone building sits on the headland before Towan Head, just out of Newquay. It's like nothing I had seen before, and I stop to check it out. It bears simple castellated features, door and window grilles alongside a tiny tower, and a flight of open stone steps to one side. It's like a miniature castle. On reading the information board, I learn that, among other things, its last recorded use was as a Huer's Hut. A huer keeps a lookout for shoals of pilchards by searching for a coloured hue across the surface of the water. The man would then raise the call for the fishermen to launch their boats, hence the term "hue and cry".

Towan Head proves to be a superb walk, although it didn't take me anywhere. As with many of the headlands, I start at a point and circumnavigate the headland. An hour or two later, depending on its length, I'll return to that same point before moving along to the next stretch of coast path. Sometimes, depending on tiredness, hunger, weather and other factors, it can be demoralising. Today is not such a day and with the views clear and far, the sun very much with his hat on, and a slight breeze in the air, it's a happy walk. I appreciate everything I experience.

With much wildlife spotted in a short time, I start noting down the creatures I see, knowing I'd never remember them all otherwise. I want to savour these special moments being face to face (or fur to face) with otherwise apprehensive animals. After walking part of Pentire East, I feel there's time to stop in Lewinnick Lodge pub for a cuppa. It gives me a few quiet minutes to think and write. I jot down about the young kestrel, sat atop the public loos near to The Warren on Pentire Point. Oh, and there had been the seal that I'm told is a regular visitor to Newquay harbour – I spotted him as I left first thing this morning. There were two baby rabbits bounding in front of me on the footpath, and two dogs. Not exactly wildlife, I realise, but these dogs made me chuckle as they looked funny, bouncing up and down in a field of high corn. They probably shouldn't have even been in the field and may have caused some angry reactions from the local farmer, but it was a comical sight.

The fulmar is a smaller relative of the albatross, and I didn't think it was that common to spot them in this area. I am thrilled, however, to have seen what I hope I correctly identify as a family of fulmars, nested on the side of the cliff, complete with two older chicks. *Are they even called chicks? How about fulmarlets ...?* I'm able to see them more clearly through the zoom on my camera. They have a tube on the top of their beaks which acts like nostrils and, as the parents fly, their wings are rigid. Such graceful birds.

As the day unfolds, I walk alongside the Gannel, still in my sandals. It's liberating for my feet, and the terrain isn't difficult. Even though I don't need them now, I'm reassured knowing my new boots are on their way, all fingers and toes crossed for them to arrive by tomorrow.

There's something about this stunning place that connects with me. The mud flats, the woods and fields on the opposite bank, the beaches, the boats. To add to this, the light makes the entire scene glisten with joy. The icing on the cake is the little egret, which proves to be the headline act for me here.

Further up the estuary at Penpol Creek, I cross a narrow wooden footbridge, only accessible at low tide. There is another footbridge, but it's much further up the creek. It does at least make the crossing possible if a high tide prevents bridge access at Penpol.

Today, I think I've met my favourite beach, at the glistening sands of Crantock. Although I don't have time to stop now, I vow that I'll come back to revisit and spend some time exploring this area more. I consider this sudden love for a specific beach, and what makes it different when I have passed so many beaches along the South West Coast Path. I decide it may be about its positioning to Newquay and the unsettling experience of being back in a bustling seaside town. It also has much to do with the way the beach is located alongside the cornfields, dunes and estuary. The complete picture is quite unusual. With the backdrop of the vivid blue sky and the creamy yellow cornfields, everything seems to glow in a way that appeals to my artistic side.

By the time I arrive at the vast beach of Perran Sands after walking along the beach for over two miles, I've reached the point where I know I can't walk any more today. At fourteen miles, I actually *want* to walk further and could walk more, especially now the chest infection seems to have cleared off, at last. With the awareness in the back of my mind that Lea and Steve are waiting for my call to come and collect me, I decide to call it a day at Perranporth. I have a lighter pack and slept in a proper bed the night before. In all honesty, I have no excuses why I haven't made better use of the day, except that I am finishing much earlier than I would usually. Other times, I'd keep walking until I was too tired or found a campsite. There's another point too. I know I need to get started on wild camping as soon as I can, or before long, I'll have run out of opportunities.

18

Coast Path Creativity

My dream and fear of wild camping can be tucked away for a while, as I estimate I'm going to be staying at Lea and Steve's for well over a week, maybe more. It'll depend on how long it takes me to find my way to Fowey. I'm sure after that, I'll find somewhere – or more to the point, I'll find my *courage* to find somewhere.

With my start at Perranporth the following day, there are more Cornish whimsies to carry my mind along the next twelve miles. I am absorbed by the old quarries and ruins of the works buildings left over from the mining era, particularly at Cligga Head. The intense red tone of the cliffs is ever-present. The building remnants are the only evidence of the area's once rich industrial heritage for tin mining.

The visual drama of the cliffs along this stretch does not disappoint, and I'm helped along by cooler, breezier walking conditions than the day before. The weather warms up as the day progresses, but either way it doesn't matter much to me as I find I get pretty hot walking these cliffs. It's my daily outdoor gym workout.

Inspiration filters through as I pass more disused quarry sites. The seed of an idea plants itself in my head. It's for an art project for my new Year Eight art classes once I'm back to teaching in September. The project would be called "Remnants" and I'll get the students to use fragmented images of their surroundings to develop into exciting new works of art. It occurs to me that when I'm cogitating an idea or need a resolution to a problem, somehow walking helps me. I'm able to respond to the need because walking provides the mental space for me to find the solution.

Sometimes, the ideas pop into my head without me even thinking about them – or at least not consciously thinking. That's the point. It's all about mindfulness. Know what your questions are, then allow your brain the peace and space to mull it over, even when you don't realise that's happening. I've had the most amazing ideas and solutions arrive in my brain at the most unexpected moments while walking this path. It makes me think I should continue with this long-distance malarkey after I've finished the South West Coast Path. How am I going to think up new stuff or sort out my life's problems otherwise? I laugh at the thought.

While enjoying a delicious, yet not so deliciously named, hedgehog ice cream at Chapel Porth, I learn from a local about their café fire, four years ago. A barbecue left in a rubbish bin close by caused the loss of the entire building. This heavenly hodgeheg delicacy takes a lot of mouth finesse to consume without covering myself, all while trying to conduct a sensible conversation with said local. They make this legendary ice cream by slathering Cornish ice cream in clotted cream, then topping it with crushed hazelnuts. Of course, it would have been rude to pass through without trying this local foodie legend for myself.

Quarry after quarry and mine after mine near St Agnes lead me to the prize of all the vestiges of industry. This is what I've been longing to see with my own eyes: the old tin mine engine houses. How I'd love to be here at sunset or sunrise and capture a golden glow bouncing from the chimney stack or a silhouetted ruin in the bluish half-light of morning. I have ancestors who were tin miners, right here in Cornwall. This knowledge prompts me to take a short detour inland, to visit a tin mining museum. Entry is too expensive for a visit this time, but instead I enjoy looking around the foyer and outside for a short break. So often, I pass through without stopping, so this is a welcome deviation.

Back on the path, another local and another story shared. They say the owners of the museum only have it because they squatted there long enough to gain the land. Once again, I take what they tell me with a large pinch of salt. I am getting used to the Cornish penchant for a good yarn.

Still surrounded by disused mine workings and varied terrain, I approach the poetically named cove, Sally's Bottom. I wonder how the cove found such a peculiar name. Was it an era-based misunderstanding? Perhaps the word "bottom" meant something else back when this cove had its naming ceremony. I conjure up all the potential reasons in my head, ruling out the playful Sally, who had bared her buttocks to the passing ships. I decide against the idea that Sally met her demise here. It's an awful thought: Sally laying at the bottom of the cove, until her body filled, stolen away by the tide, then left on the nearest shore. Maybe Sally was the daughter of a local lord, a landowner. She enjoyed using the beaches for her own recreational pastime and this cove was the lower beach of the many she frequented, her favourite. The bottom cove may have become Sally's Bottom.

I gloss over the idea that the shape of the cove may have held a striking resemblance to Sally's derrière. Instead, towards the end of my mid-walk conference, I conclude there was most probably an old ship named *Sally*. As with tradition, they named most ships after females, so this seemed plausible. Sally's Bottom? I reckon the ship ran aground here. It bottomed out and was maybe even damaged beyond recovery.

On further investigation of the cove name, I discover that the word "bottoms" is a tin mining term. Given the location of this cove and proximity to the many mines in the area, I'd have to retract my last suggestion that they'd named the cove after a ship. I accept the less romantic notion that it was relating to the industrial terms of the locale.

A couple are sitting on the grass overlooking Sally's Bottom, so I wander over to chat and ask about the marine wildlife. "I'm told to look out for basking sharks in this area. Have you seen any?"

"Yes, one spotted at Porthcurno just yesterday. Hope you'll be lucky," the man replies. I'm excited, as this is another on my list of hopeful sightings for my coast path adventure. I want to bear the memory of seeing a basking shark first-hand and not through the medium of print or internet.

Lea and Steve pick me up at Portreath, after just over twelve miles, and I am treated to more delicious food in grand portions. We engage in super conversations, and I enjoy sharing the highlights of my day with them. It's hard trying to squeeze everything in, though. There's the social aspect of staying with hosts, relaxing in the bath, and dining. Then fulfilling the admin tasks of updating the blog, social media, and writing in my logbook. To do all that before the inevitable wave of tiredness pulls itself over me is difficult. Once again, it happens. My brain instructs my eyes to close and not wake for another nine hours at least.

My new guardian angels drop me back at Portreath. There are a few clouds in the sky, a light breeze to keep the temperature down and I'm happy with this ideal walking weather. It's a simple walk to Godrevy, but I know I'll need the loo soon. I keep a close eye on the places I could use, but there seems to be no opportunity of loo spots available on the path. I need to obscure any possible visibility of Zoe's bottom (not relating to the local industry) from the nearby road.

The path today remains high, winding along the clifftops. After a chimney stack sighting just out of Portreath, it opens up, revealing the splendour of the Downs, known as Caravannel, Reskajeage and Hudder. There are many rugged coves and headlands in this section. I marvel at the aesthetic Deadman's Cove, Hell's Mouth, and particularly the wild-looking promontory of The Knavocks. It's just a short walk from Godrevy Point and on the east side of the lighthouse. I strive to capture it all on camera. The artist's heart and eye within me keep pulling at me to tarry longer. *Stay and appreciate the views more.* How I'd love to, but I know I have many miles to walk today, and I must keep going if I don't want to keep my hosts waiting.

I meet a few people today to add social interest to the journey. There's a kitschy-dressed lady who appears to be with a coach group of visitors to Godrevy. She waves enthusiastically at me as I'm passing the public toilets near to Gwithian Towans. Her outfit is colourful, as is her plastic jewellery. She reminds me of Morag Myerscough, a dynamic designer whose fashion reflects her décor. This lady is less in tune with how her mismatch of colour, material and make-up could be used to the best effect, but I instantly like her. Her smile is wickedly mischievous, and I realise I could learn much from her don't-give-a-toss attitude. We only speak for a minute, just enough time for her to ask me what I'm doing. It's a regular question to a lone woman with a large rucksack. She tells me she's been on the coach for two hours and needs to make the most of the local facilities ... like now! I laugh and share with her my predicament along the open paths that travel so close to the road, preventing me from taking my much-needed wee. I ditch my rucksack outside the toilet block and follow her in. It makes me chuckle to myself as we're still chatting through the walls of the cubicles. We're like a pair of teenagers, instead of a pair of strangers, one forty and the other at least seventy.

The Towans are Cornish dunes, and I can comfortably admit that I am a little lost among them. The path navigates through many sandy, grassy mounds. Divided into sections, each have memorable names such as Gwithian Towans, Mexico Towans, Riviere and Hayle Towans, and so on. Weaving in and out for a while, I'm walking with a guy called Neil, an IT professor. I've filled him in with the answers to all the usual questions about my walk. Then he asks, "You said you waited fifteen years to pluck up the courage to do this walk. What was it that made you think you couldn't do it?" Wow, that's an interesting question that I've not heard from anyone else before. I have lots of possibles I've talked about, like not feeling athletic or strong enough, but as I consider my response, I realise I don't really know the answer to his question. I mean, what *are* my reasons for not feeling strong enough? *This will take some careful thought, Wath.*

"I was never any good at PE at school and was always one of the last to be picked for team events. I'm just not that sporty, so assumed I wouldn't be able to walk 630 miles." Neil accepts my answer. Whether I believe it to be true is another matter. More baggage that'll need unpacking one day.

Somewhere along the way, we discover we've chatted ourselves off course. We're heading straight for the village of Phillack – which is completely in the wrong direction. A quick turn west puts us back on the right track towards Hayle. Neil and I laugh at our extended adventure together and as we bid each other farewell, he pulls out a ten-pound note from his wallet to add to my sponsorship.

Heading up an estuary and into a building site, I stop and chat to a hard hat wearing a man. He's the foreman of the site here and tells me there's a new bridge going in. "My men have dumped tonnes of hardcore into the water to enable them to work on the bridge. North Quay will look very different in a few years' time with the regeneration plan." His explanation of the works is helpful for me to understand what's happening here. "The quay was the earliest of its kind dating from the 1700s, you know." He shows me the early blocks of stone. "They used the swing bridge to let the boats through to the estuary and it's also one of the oldest in existence." I love being drip-fed all these historical gems.

The way around the estuary to the Saltings at Lelant is lengthier than I expected. I take photographs of three separate herons en route. I swear that one of them is a different type of heron, despite believing there was only one genus in the UK. It doesn't look the same anyway, even if I'm wrong.

I'm going to catch the 19.03 train back today, instead of Lea and Steve driving down to collect me. Concerned I'll miss it, I end up running the last stretch of path to St Ives. What a cracking little ye olde worlde branch line it is. Changing at St Erth, at the end of the St Ives Bay branch line, I gaze at the beauty of the station building. The railway bridge and station buildings are all original. Coming from a family steeped in railway history and tradition, it's truly a delight to appreciate. I hope it's listed.

The next train is only about fifteen minutes' journey from St Erth to Redruth. I enjoy finding my way through the town, past the bronze *Tinner's Hounds* in the shopping precinct and back to Lea and Steve's. The collection of sculptures is an artist's representation of dogs. They're casts made from earlier rubber sculptures, using the actual tin miners' old welly boots from Geevor mine. Redruth was once the central hub of the mining industry in Cornwall, so it seems fitting to install an appropriate sculpture to commemorate this. I'm pleased to see these playful hounds for myself, especially as a distant reminder of my own ancestral connections to the Cornish tin mines.

I flop down at Lea and Steve's, having completed a healthy eighteen miles for Day Twenty-Two – much better than the last few days of walking, and the most miles yet. I devour the feast Steve serves me, as always with a yummy dessert, though I'm feeling stuffed to the hilt and ready to burst. "Steve, your food is amazing, but I'm not sure how I'm ever going to walk off all this extra food." He passes me a box.

"In these, I hope?" *Yessss, at last. My new walking boots!* I smile and thank him, then pad down to my room to try them on. They're cosy and fit like gloves. I can't wait to try them out tomorrow.

Mike

19

I didn't expect to wake up with a sore throat this morning, but Lea's motherly and nursing instincts immediately make me feel better. She bustles around me with soothing words, dropping two Aconite tablets onto the table in front of me. "These will help," she says with a smile. Even from years ago, I remember Lea had a keen interest in homeopathy and alternative therapies. I use herbs and natural remedies myself, but I've never tried this one before. The tablets go straight into my mouth, and I chew, praying for the magical properties to work their wonders on my scratchy throat.

We leave Redruth by 7.20 a.m., and I'm pleased to start off from St Ives at 8.15 a.m. Any walking achieved before 8.30 a.m. (or earlier, if possible) is always a bonus for the day. I stop at a shop in St Ives to pick up some food; a bacon frazzle and a flapjack are now on today's lunch menu. I tuck both into the top of my rucksack and swish the pack onto my shoulders in a manner that I am becoming quite accustomed to. Now that I've left some of my kit in Redruth, the bag is deliciously lighter. I stride off with a mission. Within just a few steps, however, it's apparent that the route around the harbour at St Ives is not as easy to find as I had hoped.

In and out of buildings, along narrow streets, the coast path weaves its trail. I give an inner jump for joy at spotting the house of the late Alfred Wallis, a famous painter who started his artistic career in his older years, bearing a distinct naïvety with his brush and stroke.

I had learnt about him at art college, so it felt good to stand at his door, imagining his thoughts, his daily routine and his outlook, which stretched across the harbour. My first encounter with the beckoning steps of Tate St Ives also thrills me. I *so* want to skip up them and visit the gallery, to view the artworks and experience first-hand some of the great works I had never laid eyes upon before. I know I don't have time to go in, however. After a quick photo of the modern building dominating this stretch of seafront, I turn and head on my way.

Just a few steps away from Tate St Ives, I recognise the large blue rucksack and tanned legs belonging to a solitary figure. Arthur! Somehow, I thought when we'd left one another at Watergate Bay that it would be the last time we'd see each other, though I'd hoped our paths would cross again. As his pace is faster than mine, I'd assumed he'd be way ahead on the path by now. He also seemed to have a good plan of where he was going to be and when. We are both genuinely pleased to bump into one another and walk together for the rest of the day. This time, my head is ready and more sociable.

It strikes me as I walk and talk with Arthur how familiar he looks. I mull over the connections or the possibilities. He lives in North Yorkshire, so I conclude there's no way we could have met prior to walking this National Trail. He must have a doppelgänger somewhere.

Arthur's hair is a coarse, thick mop of strawberry-tinted light brown, growing strong into a swept side parting. His sculpted nose and chin create a well for a neatly drawn lip line. The lines of humour, expression and deep thought frame his small, close-set eyes. A wash of tanned skin, with ruddy cheeks and broad furrows, extends from his nose and around his mouth. It puts me in mind of a fisherman, bearing the permanence of working in the extremes of all weathers, day in, day out. Arthur worked as a skilled joiner before he retired. His weathering comes from many years of walking in the great outdoors.

If it's wildflowers you want to know about, Arthur's your man. He walks with a notebook and pen permanently about his person. If it's not in his hand, it's tucked in a carrier bag and stuffed somewhere local. Sometimes I spot him retrieving the notebook from inside his T-shirt – using the cavity between his belly and the fabric as an extra storage pouch. Within this notebook lie many scribblings that would be rarely comprehensible to you or me ... but perfectly logical to Arthur. He takes notes about the wildflowers he sees and where he spots them. "That's a rosebay," he says as we're climbing steps heading towards The Carracks. "Rosebay willowherb – it grows everywhere." He nods towards the vast stretches of tall, pink, spiky flower heads. "And this is dodder." He stops at a bank covered in pink spaghetti-like tendrils. It's not unlike a plant from a sci-fi book. I imagine how it grows, reproduces one hundredfold, smothers, chokes and sets out to take over the world.

"Dodder?"

"Yes, dodder." With his hands wrapped protectively around his notebook and pen, Arthur describes it to me. In great detail. As he talks, that sculpted nose, the close-set eyes and those lines of humour all morph together into a ball of recognition. It's him! In an instant, the man appears. The one I'd been craning myself to see for hours. Here in front of me stands the very image, a clone, a dead ringer for none other than Michael Palin. Once seen, I can't unsee and often catch myself staring in amazement. Eventually, I ask Arthur if anyone has ever told him he looks like somebody famous. "Oh aye," he replies in his North Yorkshire drawl. "It's that Palin chap ..." He grins.

It's useful having someone to walk with today as I am finding it difficult; more so than usual. For once, it's not blisters that plague me, but a bite. A little critter chomped at my right ankle yesterday, which has swollen, causing me walking problems. The humongous restriction of movement in my ankle means I haven't been able to tighten my new boot. If it's still troublesome when I get back to Redruth this evening, I'm sure Lea will have the perfect remedy.

Arthur asks me the usual questions: why am I walking the path? Which charities am I raising money for? How long have I given myself to do it? I give him the standard answers. "The thing is, Arthur, I waited fifteen years before I was brave enough to start on this path, and now I wish I hadn't waited. It's tough, but I could've done it."

"Why did you wait so long, then?"

"You're the second person to ask me that in a couple of days, and I'll be honest: I don't think I know the answer." I pause for a moment and consider the question again. "I probably lacked the belief in myself to do it. It sounds scary. It's a big thing, walking 630 miles. And then you do it and suddenly it seems more manageable and less intimidating."

We approach The Carricks, and Arthur tells me that Seal Island is the largest of the islands, just off the coast of Cornwall near Zennor Head. Sure enough, I am treated to a view of many Atlantic grey seals, lounging belly-flopped or bobbing on and around the rocks near the island. To my growing bank of wildlife sightings, I can also add four buzzards and a fleeting visit from multiple damselflies. They are so colourful and fill my world with flutterings of joy each time they pop by to say hello.

At Zennor Head, in soaring temperatures, Arthur invites me to take a quick detour inland to the hamlet of Zennor. He offers to buy me a drink at the pub, and without hesitation, I accept his invitation. I know my body. If I drink beer, in an impossible quirk of nature it'll head immediately south at the same time as going straight to my head. "I'll have a shandy, please." Arthur brings the drinks to the outside bench, fortunately shaded by the brewery-branded pub brolly. It's good respite, as there has been no shade today. With no escape from the sunshine, beautiful though it is, proves to be exhausting and we need to consider how long we're spending out in it. When walking, it's so easy to just keep going and forget how hours of the heat and those rays can completely strip you.

Arthur sits at the bench and takes a long slug of his pint. “Aye, I needed that.” He smacks his lips. “I don’t usually drink alcohol throughout the day,” he says, grinning, “but I can make an exception today.” Pulling out a ten-pound note from a wallet that looks as tired as his rucksack, he slides it towards me, almost coyly looking away as he does so. “Put that t’charities.” I appreciate his kind gesture.

“Thanks, Arthur!”

“Aye.” He nods at me. “My friends call me Artie.”

“Thanks, Artie!”

From Zennor village, we wander back towards the coast path and away from the delightful sanctuary of the twelfth-century pub, The Tinner’s Arms. Arthur suddenly throws up a hand. “Well, I’ll be jiggered!” A man in a faded red technical tee and loose-fitting cycle shorts approaches us along the narrow, hedge-lined lane. He’s carrying a scrunched and battered water bottle and wears a tatty blue baseball cap.

“Bloody hell!” The man stops in his tracks and a gleaming white, broad grin breaks from ear to ear across his face. He steps forward to give Arthur a manly hug and shakes his hand. “I thought you were long gone after Bude!” He turns to glance at me and smiles. It’s a genuine smile. Warm and with eyes that sparkle. Probably late fifties, I think.

“I took half a day off in St Ives,” Arthur replies. “I’ve already bought a couple of thousand pounds’ worth of paintings there. Thought I shouldn’t stay any longer.” Our eyes widen in astonishment. “Course,

I got no space to hang them." Noticing our open mouths, he laughs. "I didn't really buy them." Animatedly waving his notebook around, he says, "I just keep a record of the ones I fancy, so if I win the lottery I can go back and get them. The gallery owner said she could wrap it up well for me if I wanted to carry it back to Poole. But I said" – Arthur screws his nose, making his weathered face ripple into a sea of tanned, wrinkled leather – "no thanks, not worth risking it. I'll come back another day."

We all laugh, the man and I both giving each other a knowing look. A look that shows we've already made the connection that Arthur is a dreamer. A window shopper. And if he is, then that's okay. Arthur notices he's not introduced us both. "Zoe, this is Mike. We met at Lynmouth and walked together, as far as Bude."

"Yep, we got into a hostel there," Mike adds. He turns to fill me in on the detail further. "I had an ankle injury and had to stop. That day of ups and downs on the path was tough. Damaged myself and ended up staying for two nights. Thought young Artie here was way ahead by now!" Mike laughs once more and shakes his head, looking at Arthur. "Can't believe I bumped into you again." Watching the two men chattering excitedly was not unlike witnessing a reunion of childhood friends. You'd never realise they had only met a couple of weeks before. I can see some red patchiness around Mike's neck and up the sides of his face. I wonder what had happened to his skin. Maybe he'd had an accident that caused a burn, but I can't see any signs of the telltale scarring. My fleeting observation quickly fades.

Arthur mops the beads of sweat that wander down his brow with an old rag. "Gee whizz, it's hot." He stuffs the rag back down the front of his T-shirt. I wonder what else he has stashed in that pouch. "Hey, where's your rucksack?" He suddenly realises that Mike is carrying nothing more than an empty plastic bottle.

"I hid it down the lane, underneath the bushes. No one'll find it." Mike is clearly a man of practicality. "I needed water, so thought I'd jump off the path here and dive inland to the pub. No point in carrying a heavy pack all that way. Hope I'll find it going back!"

Time prods at me. Arthur has no constraints for himself, but I have an agreed time to meet Lea and Steve at this evening's finishing point. We say goodbye to Mike, heading off on his mission to find water. Once we've retreated along the lane at Zennor Head, we swing westwards at the junction with the coast path.

In the area following Porthmeor Cliff, we find ourselves above a steep gorge known as Great Zawn. What a wonderful name that is, conjuring up the image of a science fiction character in my head. Above the gorge, I stand with Artie and marvel at the sea sparkles. The sun is high and brilliant. There are no clouds, and the atmosphere remains hot with little breeze to cool off our already burning skin. As I stand here, appreciating the jewels of the waves, twinkling like diamonds amid its dance across the gentle ebb and flow, I realise it's a poignant moment. One that I'm sure I'll never forget. Arthur, despite having walked this National Trail umpteen times, admits to never having seen sea sparkles of such beauty. I take my camera out and film the performance, wondering if I'll even be able to capture the experience through the lens with authenticity.

My sore throat seems to have eased and I'm feeling much better. Unfortunately, though, these feet continue to cause me grief, even in my new boots. In addition to the bite, under and around the edge of my heels the skin is so hard, yet I seem to have gained the knack of propagating blisters underneath it. The only way I see I can deal with this is to pack out the painful area with Compeed and alter my way of walking so I'm not putting too much pressure on the sore spot. The result? An awkward gait, feeling uncomfortable over the miles, and a tired body and mind by the end of the day. Dealing with pain, mile after mile, is exhausting.

After saying a cheery goodbye and thanks to Arthur, I tumble into the back seat of Lea and Steve's little red hatchback at Pendeen Watch, six and a half miles west of Zennor Head. I know I might not see my new friend Artie again and that feels weird, as we've walked and talked together all day. Somehow, though, I am optimistic I'll bump into him once more. It's happened already, so there's no reason it might not happen again ...

Angels come in many guises. This evening, my angel is Lea, who, on seeing my pain predicament, drags a footstool over to the sofa, sits on it and scoops up my feet. She pours a wonderfully scented oil into her palms and delivers the most magical foot massage. I usually hate my feet being handled. I'm so sensitive and ticklish. But Lea's touch is firm and confident as her fingers pressure and circle every nerve, joint, muscle and bone. Today proved to be hard in the blistering heat and tiring after fourteen miles of chatter. For once, I allow myself to melt into the wave of relaxation and exhaustion settling over me.

20 Land's End

It's the last day of July and I've woken up with a sore throat, again. Lea and Steve drop me off at Pendeen Watch, but my head is not on the walk today. To make matters worse, I take the wrong path right at the start. Within the first few minutes of the day, I've seriously scratched my legs by trying to wade through gorse and bramble. On realising this is not the coast path after all, I backtrack up the road a little way and find the correct route. *Keep your eye on the path, Wath.*

I do my best to leave my sore throat and fuzzy head behind. As I walk into the miles, the applied mindset seems to work and instead I'm distracted by the wonder of the landscape. The beam engine house at Lelant is as incredible in the flesh as it is in the many photographs that adorn the postcard stands and books of Cornwall's finest authors. That today is grey and foggy only adds to the dominating mystery and visual appeal. I see aesthetic innovation everywhere. Here is no different and as my imagination works like a frenzied dervish, pirouetting through creative possibilities, it leaves trails of vibrant colours and ideas in its wake. The tingles of artistic excitement burble through me and I can appreciate how in this place films are born, artworks created, and books inspired.

The fog clags around the cliffs like sticky tape, and views of rugged rocky arches and horizons are invisible this time. Often the beauty is in what you can't see. Cornwall keeps the views hidden today, allowing me to conjure my own vision of the unknown.

There's a little bird on the road in front of me. It's struggling to move, and as I approach, it doesn't fly away. That's never a good sign. It musters an ounce of effort to remobilise, but then it falls again and onto its back. Bending down, I whisper, "C'mon little fella," and pick it up. On closer inspection, I decide it's a warbler, but I can't be sure. Still with the bird cupped safely in my hand, I look around and see a couple walking towards me. "Hi! Any idea what make and model this is?" They both walk over to me, and the man looks at the bird.

"Warbler, I reckon." He looks back up at me with a caring but definitive smile. "Won't make old bones, that one."

Sad that I can't help Master Warbler, and taking advice from my new companions, I set him into nearby bushes at the side of the road and we walk and talk together.

Deborah and Chris are here on holiday from West Dorset. They are a friendly and instantly likeable couple who are keen to hear about my walking pursuits and charitable endeavours. Our conversation moves to home life.

"I'm involved with Artsreach," says Deborah. "I don't know if you've heard of it, but it's a charity that brings the arts to rural communities in Dorset?"

"Oh my goodness, I absolutely do know Artsreach! When I lived in West Lulworth, I volunteered to help them out. I loved all the performances they brought to our village hall. Always surprised by such high-calibre artists in our intimate little venue." Deborah stops in her tracks.

"Well, what are the chances of bumping into another Artsreach volunteer on these cliffs, down here in the wilds of Cornwall?" We grin at one another, acknowledging a connection beyond the love of walking coast paths.

While the delights and challenges of walking are high on our agenda, our conversation is extra animated when we reach the topic of

Martin Clunes, especially when I learn he lives near to them. They also offer me a night at their home once I reach West Bay.

The decision to use walking poles has been one of the best choices of my trip planning. Frequently, they have helped me keep my balance or allowed me to dampen some of the impact of the vertiginous steps found on these coast paths. After all, erosion happens, and steps fall away. Sometimes volunteers rebuild them. Some risers are so high, I have to turn and climb down backwards as if I was coming down a ladder in order to make it down safely. For others, I've discovered I can lengthen the poles and use them as an extra anchor to take my weight as I lower myself down.

Through a persistent light rain, and still walking with Deborah and Chris, I ease myself down one of these many giant steps. This time, they've cut the step into the rock itself and I feel myself slip on the wet stone. *Oh shit!* I grab my pole back in a panic. As I thrust it in front of me, my wrist jars and I wind myself. But I slip no further. I'm not sure my new friends have even noticed, so taking an extra deep breath to refocus, I give myself a proverbial splash of water in the face and carry on. I hope it will appear as if nothing has happened. It's also another great way to make me forget I'm still feeling ill ... I'm working hard on those distraction techniques.

By the time I reach Sennen Cove, I know I've only walked nine miles, but I also know my miles are done. I want to give myself the opportunity to do Land's End tomorrow instead, and I'm so close. We stop and share tea and cake at Sennen Beach Café and swap phone numbers. Then, with a hearty goodbye to Deborah and Chris, I'm picked up following my early 3 p.m. finish and taken back to my guardian angels' home.

I use the extra hours wisely by resting, updating my blog, dosing up on a herbal tincture that Lea offers me and ordering some more new kit. Someone gave me a mummy-style sleeping bag before coming on this walk, but I've found I'm not getting a good night's sleep while camping because I'm *so*ooo cold. From researching this further, a down bag is what I need instead of hollow fibre. It's a simple decision. I place the order and hope it arrives before I leave Lea and Steve's in a few days' time.

The next morning it's an 8.15 a.m. start for Day Twenty-Five and I stride out, knowing two things. First: today I am going to reach Land's End. Second: I have a nasty cold. I swallow with great difficulty and sniff with a vague recognition of self-pity. It is what it is, and I know I have to walk through the cold and just keep dosing up on paracetamol. The dream of reaching Land's End, however, has always seemed so far off, almost impossible. It's a strange, pressing consciousness that this icon of my journey is just around the corner.

The sun glows to begin with and this at least creates a medicine to help my progress, but it's not long before the patchy rain and cloud returns. It hangs low and moody around the headlands, preventing any far-reaching views across the Atlantic. I strain to see beyond but can't even make out the Isles of Scilly, which are only thirty miles south-west of the toe of Cornwall.

An hour later, I'm standing face to face with the legendary white signpost of Land's End. New York is apparently 3,174 miles away and John o'Groats, a mere 874 miles. As I pause here, I bask in the significance of this moment, sniffing back my runny nose. There are few people around. The signpost shop is closed, and it's grey and blustery. But here I am. Little me, of no athletic ability and even less belief in myself. Here I am, with my size 4.5 feet that have carried me to the most westerly tip of the UK using nothing but the power generated within my legs and my body.

As I look out across the North Atlantic Ocean, knowing that America is at the far eastern edge of these waters, I allow the reflective thoughts to pass in and out of my head. *My* legs and *my* body! How is this even possible? I nudge myself. *Oi, and your mind. You'd never have got this far without some internal strength, Wath.* Of course, it takes determination and willpower to push through some of the inner battles and external conditions I've faced on this journey so far. I'm only 257 miles into the walk here and I have learnt so much about the landscape, the terrain, and my ability to cope with whatever I encounter. Alone. I think that's what warms me with pride the most. It *has* been difficult, yes. But I've done it on my own, by making my own decisions and walking this path my way.

After a couple of minutes, a woman wanders towards me with her dog. She looks lost in her thoughts, and I feel guilty for interrupting this precious time with, and for, herself. "Excuse me." I drag out a pleasant smile from this cold-ridden, philosophical head I'm wearing today. "Would you mind taking a photo for me, please?" The woman returns the smile and after checking which button to press on my camera, she obliges. "Thank you!" I beam now, the genuine power of pride refilling my soul and soothing away my body aches and sniffles.

"Not a problem," she says as she swings the camera back to me. "You can't come all this way and not have the obligatory Land's End photo, can you?" She turns to see her dog heading way off into the distance. "Gotta go. Have a great walk!" In a blink she's gone, and I am once again alone to share my moment of achievement with myself.

After the euphoria of reaching the iconic Land's End signpost, I soon discover my lift is brief. Arriving at a blot of buildings, I'm surrounded by the ugliness of what feels like a Land's End theme park, with not a coast path sign in sight. The distinct drop of mood from my earlier accomplishment is disappointing. I hurry through the complex in what I believe to be roughly the right direction and feel the relief when I pop out the other side, the wild ruggedness of my imagined Land's End now car-crashed by a developer's dream. I'm sad that they even need a tourist attraction beside such natural beauty. It caters for the whims of souvenir-hungry folk who would appreciate Land's End more for its ability to serve up the finest hot chocolate. It may supply a bargain at the shopping village or a feast for the eyes with the best 4-D cinematic experience. But Land's End will never be the raw experience of my dreams.

The coastline inspiring such literary names as Du Maurier or Graham no longer exists here. I wander away, remembering Clovelly and wondering how not just one, but two landmarks of the South West have ended up as a circus. Permitted to cash in on those wishing to witness the beauty first-hand, in a twist of irony, they are wiping away the rawness of the experience. How do you recreate nature within or around a venue full of impulse product-driven shops and entertainment? On the flip side, I try to balance my inner debate. I can see the need to monitor and perhaps restrict thousands of visitors flocking to an area like Land's End or a village as tiny as Clovelly; and it no doubt brings money into the local economy.

Wow, I'm thankful it's not too long before my disillusionment of the morning filters back into bubble mode. My enthusiasm levels rise again as I glimpse the bobbing heads of seals in the waters around Gwennap Head. Then, trekking along the clifftops, with the odd headland peeking in and out from the drizzly cloud, I spot a lizard. It glistens green like an emerald on the footpath in front of me. For a split second, it stops, as if waiting for confirmation from me of my next move. Without warning or time for me to grab my camera, it darts off into the nearby undergrowth. It may well have been a Common Wall Lizard. It's not native to the UK, but often spied in parts of the South and South West of England.

The exhilaration soon fizzes all the way to my toes as I witness my first Cornish chough. They are rare, I'm told, with only a few hundred pairs in the UK. The Welsh coastline is home to many of these, with the lower, most south-westerly tip of Cornwall also a great place to spot them. It feeds and flirtatiously glows its bright red beak and legs at me. Like a fine, colourfully stockinged lady, it's dressed in black and finished with a smack of red lipstick. It stays long enough for me to take a photo and then it's up and away with a mate.

I slide the camera back into its pouch, feeling chuffed with my chough photo. As compact cameras go, this one's not half bad. It's only a Samsung WB something or other – a little compact but with a bit more oomph than most. Having a respectable zoom is always a bonus for me as I like to see quality detail in my photographs, but having it small enough to be accessible is also an important factor. I've discovered over the past few weeks that carrying my camera bag attached to my rucksack hip belt works well for those quick grab-and-snap moments. The bag organisation layout proved itself today for catching the chough on camera, and I could not be happier.

Allowing my mind to wander, I feel no pressure to make any consideration of work, family, home life, or household essentials. This is meditation at its finest. Indeed, if I was at home now, despite being on my summer holidays, I'd be ensnared in the web of chores, duty or planning for next term. Instead, I can switch off and be at one with these sights and sounds. I've always had a strong interest in the natural world, particularly from an aesthetic perspective. Being out and about in the landscape for weeks on end has immersed me into the daily rituals of the wildlife, the weather and the people. All appear to have their expected routines, yet all can be highly unpredictable, often with comical or dramatic results.

There is a noticeable change in my feelings towards the walk since leaving the signpost at Land's End. For the first time in this journey, I have completely changed direction and am now walking eastwards ...

or at least in my head I am. Looking at the map, I realise there's more walking south to do before I can say I'm heading home proper. But from a psychological perspective, it's different. In a massive way. The sun is no longer in the same position in the sky during my mornings. Previously, it sat over the land and warmed my back or my left side. Now, as I turn this coastal corner and head eastwards, although the sun sits behind the clouds today, I can see it's over the water, to my right. From this point onwards, the early morning walks will see the sun ahead of me. It may not seem much of a change, but I've become so attuned to the daily rituals of the sun, moon, weather and nature, for it to turn upside-down now feels weird. I need time to readjust to this new land I have just dropped into, even though I'm excited.

There's another shift, too. With the passing of Land's End comes a new confidence and resolve that I *can* and *will* see this adventure to its successful conclusion. It is clearly a milestone that means more to me than I realised, and as I make these steps further away from the jarring complex of Penn an Wlas, Land's End, an unexpected pull of emotion gathers in my heart.

Jinni

21

Not far past Land's End, I meet a young lady with a compact rucksack, but it's obvious she's not just a day hiker. She's kitted out well and her rucksack displays a thin banner explaining that she's walking the coast path in thirty-nine days and which day number she's on. It's a great way to open a conversation about why she's walking the path, and her chosen charity, Oxfam.

"Hey, that's amazing, you're doing the whole coast path too! How are you getting on?" I ask.

"Hi, yes I am, thanks! I'm doing pretty good, actually. I'm sharing the miles with my dad and sister today, but mostly I'm on my own. I didn't start solo, though. A friend walked with me from Minehead but had to pull off after cultivating some monster blisters. They became infected, so he went to A & E to get treatment. Believe me, they were grim. He says he's going to let them heal and maybe rejoin me, somewhere near Plymouth." I think of my blisters and how bad they've been and suddenly feel super lucky mine haven't developed into anything worse.

"Gosh, that doesn't sound good. It'll be hard coming back to the path after three weeks or however long it takes, won't it? You'll trump him, having three weeks' worth of fitness ahead of him."

"We'll have to see. I'm Jinni, by the way. I'm walking in aid of Oxfam. It looks like you're walking for charity as well?"

"Lovely to meet you, Jinni. I'm Zoe. Yep, I'm raising money for three charities: a children's hospice in Poole – adult hospices receive funding from the government, but a children's hospice is entitled to little to no funding. They rely on sponsorship and donations to help run the unit. It's heartbreaking, but the money really helps them and the kids' families. I'm also splitting the funds between an assistance dog charity and our design technology department at school. The parents of one of our students at school set up the dog charity, so we try to support them wherever we can, and I'm raising money to buy a laser cutter for my department."

"Ah, you're a teacher?"

"Yes, I've been teaching for around six years now."

"I'm starting my teacher training in Plymouth when I get back from this walk. That's another reason I didn't want to spend too long away walking this summer. I need to be ready for September, so gave myself thirty-nine days."

"Oh wow, really? What age group? And what's your subject?"

"Science. Secondary. I hope I'm doing the right thing." A look passes from me to Jinni that says *You'll be fine, but it's tough out there.* "I've come on this walk now to lead myself into what I know will be a hard year." It sounds like she's already aware of how tricky it can be.

We continue to walk and talk together. "Who made your rucksack sign? It's clever. Eye-catching."

"My mum made it for me. She stencilled the words, ran it up on the sewing machine and stitched in a little transparent pocket so I could insert the number of days left on the adventure. It's always one of the first things people ask about my walk. You know, how far have you come? How long have you got left? How many miles are you walking? You probably get that too? It also breaks the ice and gives people an invitation to talk to me."

"Flippin' heck, yes, I do. Like *all* the time. That's brilliant!" *No, not brilliant. It's bloody ingenious. Why didn't you think of that, Wath?*

Jinni's boots look super comfortable. I notice how lithely she dances along the trail and up and down the hills. She's light on her feet and therefore pretty fast, including running down hills. "How do you do that?" I ask her, in awe, as we reach the bottom of one hill.

"I try to go down quickly and lightly, to reduce extending the pain in my knees. It seems to work." I'd not thought of that either, though I don't think I'd be capable of running down a hill – especially with this pack on my back.

With her family keeping her company, Jinni has slowed to accommodate them, and now me, too. She tells me about how she's kept her kit small and lightweight. My eyes flick to her Osprey rucksack, which is only a 34-litre pack, compared to my 68-litre Osprey. I observe how effortlessly she slides her water bottle out of the side pocket without removing the rucksack. I watch how she slips her iPhone back into a hip belt pocket after checking her Ordnance Survey map on her device. "You have maps on your phone? Jinni, what *is* this wizardry? I'd love to have something like that!"

"A friend works for Ordnance Survey and got me all the maps I'd need. It's so useful as it tells me exactly where I am right now." *Wow.*

With a fresh pair of eyes, I look down at my soft plastic map case, wedged between my hip belt and my waist. I sigh at my clumpy Scarpa walking boots. I feel the weight of my already semi-empty rucksack on my shoulders. It isn't the weight of the pack that is niggling me, it's the weight of feeling like I came here not knowing what I was doing. I researched and I made decisions, but seeing Jinni springing along the path next to me with such lightweight kit makes me think my choices were ill-founded. Even her walking boots are the smallest, lightest boots she could find on the market: Inov8. Close to trail-running boots, the low-rise ankle gives minimal support while the rest of the boot is thin but waterproof. I make a mental note to do some more informed research on my return home.

"I've just ordered a new down sleeping bag as the synthetic bag is too bulky and cold. I'm staying with friends in Redruth at the moment, so it should arrive there in a few days, ready for when I'm back out camping again."

"That sounds good. I've been thinking about how I can lessen the weight in my bag even further and have decided I might just sleep in a silk liner. They're easy to make," she adds.

"Now that's a bit too hardcore for me!" Jinni laughs along with me, and I notice how the dimples on either side of her face crease into two deep smiles. When she was a toddler, that's what Laura used to call dimples ... they were our "smiles".

I like Jinni. Despite my momentary return to imposter syndrome lurking in the background, this is my issue and not hers. A lovely young woman, good to walk and chat with, and after all, I'm getting loads of ideas from her for future outdoor gear to try out. We have lots in common, with plenty to talk about. We say our goodbyes and head separate ways as Jinni walks inland to see her family off before continuing solo again.

After around four and a half miles from Land's End, I reach the Minack Theatre. I'd heard about this incredible feat of design and determination by one woman and her gardener in the 1930s. I'm looking forward to seeing it for myself. Above the amphitheatre, I stand for a moment, marvelling at the stone turrets, the steeply tiered stone seats nestled between rocky outcrops, and the paved actor's arena, way down at the bottom with the sea as a backdrop. Pillars, steps and arches framing the mighty calm or power of the ocean. *One day, I absolutely must come and watch a performance here.* I'm humbled by this woman's dedication and legacy blasted out and carved into the Cornish bedrock.

With the knowledge I must press on, and many miles to tuck into my rucksack today, I leave my viewing station at Minack. It's now a downward game towards the beach at Porthcurno, via the steps cut into the cliff. It seems a fair estimate that although it's only just coming up to 11 a.m., half of Cornwall has had the same idea. There are bodies scrambling up, approaching me head-on, and even more behind me, carrying their buckets, spades and beach bags. Many cling tightly to tots who, unlike me, harbour no thoughts of falling, no fear; just an eagerness to get to the beach. As quickly as possible.

The flurry of people on these steps that are at best narrow and steep, and at worst, winding and ... steep, causes me a temporary panic. I freeze in the apex of one step's twist, which seems a marginally wider point in which to take a break. I wait it out until I see a gap and I feel more comfortable about resuming my slow descent. Despite being hellishly precipitous, I wouldn't have found it so hard if I'd had the space and time to tackle the steps on my own. As it is, with the insistence of people wanting to push by in both directions, I'm pressured. Exhausted with concentration and adrenalin, I'm relieved when I reach the bottom. It's time to find myself some lunch and a place to sit and regroup my tattered thoughts.

At the far end of Porthcurno beach, despite the greyness of the day, I find a little spot to nestle myself into and tuck heartily into my grub. Within moments, a rescue helicopter choppers in, hovering above the rocky area of Logan Rock and Great Goular. There's a lifeboat out there too. *Oh, my goodness! Whatever has happened?* I am caught in the moment of horror as I watch a person being skilfully winched to safety out of the water. The helicopter makes a hasty retreat, but within minutes, it's back, creating a mini tsunami across the foreshore.

It hovers while they winch another person up into the belly of the whirlybird.

Over again, the helicopter returns to collect more people. As I'm thinking I'm witnessing a tragic disaster, the reality of the situation occurs to me. I see someone being lowered into the lifeboat ... *of course, Wath, you muppet. This is a training exercise!* I laugh at my gullibility but am honoured to have witnessed these superheroes undergoing their life-saving training.

A short distance out of Porthcurno, I drop from Treen Cliff into Penberth Cove. Thank goodness – a proper loo stop opportunity! These are always a welcome sight, as opposed to the regular "find a tree or hedge to hide myself behind". I pick my way over the giant cobbles, littered in between with grassy mounds, and swing my pack off, leaving it by the door. My feet also appreciate a moment of rest in the comfort of the little girl's room. On stepping outside, I'm captivated by the fisherman unloading a stack of lobster pots from the back of his truck. His face is alight with a bright smile, and a mop of wayward white hair frames it well. The pot sits easily on his shoulders, though with his arms aloft in an Atlas pose, it reveals the unnatural roundness of his belly. Faded, stone-washed jeans in an unrecognisable state – I figure they must have absorbed at least a year's worth of lobster juice and pot stains – are wrinkled tightly over the tops of his enormous brown workman's boots. A gentle giant, I think, smiling at the fisherman while returning my pack up onto my shoulders.

The terrain becomes rocky with much larger boulders leading into narrow, steep valleys. Down one side then immediately back up the other at Porthguarnon, many boggy patches challenge my boots to a game of "Dry Toes, Wet Toes". I had been adamant I would keep my feet out of any big puddles today, but looking at the ground now, this might not be possible. The wooded area approaching St Loy's Cove and Boskenna Cliff continues the boggy theme. It's good to climb back up onto the clifftop, into open air, although it's not long before I'm descending into another streamed valley again.

Mile after mile of geographical rollercoaster, I climb steep ascents at least nine times, until I reach Lamorna – only ten miles into today's journey. As I wander down into the harbour, where I see the echoes of quarry workings, past and present, I have the urge to treat myself to an ice cream. Of course, it soon disappears with the haste of a hungry gannet. No stopping to savour the flavour here. Even so, those few seconds of ice cream felt like velvet on my tongue. My body aches have lessened as the day progresses, but my cold is still in full swing. Onwards and upwards, I stop for a moment to photograph the harbour before leaving to make my way towards Mousehole.

A roadside stand at Mousehole selling hand-tied bunches of freshly cut garden flowers gives me an idea. I choose the prettiest bunch, drop the coins into their honesty box, and stow my walking poles away as I no longer need them. It's all road work from here. With the flowers in my hand, I walk towards Newlyn, this evening's pickup point, and pause for a moment outside the lifeboat station. A pang of dreadful memory hits me: Penlee. The Penlee lifeboat disaster happened here in 1981. It may have been thirty years ago, but I vividly remember watching Richard Baker delivering the news broadcast about it on the TV all those years back. I'd not comprehended that it happened here. I was ten years old and didn't know Cornwall first-hand, yet it was one of my earliest memories of experiencing deep emotion for others lost. A sense that this was not something that was "just news". These were fathers, brothers, sons and no doubt all from the same small, close-knit village community.

Stood in front of the fitting memorial and station where the *Solomon Browne* launched, I sense the enormity and devastation of this tragedy. I'm taken aback that my early memory triggers the return of a real surge of emotion, rising from the pit of my belly to sit heavy in my chest. A tear falls, and then another. I desperately want to heave out a sob, to release the weight of the sadness, but I am self-conscious. Instead, I drop my sunglasses from the top of my head onto my face and simply allow the tears to fall as much as they need to. I hope that by the time I reach Newlyn my face isn't too streaked with tear stains, dragging gullies through the dirt of the day.

Lea and Steve are delighted with the flowers when they collect me at 7.30 p.m. This is one of my latest finish times. I worry about leaving it too much after 6 p.m. to complete the day's walking because my hosts drive from Redruth and back, besides Steve cooking dinner. With nearly sixteen miles in the bag today, however, we all know that I'm inching ever closer to their home again. From here on, the pickups will become shorter in time and distance.

After a divine shower and an exceptionally wonderful hot meal and dessert prepared by Steve, Lea insists on giving me another foot massage. Of course, I don't decline, and relish the experience while it lasts. Depending on how many miles I walk each day, it looks like I may have another five or six days with this beautiful couple. It's like they reappeared from my childhood as if by magic, to support me when I needed it most.

22

Newlyn to Porthleven

Each day I stayed with Lea and Steve, I completed another section of coast path, leaving with a spring in my step and a light rucksack. To return to familiarity, tasty home-cooked food, a shower and sometimes even a foot massage with essential oils from Lea eased the burden of my challenge. My cold has improved too, which is a bonus.

It's easy walking along the Strand with striking views across the harbour at Newlyn. The spectacle of St Michael's Mount rises from the far side of Mount's Bay at Penzance. There are fishing boats aplenty anchored here. I notice some older, larger vessels. The lack of paint and creeping rust gilds their hulls with an aesthetic quality that would be hard for any artist to recreate. There's something about the pattern of decay that is strangely appealing, and I've always found myself drawn to it. It may be a decomposing plant, a rotting tree trunk, a derelict building or boat. There is beauty in every layer of life, whether it's just blossoming or slowly disintegrating.

Over the years, I have learnt to keep my eyes open to these small but remarkable finds. It's one of my keys to gratitude and enjoyment of any place or situation. No matter how bad something appears, there is always something to be thankful for. I've heard it called the Pollyanna Effect, but whatever it is, it works for me and to be honest, it's not a conscious thing. It's inherent within me. Always noticing, always observing. I watch everything, taking my time. My mind processes the colours, the overlaps, and the empty spaces between them. I appreciate the coincidental wonder of all these forms, patterns, shapes and tonal qualities splendidly colliding at the same time.

While I'm on pavements, I don't need my walking poles, although I might as well be walking down the road naked as without them I feel bare. When I first walked with so little in my rucksack, it felt the same. I remember the first day I left Lea and Steve's. They were aghast at how much I had kept in my rucksack to walk with. I explained to them it didn't feel natural to have nothing on my back. Besides, I'd need to carry some weight, otherwise it'd be a harsh shock to my body when I get back to being "independent" again. You can't just go from walking with no gear to a full pack of 15 kg and not expect problems.

Newlyn Strand blends seamlessly into the promenade at Penzance, providing a consistent view of the bay once I've navigated past the dock. It's a small port, with colourful pleasure boats of all shapes and sizes scattered around Penzance harbour. Tiny rowing boats, some upturned on the harbour wall, clothed in a tattered version of their former glory. A range of uniform sailing-club-style boats and some largish yachts. I'm no expert and can't even begin to name them, but I like the way they look. I especially warm to the older boats that may have whimsical tales to tell from their days of being at sea.

There are no ostentatious yachts of any nauseating pomp or value, which is just as well. That type of boat does nothing for me, except to remind me of home. Yes, if I close my eyes, the clinking of the halyards, swaying against the masts in the breeze, sounds just as though I am in Poole. There are a great many more boats back there, though, than here in Newlyn and Penzance.

A large group of birds ahead of me catches my attention. They are funny little orange-legged critters. I can't identify them, but I stop and watch them on an area of beach, with great fascination. They busy themselves over the sand and the pebbles, a bumble and a bob back and forth, moving stones around with their beaks. It's mesmerising, so I pull out my camera to record a short video, as it might help me find out what they're called once I arrive back at Lea and Steve's later this evening.

It's not long before I decide to walk along the beach. Without thought or intention, I glance down, automatically finding myself treasure-troving as I go. Soon enough, my little hoard of pretty stones has grown and I'm gleaming from my finds, adorned with striations of green, black and brown. Blue-green hues to some, and others a pressed, cold white, smoothed and polished. They shine with an intensity that would fool a beachcomber into believing they've stumbled across a valuable gemstone. A vein of quartz sparkles through the centre of one pebble, and I am delighted to find a pretty green stone with a hole right through the middle. Although I'm not superstitious, I still catch myself thinking *this might be my lucky stone*. Those little mottled marine birds aren't so daft after all. They have the best pick of all these beautiful stones – and the bugs underneath.

My feet are playing up again today. There are plenty of benches to stop at, so even though I've only been walking for a little under an hour, I take a quick break. I need to drink water and readjust my socks and boots. As I approach the next bench, I realise I won't be able to stop yet, as someone is already occupying it. *All* of it. A man wearing a tatty blue baseball cap, a faded red technical tee and loose-fitting cycle shorts stoops over an empty rucksack, the contents strewn across the bench. A scrunched water bottle sits on one end, looking as close to disintegration as the baseball cap. The bottle somehow seems to hold a full quota of water.

"Mike!" The man looks up.

"Oh, hiya," he says, a semblance of recognition passing across his face. He stands upright. "Zoe?" I can tell he's hurriedly scanning through a mental stack of memo cards with names noted of three weeks' worth of various chance meetings.

"Yes, yes! How are you? It's good to see you again." Mike catches me momentarily glancing at his disarray of kit. He's quick to slide everything over.

"Here, please sit down. I'm just having a bit of a sort-out." He fusses around, making a vague attempt at being gentlemanly as he clears a space for us to sit. He tosses some of the gear on the ground. "It won't take me long to get this stuff back into my bag."

"Cheers!" I unclip my chest strap and hip belt and swing my rucksack off and down beside me so I can sit.

We both take a quick slug of water from our bottles, though Mike's plastic bottle crinkles alarmingly. He sees me notice it but says nothing. "I thought you'd be way ahead by now," I say, thinking back to when I met Mike previously. It was on the little lane walking out of Zennor, with Artie, three days ago.

"Hah, I probably would have been, but I stopped with an old friend who lives here in Penzance." For a split second, I spot a look of teenage sheepishness dance across his face. "Tony ..." Mike shakes his head gently and laughs. "Do you know, Tony and I haven't seen each other in a good many years, yet we can pick up from where we left off as if it were yesterday." Looking up at me, he raises his eyebrows. "It was a heavy night, but we didn't half have some fun, him and me!" He lifts his water bottle to take another swig but stops just before the bottle reaches his beard. "That's why I'm so late starting out today. But now I'm as dry as the bottom of a budgie cage." He gulps back at least half the bottle and screws the top back on tightly. Mike gestures with the bottle. "I'll need to pick up a new one of these in the next day or two. It's lasted me well."

"I'm surprised it's still holding any water at all!" I say, grinning. "Any sign of Artie?"

"No, not since I saw him that day when he was with you and I'd dumped my bag to find water." He bends forward, replacing his bottle on the ground, and starts repacking his kit. "I'll bet he's just around the next corner, though. I don't think we've seen the last of Artie."

"Yep!" I nod and agree.

In all the chat, I remember I need to sort out my socks. I unlace my boots while Mike packs up the rest of his rucksack. "It's okay, they're not too smelly," I say. "Just had a few blister problems, which I'm trying to keep on top of. I've been staying at Redruth for the last few nights and am being treated to regular showers and clothes washing."

"Oh, so you're not doing it properly, then?" I think Mike's teasing me, but I can't be sure. He's hit a nerve, and my imposter syndrome creeps back.

"Actually, I am." I am quick to cut in and save face. "I'm camping and everything ..." As I'm talking I see Mike look down at my saggy rucksack. *Damn.* "While I'm staying with my friends, I'm leaving some of my kit there. I carry enough so I don't get too used to carrying a lighter weight. It would feel weird walking wearing nothing." Those eyebrows raise again. "On my back," I hastily add. We both laugh at my slip-up.

With my socks and boots back on and Mike's rucksack squeezed to the hilt, we're both ready to set off again. Mike takes three paces forward and then swings around sharply. "Got to make sure I've not left anything behind," he tells me. "I've left too much stuff in the past, and all because I didn't make that check." It's a brief glance and after a second, he's happy that we've both cleared the bench of our belongings. We can officially make headway again.

There's no question that we'll walk with one another, for today at least, although during one of our many random conversations, Mike voices it. "I ought to check if you're happy walking with me? Sometimes people prefer to be on their own."

"No, no – it's absolutely fine. It's good to have some company," I reply with a smile. Conversation is easy with Mike.

"So when did you start walking the path?" Mike asks me.

"I set off on the third of July. This is my twenty-sixth day." He looks at me, shocked.

"Hold on a minute, I started on the sixteenth of July, so what have you been doing all this time? How come I've caught you up when you started nearly two weeks before me?"

"It doesn't sound great does it, but I've been poorly, so started off really slow. I had a terrible chest infection and cough, which lasted around twelve weeks. I almost didn't come because I was so ill." I look at Mike to see if I'm boring him, but he's nodding and looks like he's taking it all in.

"I also left the path for five days. My grandmother died." Mike stops walking, turns to look at me.

"Shit, I'm really sorry to hear that. I'm so sorry. That must have been hard?"

"Yes, it's been up and down. Quite literally. You know, the path and my emotions."

"So, have you done a long-distance walk before?"

"Nope, this is my first. I'm doing it to mark my big birthday, which was a couple of months back. And I'm walking for charity. How about you? Why are you walking the coast path?"

"We owned a pub in South Wales, but me and my long-term partner split a few months ago. She bought me out, and so I came down to stay at my sister's house in Weymouth. I was thinking about what I should do next and was like, why don't I go off on a long walk like the South West Coast Path? Joan said she'd drive me to the start in Minehead. I popped into an outdoor shop, bought a few bits, and here I am!"

"Not much planning, then?"

"What is there to plan? You just take your bag and go. As long as you have a sleeping bag, tent, and something to cook with. What more do you need?" I laugh as Mike says this, thinking of all the gadgets I bought and ended up sending home because they added unnecessary weight to my pack. There's the solar charger that never works, my infamous egg box and frying pan, and even the camping chair, though I still have that with me, at the moment.

As Mike talks, my thoughts turn to the months I'd spent planning this walk. The research for the kit I thought I needed. The fear of walking on my own, of camping and crossing rivers, prickles across my neck and I realise that as a man, or at least a confident man, Mike probably wouldn't get this. I choose not to mention it, but wish I could bottle an ounce of his can-do and get-it-done approach to save for another day.

"Have you done a long-distance path before?" I ask.

"Bloody right I have. I've been walking and camping since I was a kid. Did some longer routes in the past few years, some with my sons and others with friends. I'm used to it, but I've done nothing as long as this one."

"That makes sense, and why you're more confident about this path. I didn't know what to expect. I wasn't sure how many miles I could do in a day, even. My partner came along for the first two weeks with my campervan, and we slept in that each night. I do think I lost miles on those days, though."

"You would have done, yep. So you're staying in a friend's house right now *and* you've had two weeks in a campervan. You've not roughed it at all, have you?" I feel like I'm being grilled now.

"Actually, yes, I have. I've camped at a few sites. I just haven't wild camped yet. In all honesty, I'm a bit nervous about it."

"Well, I meant wild camping. Camping at sites is so unnecessary." I throw Mike a look. I don't know him very well, but I'm certainly not about to have him knock the way I've chosen to walk the coast path.

"It might seem unnecessary to you, but when you have no other option or you're learning how to do this thing, it's a blessing. We all have to start somewhere, and I've had a lot of support from the campsites I've been to."

"Yeah, sorry. You're right. We've all started somewhere, even me. Are you going to wild camp soon?"

"It'll depend on when I reach Fowey. That's how long I'm staying at my friend's house."

"You'll be fine. You just need to pick the right spots. It's all about the spot. Once you've done it, you won't want to camp any other way."

I think I believe him.

We cover a multitude of topics on our tour along the prom, ever closer to the picturesque and dramatic detail of Mount Bay, and the star of the show: St Michael's Mount.

Over the years, my head has shrouded this place in fairy tale or mystery. I have never seen it first-hand, and I guess I hadn't realised just how like Mont-Saint-Michel it is. As a teenager, I visited Brittany and have a clear memory of reaching the place via a tidal causeway. I remember being struck by how Mont-Saint-Michel appeared as a volcanic-looking isle of granite. It seemed so far removed from its surroundings, as if placed there by some higher power.

Now in Marazion, I stand for a fleeting moment, shoulder to shoulder with my new walking buddy for the day, looking back. It's important not to focus wholly on the path ahead; it would be so easy to forget the path trodden. As we admire the views back across the bay, we pass comment on our personal experiences of the features that pique our interest. We marvel at the distant view of the South West Coast Path walked from way before Mousehole, through Newlyn, Penzance and to this point where we now stand. With the imposing presence of St Michael's Mount rising through the greyness in the foreground, we turn and make for the next stage of our journey. We both promise ourselves to return and take the time to walk across the causeway and visit St Michael's Mount another day.

Opportunities to walk and talk are a super way to pass the time. The miles gracefully evaporate underneath muddy boot marks, long before you've heard where your new friend is from and why they're walking the trail. It's like therapy and before long, we've shared our life history in snippets. I found the same when walking with Artie and Jinni. Just as a book transports you off into another world, I can say the same for conversation. Nothing else matters except for those reciprocal exchanges of learning, sharing and social communication. That is, until you realise you have been talking for an hour and not paid any attention to the whereabouts of the National Trail white acorn, wooden fingerposts or waymarkers. Fortunately, we haven't gone far out of our way. We easily rectify our neglect of the route by taking the next turning right, back to the coast path instead of heading inland towards Perranuthnoe.

Beyond the private estate of historic houses of Prussia Cove, my mobile rings. Mike walks on ahead. I'm surprised as my family usually calls me in the evening, or Ross texts me if it's during the day. Scrabbling into my hip belt pocket, I find the phone, pressing the green button just in time. It's a police officer from Newquay police station. My heart thuds. *In* an instant my head is frantic, considering all the possibilities of what this could mean.

"It's okay," the female voice at the other end reassures me. "We just need to take a statement regarding the accident that took place on the twenty-sixth of July at Newquay harbour." *Accident? What accident?* I sweep through my memory of my arrival at Newquay harbour and remember that was where Lea and Steve first collected me a week ago. The dawning takes a few seconds.

"Oh, yes, I remember. I'm so sorry. You'll have to excuse me as I'm currently out walking. I'm on a very long walk, away from home. I'm miles from Newquay now. Up on a clifftop the other side of Penzance, in fact! Can you hear me okay? I live in Dorset." I'm making no sense.

I'm sure the police officer utters a faint noise that could be mistaken for a chuckle.

"Hmm, that's different," she says flatly, and then asks some more formal questions and goes on to take my statement. It takes about fifteen minutes.

"That's fine. I think I have all I need now," the officer says. "I'll give you a case number, so if you think of anything else, you can let us know." After ferreting around for a pen and my notebook, I jot it down roughly, though I doubt I'll need it. "Thank you for your time," PC Neutral says, "and happy walking!" *Well, I'll be ...* all that while I thought she wasn't really interested but I guess her need to be formal was about her doing her job. Back on my walk again for the day, I head off to catch up with Mike.

It's 5 p.m. and the grey, cloudy day that we left behind in Penzance has become strangely hot. An hour later, as we walk down the cliff path towards the harbour at Porthleven, the heat is building up even more. The heavy atmosphere whispers of thunder to come as it closes in around us.

Sixteen miles accomplished, Mike and I say goodbye at Porthleven and share thanks for a great walk and ideal company. We agree to keep an eye out for one another tomorrow, though at this stage I'm not sure what time Lea and Steve will drop me off. The miles are certainly easier as each day progresses. Although I'm not carrying as much kit in my rucksack, I note that I'm feeling fitter than I have done for a long time.

Lizard Point

23

It's a bright and cheery start to my day. Although hard to believe, this is already my twenty-seventh day on the path, and tonight will be my ninth staying with Lea and Steve. I've noticed a stark difference in the miles I can bag each day now and will have accumulated over one hundred miles for the week if I keep progressing in the same way. This is great news, as I still have around 345 miles to go. That means in twenty-seven days, I haven't even reached the halfway point. My fitness is increasing daily, but timewise, it's still going to be a squeeze. At least staying with my friends has made a positive impact towards giving me a better chance of finishing in the time I have available.

I'm thrilled to see three more choughs – this is the first time since my sighting of them back near Land's End. I also learnt last night through Lea and Steve that the birds I spotted near Penzance were turnstones. As with the choughs, this is another new bird to add to my internal catalogue of feathery sightings. As I walk, I lose myself in thought for nearly an hour, only stopping when I'm nudged out of my headspace to capture more photographs of the beauty surrounding me. I'm thinking about all the people I've met over the past four weeks. The chance encounters. The arranged visits. Those who are walking the full 630 miles of coast path, and those who were out walking their dogs, holidaying or working in the area. I hadn't expected a solo walk to be so rich with personal encounters, and the kindness from friends and strangers alike has touched me. I'm getting it. The experience is not just about putting one foot in front of the other and the physical demands of the walk. The people I've met have added to this adventure in ways I could never have prepared myself for.

Loe Bar is unlike anything I have seen. It's effectively a wide wall of sand that dams off an area of inland water from the ocean, known as The Loe. This haven for waterfowl and other wildlife sits to my left, stretching long with the appearance of an island in the middle. The sea to my right, although warm and summery, holds a look of command about it today. There's something brewing.

Ahead of me, I spot a blue rucksack. *That must be Mike!* I step up my pace as best as one can on the sand. Apparently, it's a good workout for the muscles – not that I need a workout right now. Four weeks of walking and my workout has been a daily routine of up hills, down hills, sand, prom, and repeat. Despite the niggles of troublesome blisters, I feel the benefit of that routine now. *I hope you can keep it up on your return home, Wath.*

At last, I've almost caught up with yesterday's walking companion. His baggy shorts droop slightly below his rucksack, and his calves, defined in the sunlight, look strong. I call out and Mike swings round.

"Aha, I wondered if I might see you today. Late start, was it?"

"Oi, cheeky, I can't leave too early as I get dropped off. It wouldn't be right to expect Lea and Steve to come out at the crack of dawn."

"Ohhh yes." Mike nods with a thoughtful smile pursed across his face. "I forgot you're not a real camper."

I screw my nose up and shoot him a telling glare, which promptly breaks into a grin. "Now look here, I didn't rush all this way for you to poke fun at me." I give him a look that says *You can either walk on your own today or you can be nice*. Mike smiles apologetically, leaning in slightly to make eye contact.

"Sorry, I was just playing."

"I know. That's okay."

"Sorry," he repeats. "I was teasing. I only do it to tease, sorry."

"It's fine, really. I don't have a major problem with it."

"Okay, sorry. Sorry." Mike pauses and looks down again. "Sorry, I say stuff sometimes, sorry."

Laughing in exasperation, I say, "You can stop saying sorry now! Let's get on with this walk, shall we?"

Mike smiles again, relief plastered over his face.

"Righto, c'mon. Let's be off then!" Pushing a walking pole into the ground, he propels himself forward with gusto.

We soon descend from the cliff to walk closer to sea level, which leads us into a pretty cove. To our left, we are astonished to see a small church, nestled into the sand dunes. With a step off the beach, we're straight through the gateway, where I read the church sign: "*Welcome to St Winwaloe, Gunwalloe*". So this is Gunwalloe. *Even if the church didn't appeal to me, the name would have me every time.* Mike looks at me, searching my face for any sign of interest in the building. I think my expression gives it away.

"Wanna go in?" he asks.

"Yeah, definitely!"

The small graveyard is well kept and houses a wide variety of headstones. Close to the building is a raised table tomb sat atop eight pillars. It looks grand. From the outside, there are three well-defined sections or halls to the church, side by side. They have steep apexes in the gable ends, above each of the three windows. A broad square tower, raised a little above the level of the church, sits just behind the main door but is separate from the church. It has two louvred slit windows, and a steep, pitched pyramid roof.

"I'll bet that's a bell tower," I say to Mike.

"Could be. What makes you think that?"

"Those louvres in the window slits make me think of bell towers – keeps the birds out ... sometimes. I used to be a bellringer in my younger years. There are many churches that are so old, they weren't able to add towers to the main building retrospectively, so they just built a separate bell tower instead." Mike looks impressed.

"Hmm, good call, I'd say."

As we approach the main door, there's an unusual statue sitting above the pathway at the edge of the churchyard. Someone has draped flowers in the outstretched hand. It's a representation of the church's dedicated saint, St Winwaloe. The church dates from the thirteenth century and is one of the oldest in Cornwall. Its unusual siting on the beach is the only one of its kind in the county, and we read on an information leaflet that some historians believe it's built on the site of a fifth-century place of worship. Inside the porch, there's a plaque that reads "St Winwaloe. The Church of the Storms". I don't doubt it. This place would see it all. Weathered, battered and repaired. Remarkable that it's still standing. I'm sure there is an intended and profound message in that somewhere for the parishioners.

Mike turns the ring with care to lift the latch on the historic door, dressed with traditional, ornamental wrought-iron hinges. We enter the building without a sound. It's odd how one can be full of chatter and jokes, and yet the silent power of a church holds the ability to reduce all but the unknowing toddler to a respectful whisper. We both make low, appreciative sounds inside this medieval building. We note the old floor tiles still in place, the delicate carvings found at the pew ends and the wooden rood screens. Mike is particularly interested in the structure and intricate carvings of the exposed wooden beams holding up the roof. Two preserved doors, bearing rich paintings of eight apostles within the arched and carved panels, stand retired. Now stationed as decorative artefacts of the church's history, for me these are the highlight of our visit to St Winwaloe. For those seeking quiet reflection, the place is perfect.

I find the visitor's book and sign it. You never know, I might come back here one day, and it would be fun to look back at my thoughts. It's time to move on, however, so we pick up our rucksacks that we've left by the door and return to the equally peaceful beach of Church Cove. Although it's now the summer holidays, this area isn't as busy as I had expected it to be. We are in the deepest, most southerly point of Cornwall. Well, almost. Gunwalloe is part of the Lizard peninsula. When we reach Lizard Point later today, I'll be able to say I have stood at both the most westerly and the most southerly points not just of Cornwall but of mainland Great Britain.

"Why did you choose to walk the South West Coast Path specifically?" Mike says suddenly. "As a first walk, it's long and can be a slog if you're not fit enough."

"I've wanted to do this path for years ..." I begin.

Mike cuts in quickly. "Sorry, I didn't mean you're not fit enough. I hope you understand that? Sorry. I don't want you to think I was suggesting that."

"Nope, I didn't think that at all. It's okay!" I reply, laughing. "You can stop with your 'sorrying' too."

"Yeah, I know. I'll try." Mike stops himself from saying sorry again, and his broad grin stretches across his face as he rolls his eyes and tuts. "I interrupted you ... you were going to tell me about why you chose this walk."

"Oh yeah, well I first heard about the South West Coast Path around fifteen years ago. It felt out of my league then. Didn't think I was capable."

"What made you think you couldn't do it? You were younger back then, so in theory would have been more able."

"I had a young baby. I was in my mid-twenties, and I hadn't geared my life up to walking as I had when I was a teenager. Laura's father wasn't really into the whole outdoor scene, unless it involved cricket or football. Someone gave me a baby carrier and so I used to take her out into the New Forest on my own for mini adventures. I have loads of photos from those times." I pause, thinking more about my answer. "It's never occurred to me why this path. I guess it's probably because it was the trail that I'd filed away for a 'one day' walk. Never classed myself as super-fit or athletic. Neither did anyone else, as I didn't get picked for team sports. I just didn't think I was strong enough."

"That's not a reason, though, is it? You think about what you were doing with your baby. Lifting, carrying her around. Women are stronger than they realise. I know that from my first wife and having two sons." He raises his eyebrows at me, bidding me to think of a better reason I didn't walk this path sooner.

We walk for a few minutes, each lost in our own memories of young children and lives past. "There *is* something else. Me and Laura's dad, not long after marrying, we emigrated to Australia."

"That's a big thing to do. I like to visit places, but I wouldn't want to live anywhere other than the UK. What happened?"

"We left the UK four months after our wedding. I was only twenty-one. For many months, maybe a year beforehand, I'd been getting a weird thing that happened with my body. It's so long ago now, I'd forgotten all about it, but it may also explain some things about why I didn't think I was strong enough." Mike listens intently as we walk, so I continue. "At random times, I would get a painful swelling that could occur anywhere over my body. It usually targeted joints. Knees, knuckles, toes, elbows. Sometimes it would break out on my lip too, though I realise that's not a joint." Mike's eyebrows raise again. I thought he was about to sympathise, but after a day and a half of walking with him, I should have known better.

"Some people have joints in their lips, or double-jointed even ... Does that mean they can talk more?" His look is playful, like he's goading me to react.

I smile and carry on, ignoring his quip. "My grandmother on my father's side had severe rheumatoid arthritis. She used a battery car to get about. I got scared that I may have the early stages of that."

"So, what was it?"

"I'll never know. When I became stressed, it flared up. It got so much worse when we flew to Australia for the big move that I ended up with a wheelchair between LA and Melbourne airport. It was a painfully debilitating thing, I can tell you. We gave it the nickname 'elephantitis' because my affected joints, lips or eyebrows would double in size. The tests continued while we were in Oz and the doctors had whittled it down to an autoimmune issue. It was the Australian recession, and we struggled to find work, so after five months, I came back home to the UK without ever finding the answers. My husband followed three months later. The most bizarre thing is that at twenty-four, I gave birth to Laura and I've never had elephantitis since. In fact, not since falling pregnant."

"That is weird. I wonder what caused it?"

"My guess is hormones. Who knows? At least it's not an issue now."

"And how's your grandmother? The one with the battery car?" Mike asks me.

"She died, sadly. While I was in Australia. It hurt me I couldn't even get to her funeral." I explained to Mike about my adoption and the family set-up with Mum and Dad, Lorraine and Lyndon. "Luckily, I had twenty-two years in which to build up a good relationship with Lorraine's mother, Mary, who I called Nan. It was Nan's funeral that I went to a couple of weeks ago. I'd loved to have had longer to get to know my gran Jane, Lyndon's mother. We got on well and we used to write, but I only knew her for three years before she passed."

"Sad. I never knew my grandparents either," replies Mike. He looks back at me. "You won't grow a trunk or anything, will you – you know, with your elephantness?"

"Elephantitis. And stop it! No, I won't. I haven't suffered with whatever that was in over seventeen years."

As we walk, I lift my arm in front of my nose, walking pole extended at arm's reach, and trumpet like a pachyderm. We both crack into peals of laughter.

At about eleven and a half miles into today's journey, we reach the haunting splendour of Kynance Cove. Steeped in mystery, and legends of pirates and smugglers, this collection of rocks, coves, cliffs and pools is exquisite. Lea reminded me last night that I would pass through Kynance today. She said to keep an eye open for the green pebbles of serpentine that it's famous for. The rock formations are striking and even the colour of the sea looks much greener. I wonder to myself if this is down to the colour of the serpentine rock reflecting through the water, or just my head playing games.

There's a group of four people sat at the side of the path, and they're interested in what Mike and I are up to carrying bigger packs than most regular walkers. I laugh inwardly as I soon realise they think we're together. I know we're together as walking companions, but I hardly know the bloke! This is only the second day of walking with him, and these people have made assumptions. Mike is a chatty guy and appears to get on well with talking about his journey to strangers. He kindly introduces my story too, leading me with ease into my charity spiel. Karen, David, Sue and Tony are also friendly and chatty. Like me, David is a teacher. He suffers seizures, however, so feels some limitations about the activities he's able to take part in. I give them one of my leaflets, explaining about my blog, why I'm walking and the fundraising projects at school. At last, Mike and I peel ourselves away politely, by telling them we need to get to Cadgwith at a specific time as I'm being collected by my hosts. I'm grateful, though, and thank them for taking the time to listen to our stories.

I'm not sure what I was expecting to see on reaching Lizard Point itself. It's incredibly scenic, but I think the beauty of today and the previous days has overwhelmed me. Without the rugged definition (or the sweetness of the incredible blackberries) of Mullion, or the wild artistry of Kynance Cove, it could easily have blended into anonymity. I appreciate being at the southernmost point, and say hello to the local ponies grazing here. If I'm honest with myself, I also think I'm weary now. After at least fifteen ascents since Porthleven and around thirteen miles, I know I have another four and a half to go before we can consider today wrapped up. These are going to be long miles.

The weather has, as I predicted earlier, now taken a turn for the worse. The cloud increased after we left Gunwalloe. By 4.30 p.m., the grey sky that has squeezed out a bearable drizzle on and off suddenly makes its presence known with what I can only describe as "fat rain". It drops with a heavy, invisible impetus that seems to prevent it from letting up at all. There's no wonder that Lizard Point had little positive impact on my soul today. All this, and yet I am garnering an awareness that whatever the weather throws at me, by the time I've come through it, I feel on top of the world. It's a strange phenomenon.

Soaked to the skin, I lift my bag dripping with the wash of rainwater onto a plastic sack that's spread out to hold my gear in the boot of the little red Citroën. I'm grateful that Lea and Steve are happy to collect me later than they used to. It gives me more time to get the miles in – and today, at seventeen and a half gruelling miles, I certainly did that. Every step further away from Land's End has brought me closer to their home. For them, leaving to pick me up or drop me off is less distance and therefore, for a couple now in their seventies, it's not so tiring. My destination tonight is still twenty-one miles away from Redruth, so it's forty minutes there and forty minutes back.

Who knows if I'll see Mike again? It's been a good couple of days' walking. I'll admit he's probably pushed me to churn out more miles today than I might have done otherwise. As we leave the village of Cadgwith behind, truly spent, my body has nothing left this evening. It'll be a shower, food, then bed. Oh, and I must remember to find some energy to write my blog too. That won't be easy. With any luck, I'll wake up a bit later. Social interaction when I'm this tired is quite challenging. In the normal way, I'd just climb into my tent, shovel some grub into my mouth, slide my body into my sleeping bag, write a few lines and fall asleep. The engagement of mouth to brain to create any coherent speech after walking for over eleven hours is a feat in itself. I consider this carefully, as the flashing sights of inland Cornwall diminish past the rear passenger window and my eyes close, for a while at least.

24

Steve and Liz

After torrential rain overnight, it's still raining this morning. I may have started my day off wet, but I soon need to strip off the waterproof trousers and Páramo smock. My workout is enough to get the heart rate going and steam rises from my clothing within ten minutes of returning to the path. Within the first quarter of a mile above Kildown Cove, climbing upwards to over 200 feet is my early induction into understanding the path's pattern for the rest of the day. The contour lines on my map are exceptionally fancy, warning me to expect plenty of ascents and descents to conquer before being picked up at 6 p.m this evening.

Steve dropped me off in Cadgwith at 8.30 a.m. Here is yet another quaint fishing village. I am used to this now, as part and parcel of the Cornish edition of the South West Coast Path. Once you've seen a few, it's hard not to take these chocolate-box hamlets for granted.

As I'd walked past the cove earlier, the hub for those in the local fishing circles, I'd spotted a man sitting outside a stone boathouse, just off the beach. I offered him my usual smile and a cheery "Good morning!" He'd lifted his hand and waved, with a slight nod of his head. There's a rickety old bench on which he savoured smoking his morning pipe. As the puff billowed from his lips, I noticed how they formed into a flexible sideways shape, serving as both his pipe funnel and fresh air duct. I found myself fascinated by his ability to keep his mouth held in such a position. I figured it must be because he's a fisherman. His skin is so weathered it's become extra malleable and can hold any shape he wishes.

When I hauled myself up out of Cadgwith, I berated myself for yet another missed photo opportunity. This one, I realised, would have been a striking image with his slightly shabby appearance, twinkly eyes and pipe-moulded mouth. *Dammit, Wath.* I must work on these fears of worrying about what people will think of me or say if I approach them. I'll not get that chance back and one never knows where a missed opportunity may have led. Random conversations with people, especially on this adventure, have opened many doors over the last few weeks. Despite being thought of as extrovert by most people, this little demon is the introverted side of me that plays unkind games with my head when I least expect it.

"Mike!" I spot his signature blue rucksack and red T-shirt. "Mike!" I shout again – this time louder. He's across the other side of the valley at Downas Cove. Back at Butter Cove, I must be too far away, as his body language made no response to my calls. *Dang.* Either he is as deaf as a post, or I'm unable to carry my voice far enough. It would have been good to catch him up. I attempt pursing my lips to muster up the best high-pitched whistle but end up sounding more like I've swallowed the ball from inside a whistle instead. *Dang.* And now double-dang, as I almost step on a frog. Or is it a frog? *Crikey, that's huge!* I look closer and a frog it is, but of ginormous proportions. *That's no frog,* I grin to myself as I carry on. *It's more Teenage Mutant Ninja Turtles ...*

Along this part of the coast path, I stop in my tracks to witness an exciting air-sea rescue. I watch them dump a live body into the sea and winch it up into the aircraft a multitude of times. Then the realisation hits me. This is another air ambulance training exercise. I still find it interesting to watch, until I remember not to hang around, to avoid delaying my pickup later.

At Dean Quarries, an area on the coast used for landfill, the coast path turns inland. Coastal landfill sites have never made sense to me regarding erosion, losing waste and the leaching of toxic substances into the sea. But that's a whole other book. It disappoints me to see the shape of the terrain on the map hugging the coastline, which should be stunning. There are many tightly packed contours, but I won't see it. The detour is necessary to avoid the quarries of Dean and Porthoustock and after one and a half miles, I descend a steep hill into the cove of Porthoustock itself. Back up the other side on another steep climb, I have a further one and a half miles of inland detour, this time to avoid the large disused quarry of St Keverne.

It's been way too long walking inland, so it's with great relief to descend at last into a small, wooded valley. This is Porthallow. *Halfway! At last!* I jump up and down inside with excitement. I am twenty-eight days into my walk, and I've finally conquered half of it. A whole half. *Dad always laughed when I said that* – his smile fleets through my head. Every step from this point on will be a step homeward. I know that all the way, I've been walking home, but the adventure is so big and incomprehensible that I simply couldn't take on board the idea of heading home when I was seven weeks away. Now it's in my sights and I feel like this is totally achievable. It's almost like I have a new goal which has refocused me. *Ha, so this is what a reboot feels like then ...*

As I walk down towards the cove at Porthallow, it doesn't seem like much of an area for celebrating the halfway point of this well-trodden, epic path. There's an extensive building on the west side of the cove and just an open space with an area of randomly parked cars looking out to sea. And then I see it: the halfway marker. At 315 miles into the walk, it's a three-metre-high rectangular stone sculpture. The long inscriptions detail lists of wildlife, birds and plant species one can expect to encounter en route. *Bet it doesn't mention the mutant frog.* It lacks the splendour and pomp of the starter marker at Minehead, but

I welcome this opportunity to recognise the achievement of reaching the midpoint of my journey.

A photo. Well, of course I need a photo. I could set the camera up on a self-timer and take one, but then the angle from the ground looking upwards at the full height of this marker would look peculiar. There's a couple perched on a seat in the area near the building. Both are wearing rucksacks, but the man, who appears exceptionally tall, wears a much larger pack than the woman. I approach them and ask if one of them could take a photo of me. The woman obliges with a wide, radiant smile, her eyes gleaming from behind her glasses. I notice a few of her tight ringlets that fall around her face, clinging to her shoulders like a silk scarf. *Beautiful*. I know I have tight curls, but these are such springy coils. *I'll bet it takes ages to dry*. "Thanks so much," I say as she returns my camera. "Would you like me to take a photo of you two?"

"Yes, please!" She beams gratefully. I take the snap and then stop to chat with them both for a while. "I'm Liz," she says, "and this is Steve, my boyfriend. He's walking half of the path and I'm walking a little section of it with him too, before going home."

"Are you going all the way?" Steve asks.

"I am indeed."

Right here, in this moment, I feel proud that I can say I have travelled 315 miles on foot, solo. Steve looks as clean and as fresh as only a walker can in their first days of a multiday hike. At least I have been staying at Lea and Steve's, so I don't look or smell as bad as I could have. It turns out that Liz and Steve have travelled all the way from Anglesey, North Wales, to walk this half of the South West Coast Path. Steve is a housemaster in an independent school in Llandudno and Liz a marine biologist living at Menai Bridge. I like these people, and I'm sad Liz can't stay for more than a few days of walking as she has work to return to. They both seem like the sort of outdoorsy folk that I can relate to ... and I reckon they can relate to me. Hopefully.

After walking together for a while, we part company as I have a ferry to catch at Helford and have noted that the last one leaves at 5.00 p.m. I can't afford to miss it as I'm meeting Lea and Steve at Helford Passage at 6.00 p.m., the other side of the river. Steve and Liz are taking a slightly different route, so we say our goodbyes at Gillan Creek where they head off to walk or bus the road route to Helford. Being a purist about this whole National Trail thing, I have made a rule that I must never veer off the actual path – not intentionally, that is; there's always the possibility that I may get lost or miss a turning.

The stepping stones here at Gillan Creek are fun and quite picturesque. It's hard to imagine this area being overwhelmed by water at high tide or during a storm. I'm grateful for the crossing, created for the benefit of walkers. Out to Dennis Head, past Ponsence Cove, and along the foot of a steep cliff, I am aware my time is truly ticking on. *Bloody hell, I need to make that ferry.* On the road at Helford, the time is so close to 5.00 p.m. now that I find a pocket of energy with much power-walking and run-walking, intermingled with dance-like walk-jogging and power-shuffling to reach the ferry in time. I even overtake a couple of women slowly pushing buggies who give me the strangest of looks, as if to say, *What's the hurry?*

"Ferry to catch!" I call behind me as I whizz past. It's almost like I'm heading for a cruise to carry me to distant lands, more than just taking me over the Helford River. It's not wider than about half a mile across. Hilarious.

Huffing and puffing, I make it to the ferry "terminal", which is nothing more than a short footpath leading to the side of the river. I can see a boat already partway across the river, heading away from me. I check my watch: 4.56 p.m. Thank goodness I've made it – I hope that wasn't the last one. The powerful release of relief flushes through my body and I realise simultaneously that I need a wee. Now. With all that power-walking stuff, I hadn't paid attention to my body and its frequent waterworks. I hope above all things there will be somewhere on the other side of the river where I can resolve that minor issue.

The tiny blue-and-white boat with the little outboard motor on the back has the word "FERRY" painted on each side, just in case you were in any doubt about the purpose of this vessel. After around thirty minutes patiently waiting and practising pelvic floor exercises, I finally climb aboard. I flop down on the nearest bench and look up at Captain Helford, with a "Thank goodness for that, I thought I'd missed you!".

"There'd have bin 'nother in a few moments," the ferryman replies in his endearing Cornish drawl. "Last ferry ain't till nine o'clock." I'm not sure whether to laugh or cry at that revelation. It turns out that although for most of the ferry season, they run until 5.00 p.m., during the months of July and August, they do indeed run until 9.00 p.m. He kindly declines my offer of payment when spotting my charity banner hanging from my back. *Excellent!* There has been so much kindness and support on this walk. The ferries, taxis and buses that have offered me free rides have been hugely welcome.

The ten-minute crossing is smooth, and as we berth at Helford Passage, I spy a veranda outside a pub. It's literally on the water's edge, just above a small flight of steps.

"Zoe!" It's Mike. He's sat at a bench on the veranda, with a pint in his hand and a sparkling white, tooth-filled smile etched from ear to ear, alongside none other than Liz and Steve.

"Wow! You all made it before me!" I turn to Mike. "I've been following you for miles but never been quite close enough to catch you up or make you hear me!" He grins at me. "I see you've met," I say, smiling at Liz and Steve. "I didn't think we were going to meet up again, but I'm so glad we have!" We all laugh, each pleased to see a familiar face. "How are you?" I ask Mike.

"Happy as a pig in clover, mate," he replies, knocking back a huge gulp of his beer. "Fancy a drink?"

"Do I ever!" I'm eager for a drink. "But first, I have business to attend to ..." I dump my bag and trot off to find the ladies.

Liz and Steve chat with me some more about the charity side of my walk, and Liz pulls a fiver out of her rucksack and hands it to me. "There you go, Zoe. Pop that towards your funds." Another kind gesture. This time, I sense this isn't just a chance meeting that passes after a few minutes of chit-chat, sealed with generosity. Liz's hair, now released from its band, fully frames her face. Her freckles contour her skin and dimples attractively. Steve carries a thick mop of extra-dark hair and wears a pair of black shades. He looks chilled in his crisp grey cargo shorts and lightweight rain jacket, rolled up at the sleeves. Pint in one hand and mobile phone in the other, he occasionally looks up to hear about the parts of the path we have already experienced. He's planning to camp all the way back to Poole. It's possible we might see him again, then. That'll be good.

It's not long before Lea and Steve arrive at the pub. On seeing I've connected with some new friends, they tactfully agree to stop for a quick drink, which I'm so grateful to them for. Sometimes, these moments are spontaneous, though it's always a little awkward when you're relying on someone else's kindness to collect you.

25

Boats, All Shapes and Sizes

I start my day at the hamlet of Helford Passage at 8.05 a.m. after Lea and Steve dropped me off. The first thing that hits me is how the morning air smells of the unlikely combo of salty coffee and seaweed. New ice cream flavour, anyone? As I begin my walk, the tiny village still seems to be waking up. The path is serene, winding along a quiet lane that nears the water's edge but soon leads up into pretty woodlands, which rise and fall with the gradient of the landscape. Despite being higher above the sea than at Helford, I can still hear the gentle lapping of waves below and they set a peaceful tone for the day. The views from Rosemullion Head across into Falmouth Bay give me much to look forward to, especially as I can see beyond the bay to the next couple of days' worth of Cornwall.

Two hours spent on my own in perfect weather is good thinking time. I drift into thoughts of how in just two days I'll be back to doing this path in a way that offers me a routine of my own making, yet with a level of unknown endings that still unnerve me. I ponder over how each night, from here on, I won't have the comfort of a bed and shower, or the luxury of a foot massage. Instead, I'll need to search for suitable places to sleep, and while it scares me, I know with a renewed urgency that I must conquer my wild camping demons.

By chance, after around four and a half miles, I catch up with my new walking companion at Maenporth. As Mike and I walk together, the sight of an old-fashioned ship with black sails drifts into view, its dark silhouette striking against the smoky blue expanse of sea and clear blue sky.

"Wow, that's an unexpected ship to see. It's beautiful," I say. "Think of all the stories a boat like that could tell." It's already stirring my imagination.

"It's cracking!" Mike is more animated than usual. "I love to see a traditional boat, wooden, of course. I've done a little sailing – I mean, there was the time I joined the merchant navy but that doesn't count. I got left behind anyway."

"Really? How come?" I ask him.

"Probably out drinking. I don't remember, to be honest. All I know is I got into a lot of trouble and the ship left me behind in Costa Rica for two weeks, until they flew me home."

"Ooops, that's a hard lesson to learn!"

"Yep, I returned to carpentry after that – on dry land." Mike rolls his eyes at me. "My short experience of sailing was on a seventy-foot yacht with a group of friends, around the Isle of Wight. Bit choppy. My role was the yacht cook."

"Did you suffer with any seasickness?"

"Oh, yes. For the first week in the merchants, I was as sick as a dog going across the Bay of Biscay, and then I was fine. On the boys' sailing holiday I didn't suffer at all, bizarrely. The yacht was at forty-five degrees at one point, and we were all holding on, but I had no issues with sickness on that trip. But when it happens, you've just got to get on with it and it soon passes."

We both look back out at the black-sailed ship. It seeps an air of menace with a wash of regal pomp for good measure. It doesn't escape my camera, and for the first time, I see Mike enthused enough to take his camera out too.

"Well, I'd love to sail one day. I've never seen a boat like it before. It's a beauty."

"Me neither," Mike says. "Makes me want to get back out onto the water. I mean, I do have a boat nowadays, but nothing like that. I have a forty-foot narrowboat, moored on a landlocked canal in South Wales."

"Ah nice! What's it called?"

"*Alys*. If we'd ever had a daughter, my ex-wife and I were going to call her Alys. I have two sons, Ben and Sam, so I have a boat called *Alys* instead. With a *y* and an *s*, the Welsh way."

"Lovely."

"You and Ross can stay on her one day if you like? I've let lots of people borrow her."

"Wow, we'd love that. Sounds like it would be fun, thanks!"

In Falmouth, once again we bump into holidaymakers Karen and David. With just enough time to share some more stories from our experiences since seeing them last, we soon say our goodbyes. The moment they are out of earshot, we laugh at the absurdity of them clearly thinking we're a couple. With another five and a half miles in the bag, we reach the ferry that will take us from Falmouth to St Mawes. It costs a whopping eight pounds and for three miles. That feels steep, but it's necessary to continue our journey. With St Mawes harbour now to cross, while waiting for the next boat Mike spots a pub and suggests we stop for a drink to pass the time. Of course, it would be rude to refuse! A warm and cosy atmosphere fills the bar, along with the chatter of locals, holidaymakers and the clinking of glasses. It's a comforting contrast to the cool breeze that's stirring outside. I've noticed how friendly and confident Mike is with striking up conversations with people in pubs and those out and about too. It's a pleasure to watch and be a part of; he has a knack of drawing people together.

The tiny ferry from St Mawes to Place feels like a step back in time. We cross the half a mile of water, to a peaceful, secluded section of the Roseland Peninsula. The beautiful St Anthony in Roseland church beckons us to stop and tuck into our rucksack snacks. As we sit and eat, Mike points up at the roof.

"See those tiles, they're glass. In all my years of roofing, I've never seen glass tiles that shape before. It's known as a Roman tile." Each tile glistens as it catches the sunlight.

"That's clever," I reply.

"It is. It's what they called 'borrowed light'."

"I'm guessing there's a darker part of the church and that's a way of allowing natural light into it?"

"Yep, it's used a lot on landings and in attic spaces, where it has a tendency to be darker."

There's a sign on the wall, so I wander over to read it and learn that the church is now maintained by the Churches Conservation Trust. It's essentially decommissioned and no longer in use for parish services. "If it's not used now, perhaps the borrowed-light tiles on the roof mean they don't need to use electricity when people do go in?"

"Maybe. It seems to be well looked after anyway, which is good."

We both talk about how much we appreciate the fine carved details around the Norman stone arched doorway. "That's effort," says Mike.

"Yeah, a lot of work went into that."

Miles disappear quickly when I'm lost in conversation. It doesn't feel one-sided either. I know Mike is listening, because he asks relevant questions, and we've probably covered both our life stories by now. Before we know it, five and a half miles have passed and we're in Portscatho already.

We decide to stop for one more drink in a pub in Portscatho, where we call it a day at fifteen miles. The pub oozes quirkiness, with rustic wooden beams and a stone fireplace. It didn't need to be lit on a day like today, but somehow, sitting beside it still provides a welcome end to our day's journey. Mike tells me how he loves to relax in front of an open fire, happily watching the flames dance, periodically poking the wood, adjusting the position of the embers, or chucking on another chair leg. He chuckles as he tells me about how many great thoughts and ideas have been hatched in front of a roaring fire, and many a glass of whisky sunk, as the crackles die down and the sun rises.

Last night, my eleventh night with Lea and Steve, I felt a tumbled mix of sadness, gratitude and excitement for the days ahead. I'm aiming for Mevagissey today, a healthy nineteen and a half miles away. Together, we discussed the options and associated logistics this morning and decided that tomorrow will be their final day of dropping me at a start point, to head out from Mevagissey, back on my own.

The morning feels tough, my muscles stiff from the previous day's walk, but I start just after 8 a.m. once again. As I consider how the days have panned out, I note the consistency with which I've covered more miles each day. Mike has also probably pushed me further than I might have walked on my own, so my legs are feeling it today.

With a stroke of luck, within minutes, I catch up with Mike, and, to my delight, Jinni is walking with him as well. "Hey peeps, lovely to see you both!" They each get a morning hug from me.

"Mike said he thought we may see you today," says Jinni. "I've heard about some of your day yesterday. Sounds like most of it was spent in the pub."

We all laugh together. "Haha, yep. We did have a few pub stops yesterday!" I say.

"Nice morning, eh?" Mike says.

"Gorgeous. Legs are a bit sore today though. Something to do with all those miles we churned out yesterday." Sunshine fills the morning, making our walk pleasant and lifting our spirits, and I quickly forget about my aching muscles as they warm up and settle into the terrain. In under three miles we reach the beautiful beach of Pendower. Jinni says it's well known for wild camping now. It looks lovely, although the old hotel and restaurant nearby has closed. It seems there's a problem with footpath erosion. I hope it gets a second chance. Everyone needs a second chance.

The route is up and down, hugging the clifftops and giving my head for heights a testy nudge every so often. Because I'm chatting with friends, I seem less inclined to vocalise my fear, but it helps seeing others breeze along these narrow paths without drama, even with the drop to their right. Along the way, we are visited by more choughs, or rather, we visit them and they choose not to fly away immediately. On a short pit stop, I note down in my logbook how their distinctive calls and acrobatic flight have added a sense of excitement to my day.

At some point in the afternoon, Mike surprises me and Jinni with flapjacks. What a friendly gesture! We have our photo taken with our treats, looking smug.

As the day progresses, the clouds roll in and by 6 p.m., we're caught in a heavy rain shower. The sudden downpour soaks us to the bone, but we're not too bothered, choosing to laugh it off. We decide it's brought a refreshing coolness to the air, after the day's warmth.

Ross headed off up to London today, to see Iron Maiden at the O2. We both have tickets, but I've chosen not to leave the path again. Having already taken time off to attend Nan's funeral, I can't afford to lose more days if I want to finish before returning to work in September. I'm not envious that I'm missing out, which I thought I might have been. This trail has flicked a switch turning off all the commercial distractions, focusing my head wholly on the simplicity of putting one foot in front of the other.

In Mevagissey, there's a dead seagull on a front doorstep. They are huge birds when you see them up close and I'm compelled to photograph it. This harbourside fishing village has a sombre feel under the grey skies, with the rain and the deadness of the bird adding to the melancholic atmosphere.

Our day is done, with our nineteen-and-a-half-mile target achieved. Pushing for more miles with a lighter pack proved to be a great idea. Tomorrow, however, will be very different. All my adventure belongings need to be stuffed back into my rucksack in the morning, making the pack heavier and the journey more challenging. My tummy gives a little flip-flop as the thought crosses my mind.

With the beautiful wild camping spot at Pendower miles behind us, Mike and Jinni decide to head off to The Ship for drinks and think about their camping plans, while I wait for Lea and Steve to pick me up for the last time.

Going Wild, At Last

26

Enter stage right ... The Shitty Committee. It's back, and this morning is the biggest head struggle yet. Today is the day for farewells and endless thanks to Lea and Steve. How I love these people. However, the realisation that I will be on my own again has weighed heavy on my mind overnight. Somehow, I've allowed the limiting self-belief and confidence-crushing voices to creep their way back in. During these twelve wonderful evenings of sleeping in a proper bed, being fed delicious food, pampered and taken care of, from every angle, I hadn't realised how hard it would be to retrieve my adventure mindset again, or how fast my courage had retreated. I spend a few minutes on my own and give myself a good talking-to. Positivity laps at the edges of my consciousness ... I think.

I set off around 9.30 a.m. and while there is a little faffiness, in fairness, this time I'm loaded back up again with all my gear. To knock me back into shape, I quietly hope that I might bump into Jinni and Mike again, but I had a late start, so it's unlikely that I'll see them now.

As I trudge out of Mevagissey, along the coastal swings and roundabouts of inlets, headlands, high points and valleys, I lift my head for a moment. I spot a figure in the far distance, about two valleys ahead. *Mike!* The prospect of a familiar face and companion to walk with again injects a cheerful spring into my step. We dip and dive in a choreographed dance along the rollercoaster of clifftops. As Mike's figure drops away into the next valley, I set about making the slow climb up the preceding ascents. Just as I reach the crown of the hill, that determined figure disappears with speed, down into the valley, two hills ahead. And that is how I continue to follow him. Never quite catching him up, but always hoping that for a one moment he might hear me, stop for a quick break or turn round to see me, half a mile in his wake.

The views are exceptional, but the folks I bump into are the real spice of life out here. I never know who I'll meet, the kindness they might offer me, or the wacky stories they'll share. That's what makes this well-trodden path so exhilarating. As I follow Mike, I think about some of these people. It causes the dimple in my right cheek to ripple into life. Out of the hundreds of tourists, locals and walkers I've met, I smile the deepest thinking about my new walking buddies. Four super special individuals, each walking the South West Coast Path solo, and every one of them I stumbled across independently of the other. They know their stuff – more than me, at least. Between them, they are gear savvy, and exude the spirit of outdoorsiness, which is how I aspired to walk when I first planned this journey. Yet even in the absence of Artie, Mike, Steve and Jinni, I draw comfort and reassurance as I consider what any of them might do: in confidence, nature knowledge, navigation skills, and how they are happy to sleep wherever they drop their rucksack. Without them realising, they have proved to be of significant support to me.

Right now, though, I am alone.

And here's the truth: so far, in the thirty-one days that I've been walking this challenging National Trail, I have only ever set up Harry, my trusty tent, at a campsite. It irritates me that I've not yet fulfilled my promise of wild camping solo. If I'm totally honest, it terrifies me. I am fearful of making the step to camp out there, alone, without protection of campsite wall or fence, toilet block, and other humans around me. Deep down, I know I am fearful of going back home, back to the school where I work, and to my family and friends, carrying the weight of a failed mission to be a solo backpacker and wild camper. *Pull yourself together, Wath. What is your problem?*

Today then? *It has to be today*. I sniff in disgust as I've lost count of how many times I've told myself this. By the time nightfall comes around, my courage hangs in tatters and other excuses filter into my head. *This spot isn't suitable. I'm too close to a town. There are cows in the field. I'm too far away from civilisation. It's too lonely. Nope, it's way too dark. Who do you think you are, Zoe? You're not a wild camper. Leave it to the experts.* This is me. Me and my Shitty Committee. My inner excuse-makers, plain ole Doubting Donnas and naysayers. How the heck do I shift this chorus of critics out of my head and out of my life? "Get lost!" I scream into the sunny morning sky. Checking myself, I glance around wide-eyed and astonished that I'd made a stand against so many on the committee. *Well done, that felt good*. That was indeed promising. *Houston, we have made progress*.

With an awkward wiggle, I shift the weight of the pack around on my shoulders and stride onwards with a small fizz of anticipation germinating in my boots. Will today be the day?

For almost three miles, Mike remains steadily ahead of me, never dropping back for a moment. On reaching Pentewan, I'm relieved and delighted to see that he has stopped at last, probably for elevenses. The grin plastered over my face speaks volumes, and the promise of company for the next few miles is a real lift. My delight disintegrates into dust as I approach and realise this person I've been following for the last two hours is not my new walking buddy. While unimpressed at my daftness, on the upside I suppose at least it had given me a focus, even if a false one.

The views are always changing. Despite being a coastal route and holding vague similarities to other stretches of coast path, it still stops me in my tracks. The visceral, untamed beauty takes hold of me, as I marvel at the wind-shaped form of the trees, the jagged rocks and the unpredictable conditions of the sea. I am lured by its sound, the salty sweetness of the air and the colours. As I descend steep steps heading northwards towards Porthpean, a SodaStream of bubbles and waves created by a powerboat racing event snaps me back from my mindful moment. As exciting as it might be out there for the competitors and spectators, I quietly acknowledge it, doing my best to ignore the aggressive sounds of the engine rattle and forced throttle.

The path has taught me to pick my way down steps with care. Part way down, I meet with a pleasant couple who are happily watching the races from a bird's-eye vantage point up here. I stop for a chat and as I answer their questions about my adventure, Kathy reaches into her handbag for her purse. She pulls out a five-pound note and hands it to me, smiling kindly. "There you go, dear. I think what you're doing is so inspiring. Put this towards your charities." Lifted yet again by the belief that others hold in my mission, I thank the couple and squeeze down past them, cringing inside at how precariously perched they are on their viewing ledge.

My bank of skills as I walk and learn about myself is ever-growing. Who would have thought that weather-watching would have been one of them? Indeed, I am proud of my new ability to observe the clouds and forecast the likelihood of rain and how long before it reaches me. Behind me, I notice a mass of heavy, black clouds rolling in and know full well to expect a deluge in a matter of minutes. As predicted, within five minutes, I find myself amid the rinse cycle of an industrial washing machine. At the bottom of the steps, steeper than the Stairway to Heaven, I decide to shelter from the cloudburst under a small grove of trees. Well, as sheltered as one can be in biblical rain. *Pasty time*, my belly tells me. What a great idea! My home belly always appreciates a bite to eat, but my coast path belly seems to have mutated into an eating monster. This home-made pasty full of peppery potato and tender beef tastes so good and gives me the energy and motivation I need in bucketloads to continue onwards towards Charlestown.

On the outer fringes of St Austell lies this small harbour village. Today, with its localised monsoon and more dark clouds looming, Charlestown has less of a welcoming appeal about it. One corner turn towards the harbour, and I am in awe of a historic tall ship anchored at the quay, rain and clouds forgotten. As I absorb this immense wooden beauty, with its masts, folded sails, and figurehead, there is an almighty clap of thunder. Within seconds, the heavens are open once again. I search for somewhere to shelter, but every pub and café I peer into is full. In fact, in this moment, every person and their dog who are holidaying in Cornwall seem to have descended upon this one tiny fishing village. I spot an empty beer garden; I sneak in, plant myself underneath a beer table brolly, and wait for the storm to pass.

Even though the rain stays put, it eases up and I am happier now. I hear the thunder rolling away as it distances itself from Charlestown. My afternoon continues on much gentler paths than those of this morning, though I am disheartened by the building site that is Carlyon Bay. While I understand the need for tourism, I find this style of commercial approach too much of a concrete jungle. I speed up to pass through into a more natural setting as soon as possible.

Within a few miles, I reach Par. It's another fishing port and still not inspiring me in whatever way I was expecting. *Perhaps it's me? Is it my hormones?* I usually appreciate most things and accept them for what they are and what the view offers, but today I simply cannot see the attraction to Par. The awful view of a holiday park plonked near the coast doesn't help. That's never going to enthuse me. But before I write Par off completely, I arrive at its sands. Wow, what a contrast! The creamy white stretch of beach, reaching off into the distance, calms my mood and if it *is* my hormones playing up, they get the magical settling treatment too. *This is more like it. It's delicious.* For once, the internal dialogue I have with myself is reassuring and soothing.

With my head in a better place now, I consider this evening. I know I can't avoid it, but with the lack of campsites on the path in this area,

I realise that the prospect of having to wild camp solo is becoming a stronger possibility. There's a campsite off the path, but this would require me to walk inland at least a mile in the opposite direction. I'm coming around to Mike's way of thinking that creating unnecessary miles in my day isn't sensible. Not when there is a perfectly good camp spot right on the path itself.

I wander into Polkerris with its pretty little cove and harbour soon after Par Sands. It gives me an ideal opportunity to stop for dinner. I'm still not comfortable dining in pubs on my own, but needs must. *The Rashleigh Inn*. I eye it up and down. It looks like a decent sort of place, and it's hardly the Wild West out here. I coach myself to avoid any attention being drawn to me, making me feel uncomfortable about taking myself out for a dinner date.

On scanning the menu, I'm disappointed there's no traditional hearty pub meals. Lasagne or fish and chips would be perfect after all those stormy miles I had put in today. Instead, I settle for brie and bruschetta. Tasty, but not much of a meal. In honesty, I should have had some meat. My concern was that as a gastropub, the meat would arrive as one rib, lost on a square white plate the size of a tray, with a dangle of wild samphire and a drizzle of bluecurrant jus, all MasterChef-stylee.

Deep down, I also sense my anxiety rising. It's been bothering my subconscious and therefore I'm not responding to the appetite I know I should have by now. The wild camp must happen, as I have no other option this evening. I never caught up with Mike this morning, so it's just me and me tonight. I pay the bill, haul my pack onto my shoulders, and walk outside. Ten seconds later, I walk straight back in and over to the table again, to collect my lonely walking poles. I smile at the diners sat at a nearby table, who give me glances echoing a mixture of both pity and astonishment. How many more times will I leave these poles behind?

After a couple of steepish climbs heading out of Polkerris, I contour along the highest edge of the cliffs towards a headland. The light is dimming, though not too quickly. August still blesses us with an adequate level of daylight until around 9 p.m.

The views behind me are superb. I'm always stunned when I look back at how far I have come on foot. In equal measure, when the cliffs stretch out ahead of me, sometimes for many miles, I can see a great number of days of walking. This isn't always a good thing, as it can feel daunting if not broken down into smaller, more manageable snapshots. To see twenty miles ahead is way better for my brain to take on board than to see fifty miles stretching into infinity.

For about one and a half miles, I walk in the twilight. I reach a point on the headland where I can make out a small wood just a few metres ahead. The options spin around my head like a vomit-inducing funfair ride. I'm worried that I won't find anywhere to pitch my tent in or beyond the wood. The evening light is fading fast, and I don't relish camping amongst the trees. That may be a childish imagination running away with me, but there's something eerie about the woods at night. While this walk has prepared me to face a lot of things, I'm not prepared to sleep in woods on my own. At least, not yet.

Right where I stand, I look at the surrounding space. I can see there's a tiny patch of grass between the kissing gate I had just walked through and a five-bar gate that leads into a field. The field stretches into the distance, sloping downhill. Beyond is the vast expanse of sea and above that, not the sky as one might expect, but the undulating outline of the coast I walked earlier today.

Shaped like a horseshoe, the coastline of St Austell Bay stretches approximately three and a half miles from the west headland to the east. Within this, the bay where I had watched and promptly tried to shut out the sounds of the powerboat racing this morning. The commercialised Carlyon Bay, the storm magnet of Charlestown and the steep steps of Porthpean. They are all there, and in reverence I look across at the outline of the cliffs, wondering how on earth my feet, my little size 4.5 feet, had carried me this far. Not just today, but every day for the past thirty-one days. It's truly mind-boggling.

This is it, then. This is going to be my first wild camp spot on the walk. I remind myself that I'm an expert at setting up my tent now, although my twelve nights at Lea and Steve's means I'm less finely tuned than I had been. I set my bag down on an area of grass, after scouring it with my head torch for dog, cow or horse poo. Quick work to detach my side dry bag that contains Harry Hilleberg. I follow the system I had established previously to the letter, to ensure not to lose or forget anything. I lay Harry out as best as possible in the cramped space of grass available, pushing the four ultra lightweight pegs into the loops at the four corners of the tent base.

Next, I secure the fly sheet and the guy lines, to add tension to the fly. The storms have passed now, but I'm not taking any chances, so install my full set of pegs into the ground to secure Harry from damage by the elements. In my head, it's as though wild camping might render my trusty tent helpless. The truth is, there's little that could wreck Harry and I am proud he's been my faithful camping companion and shelter when I've needed him.

With the tent up in a few minutes, I note it looks peculiar, squeezed neatly into this tiny gap at the side of the footpath like a triangle of sandwiches snugly squished into a lunchbox. I pull my pack inside and prepare to rest.

The quick trip outside to have a wee before bed is simple enough as it's still early, by summer standards. Not even ten o'clock and it's only just reaching full dusk. I admire the gorgeous indigo blue of the sky, brushed, washed and blended with the last salmon hues of a late sunset. I wish hard, beyond all hopes, that I won't need to go to the loo again in the night.

This new experience makes me a little edgy. I scramble back inside the tent and thrust my feet into my sleeping bag as swiftly as I can. If I could get my head down and find sleep soon, then at least I could pack off any worries about this whole wild camping malarkey.

During the small hours, I stir. My ruffled senses take a moment to establish where I am. Even with so much angst beforehand, I had drifted off to sleep with ease. Right now, though, I have that telltale tingle in my bladder, warning me I don't have long before action is required. There are no signs of the sun rising, so it must be early, around 3 a.m., I guess. I think hard about what I should do. My heart thuds wildly, and the blood drains from my feet.

As I lie in my sleeping bag, looking up at the tent fabric just centimetres above my nose, I wonder what is out there. *You can't go out.* I know I need to, as there is no way I can hold on for another three hours. My bladder isn't that efficient. *Someone might be out there.* God, what if someone really is out there, just waiting for me to clamber out of my protective Harry haven and straight into their trap? I'd have to run. *You won't be able to run fast enough.* I'm going to have to get up and go. *It's too dark out there.* Who knows what might hide in that blackness? I consider the option of holding on. It'll be great for strengthening my pelvic floor. *You're going to pee in your new sleeping bag ...* Arggh! I fight with myself for what seems like an hour, all the while squeezing my muscles as if in an antenatal class. I argue back and forth with myself until I can stall the inevitable no longer.

I slip out of my sleeping bag and into my walking boots. My heart bangs and I'm very much awake as the anxiety about who or what I will find outside races through my body. I'll have to be speedy, as the urgency within my bladder now hurts me. With a deep breath, I take hold of the tent zip. *You can't do it, can you? I knew you'd bottle out ...* Enough is enough. I deftly unzip the tent without further nonsense and stop dead in my tracks with a sharp gasp. Shock replaces my fear, which falls away in an instant. I am treated to a sky so vast and so exquisitely decorated with stars that for a split second I even forget my extreme need to answer the call to nature.

Wow. It is wow, indeed. Never have I witnessed so many stars in the sky. *This is phenomenal.* Oh god, suddenly my brain sends repeated messages to my bladder that we have to act ... NOW! Diving out and finding a suitable patch, I squat and smile. Not just because I feel the wild relief of peeing with a view, but because my eyes are now fully open with the awareness of what this adventure means to me. In this moment, I promise myself never to pass up the opportunity to walk or wild camp solo, ever again. I know it's not just about getting out of the tent sooner. My eyes are wide open to the fact that I should have done this walk years ago. Wide open to the consciousness that there's nothing to fear except my self-limiting beliefs.

27

Crossing into South Devon

Waking up on my borrowed patch of Cornwall takes me a while to digest. I did it. Piggie, we bloody well did it! *Well done, Wath, you wild camped solo, but don't get cocky. There's more to learn yet.* There *is* so much more for me to conquer on this walk, but although slow to wake this morning, I also sense a burgeoning within me to wild camp again tonight. The promise of this experience I'd missed out on for so many years has risen to the surface, and I am suddenly very alive, despite the sleepiness.

I heat a pot of water and enjoy a porridge with my view, chat to Piggie about how proud I feel and then pack up my tent, still thrilled with my achievement. Granted, I could have selected a better location; the site between the five-bar field gate and the kissing gate was a tad on the bijou side. But I can work on that.

Bag zipped, clipped and hoisted onto my back, I walk away and catch myself to turn and check the area. A great tip from Mike. Good, there's nothing left other than a few flat blades of grass in a Harry shape. I look across at the woods and am happy I didn't opt to sleep there last night. Two minutes on and the narrow path opens out onto an area of what looks to be common land. It slopes away slightly but in the middle stands an enormous daymark tower. It must be around seventy or eighty feet high, painted in vivid red and white stripes. I laugh at myself to see all this wide-open grass; I could have been far more selective and less obtrusive.

For around an hour, I walk, think, hum songs and admire the approach to Fowey, feeling lighter than I have since leaving kit at Lea and Steve's. The reason this time: not kit, but the weight of a failed mission now lifted from my shoulders. I still have the river crossing to tackle, but I have a few days before that happens. As the thought passes through my mind, my tummy gives another flip as I allow it brain time. Despite my fears for months beforehand, I'd pushed it to the back of my head since starting the walk. Now, suddenly, it's peering around the metaphorical door at me and poking its tongue out.

From Fowey I take the ferry across to Polruan and decide to stop in a corner shop for some snacks. In a shop that can't hold more than a few people at a time, I jump for joy at finding it full of my friends. Artie, Mike and Steve are all here. What are the chances?

"Guys! This is amazing! How come you're all together?"

"We camped together last night. And Jinni. You should have been there," says Steve.

"Where did you stay last night?"

"I camped just before the Gribbin daymark tower. I had a little spot all to myself. It was my first wild camp too!"

"You did it? Great stuff, Zo!" Mike cheers. "How was it?"

"I was nervous at first, but once I'd popped out in the night for a wee, it all changed from there. I can't believe I left it so long. Looking forward to more of the same now! So, where's Jinni?"

"Jinni's gone on. She has to be back on a specific day and wants to make sure she has enough time to get to Poole," Artie tells me, as he stuffs his bag with purchases from the corner shop.

"Awww, that's a shame." Deep down, I'd hoped I might get to walk with Jinni again and maybe even camp with her, too.

Across two hot and breezy days, I walk with the boys and see the threads of a team tightening up around the edges. Steve fills me in with his knowledge of all the up-to-date, high-spec gear. "Did you see Jinni's boots?" he asks me.

"Oh yes! They were one of the first things I noticed. I asked her about them and wrote the details down, so I wouldn't forget. They look very lightweight."

"I'm going to order some for myself. They're the lightest boots on the market."

I walk with Artie for a while, and he shares more about the plants he's seen this year. "Aye, I've got plenty in my notebook, but I've still not seen a corn marigold. I keep looking but not yet spotted it. I saw a picture in a book in the library and it was gorgeous. It'll be right lovely when I see them for myself." Artie has a wonderful way of enthusing about things.

"Are you likely to see them on the coast path?" I ask.

"Maybe, depends on soil. It's hot now, but I can smell shades of autumn. It might be too late for them."

"Wow, Artie, say that again!" I'm mesmerised by the rhythm of his poetic language.

"Which bit?"

"The bit about smelling autumn."

"I think I said I can smell shades of autumn?"

"Yes, that's it! That would be a glorious name for a poem ... or a book, even."

"Aye, I'll give you that. You can have that for nowt."

As we all walk, sometimes together, sometimes dropping back to our own pace, to be in our own thoughts, a very short but large chap stops to talk with us. He's speaking to us, but all I can see is the size of his rucksack. It's almost as big as he is. Must be at least eighty litres. He tells us he's walking the whole of the South West Coast Path but doing it from Poole back to Minehead. This is the first person in all these days and miles that I've met doing a reverse route of the path. Then he looks at me and says, "You must be Zoe?" I nearly fall over in shock. "I met a young lady up the path a few miles, and she said about these other Coasters who are walking, and she mentioned you by name. Said to look out for you."

"Ah, that's nice! I like the name Coaster, too. I may adopt that."

"I'm Shaun, it's been good to meet you all. I best be off now."

We chorus our good wishes between us. Once Shaun has gone, Steve comes up to me. "Shit, that was a whopper of a rucksack. Nice guy, but what on earth was he carrying to need a pack that size? His back won't thank him for it by the time he reaches Minehead," he says, "if he makes it that far."

Steve soon strides ahead. It's not that he walks any faster than us, it's more that his long legs naturally carry him further, quicker. He likes his own space too, I notice. Often perched on a bench waiting for us, having a quick smoke or off on a high point somewhere, either searching for a drop of 3G for his phone or on the lookout for a picture-perfect photo opportunity.

I drop back to walk beside Mike. He's slower-paced than Artie and Steve. "How's it going?" I ask.

"Yeah, all good thanks. Thirsty work today, though. I overheat easily and I've got to make sure I don't burn too. I damaged myself a few summers back while out walking in Scotland with friends. Burnt all the skin off my neck and round the sides of my face." He points to the patches I'd spotted on his neck that day I first met him with Artie, on the lane leading out of Zennor.

"I see you've got yourself a straw hat. That must be keeping some of the sun off. Have you got any cream to put on too?"

"Yes, I need the hat, otherwise if I burn my head again, it'll stop me from sleeping. It was agony last time and then I had weeks of itching as it healed. I've got cream, but I've not put any on since this morning. I suppose I should do that next time we stop."

"Hah, yep, it would be a good idea. Sun cream doesn't work when it's in the bottle," I banter with him. "I liked the term 'Coaster'. What do you think?"

"Is that what that Shaun guy said?"

"Yes, he referred to us all as Coasters. I think Jinni may have said it to him, though I can't be sure."

"I reckon that's what we should call ourselves then. C'mon you Coasters, let's do this." Then spontaneously, Mike shouts, "C'mon you Coastal Walkerrrrs!" Steve and Artie turn around, both smiling.

"C'mon you Coasterrrrrs," we all sing-song in a jolly response. It appears we have a team.

It's my thirty-fourth day on the South West Coast Path. We set off at 8.30 a.m. from a wild camp near to the coastguard lookout station at Rame Head. Mike is getting cold, hanging around for us slowcoaches, so announces that he's going on ahead to keep himself warm. Steve, Artie and I opt to take a slow walk to the Cremyll ferry, where we'll meet up with Mike again later. It's a warm day when the sun is out, but many clouds scumble across the sky and the keen breeze adds a chill to the air. It's hard to decide whether I need my waterproof smock on. We miss the next available ferry, so end up waiting for half an hour. In the grand scheme of things, however, this doesn't make much difference, as I later discover that we're unable to move on further, anyway.

With more serious blister issues again today, I stop after just a mile of hobbling to attend to my foot. Using a dressing and tape, I pack it out well, hoping it might relieve the pressure and reduce the pain.

I'll tick off another milestone today – the momentous crossing from Cornish soil, back into the Devonian lands of Plymouth. Steve,

Artie and I walk and talk lots. The paths are mostly wider now, so it gives us room to walk side by side.

"What walks have you done then, Artie?" Steve asks.

"Oh, so many, I can't even list them. I've walked in England, Scotland and Wales. This will be the fifteenth time of walking the South West Way, though. It's the best."

"The South West Way? Where's that?" I ask.

"Hehe, it's here! That's what it used to be called. I'm still in the habit of calling it that," he says. "I'm planning to get all the National Trails done but would like to do them in one go. It's hard trying to figure a route where you don't cross the same path twice. I'm sure there's a man who's done it. When I get home, I'll email the Long Distance Walker's Association to see if they know. I'm away walking for about seven or eight months of the year, so should be able to fit it in." Artie's a retired joiner, so without the responsibility of work, he's able to suit himself when he comes and goes on a trail.

"That'll be incredible, Artie. Let us know how you get on," I say, enthused by his plan.

"I fancy doing the new walk opening up along the Wales coast next year," Steve says. "It's longer than this one by 240 miles. Linking to Offa's Dyke, it'll make it the first ever country where you can walk all the way round."

"I remember Offa's Dyke, nice walk that," Artie adds.

"Wow, it sounds like a fantastic walk! Unfortunately, I wouldn't have time to walk 870 miles during my summer holidays though. I've already taken two weeks' unpaid leave from school to fit this one in. School certainly wouldn't give me next July off again." Despite sweeping the suggestion away, I can feel the edgy rumbling of an idea in the background.

"If you're going to do all the National Trails next year, Artie, you ought to think about treating yourself to a new rucksack," Steve says.

"Aye, I know I need to do that. I could do with another sleeping bag too. Like that one Zoe's just got herself. It looks right small and so lightweight. Don't take up room in your bag like mine."

"After seeing Jinni's small rucksack, I think I'll be treating myself to a new one too." I laugh. I'm not joking either. I've realised that 68 litres is the size I'd probably need if I was doing an expedition in the Himalayas. There's little I actually need to survive on paths like this. I love learning more about their experiences of wild camping. Like a sponge, I'm ready to absorb all the tips I can.

The time passes fast with walking companions, and we particularly enjoy the section through Mount Edgcumbe Country Park. We all agree it's rather pretty. It's a shame we don't have more time to spend here and appreciate its offerings. Steve makes me laugh – he's always on the lookout for a new, unidentified wild camp spot. His chirrup of "Nice spaht" often echoes around the landscape. Together, we'd all respond with the extended drawl of "Nice spaht". I think this catchphrase might stick.

There is boundless wildlife around us most days, but over the course of a few hours, I've seen four peregrines today. In Mount Edgcumbe woods, we're surrounded by old beech and ash trees and I'm enjoying listening to the call of the crows, the shrill twitterings of the smaller birds, and the low rumble, wash and crash of the waves on the rocks, around fifty metres below us. We catch sea glimpses through branch-lined viewfinders. With the sun strong on the horizon, it creates a runner of sea sparkles reaching for the shore. A monster butterfly passes us, pauses for a moment in mid-flight, as if to figure out which way to go, and then flits onwards. It's unusual and one I must look up.

"Gee whizz, that's lovely," Artie says. "I think that might be something like a lion or leopard butterfly."

"I haven't heard of either of those. I think there's a rare High Brown Fritillary, which if it *is* this, would be amazing to say we've seen it." The only known pocket of these butterflies in the South West is sixty miles north-eastwards, in Exmoor's Heddon Valley. That's back where I stayed at the Hunters Inn and received the news about Nan's death.

The thing that strikes me about these woods is how characterful the trees are. Every bough or trunk deformity creates a canvas of shapes and patterns, causing a gallery of animals or faces to spring out of the trees at me. Roots, like tree feet, spread their toes wide into the earth, moss nestled in between the toes, clinging to the fractured stone banks. Red earth spills from the cracks.

To get me through the hours, I decide that more singing is in order today. These blessed blisters are at worst unbearable, and at best, debilitating. I do what I can to ensure my feet are comfortable, to avoid any unnecessary pressure on the blisters. Singing helps my mindset and helps me to forget their punishing pain.

The woods open up to well-trimmed grassland, where sheep graze and children picnic with their families. The view extends wide over the harbour to Plymouth. Central between the banks of Cornwall and Devon, I see a small island, edged black with seaweed and littered with a few buildings. I wonder about its use. The path skirts around the outer fringes of the country park but holds so much interest as we pass an ornate temple and a small lake. Dusted with a short stretch of beach, the path leads into the historic formal gardens where cannons guard the grounds.

As we approach the Cremyll ferry, we catch up with Mike. Once we're aboard, we have a seven-minute breather to relax and I'm told the island, now seen from another vantage point, is called Drake's Island. It sits to the south-east of the ferry point, while a naval base dominates the area upstream towards the Torpoint ferry. I've found it an attractive introduction to, dare I say, a city of little promise. Nothing I had heard about Plymouth until now had made me want to stay and investigate it. On landing at the embarkation point on the other side, however, I discover I am pleasantly surprised. It's a strange feeling, being back in Devon, with only this county and Dorset left to walk through. I feel a small pinch of sadness in my chest, muddled up with the achievement "tick" of another county completed.

Passing through Plymouth is a simple and cheery walk. The path is straightforward to follow, thankfully. I snap a sneaky shot of two biker guys on the harbour wall, looking cool in their shades and leather. Piggie poses for a fun photo next to a "No Tombstoning" sign. *You gotta watch these l'il pigs, y'know ...*

Tomorrow will introduce me to my most intimidating section of the entire walk – crossing the River Erme. I push the thought and my fear away, as we're making our way out of Plymouth and the focus is on where we'll stay tonight. We'll consider how long we feel like walking and how much daylight is left. On this occasion, we have to negotiate our walking day around tide times and ferries. We know that to cross on the Noss Mayo and Newton Ferrers ferry, we'd have to arrive before 4 p.m. There is no chance of that now, so we can just take our time.

On reaching Warren Point, I'm pleased that we've still made a healthy eighteen miles – and me with these blisters too! As a group, we decide on a wild pitch, as this is the furthest we can go without crossing the water. This perhaps isn't the best *nice spaht*, like those seen earlier in the day, but it'll certainly do. High up here on the warren, the breeze from the day's walking develops into something way windier. So much so that in any exposed parts of the warren, we would have been opening ourselves up to the potential of a noisy, chilly night with little sleep. Harry Hilleberg tucks in well behind some gorse bushes, giving me perfect shelter. Like gentlemen, the boys pitch their tents elsewhere, until I usher them over to come and use the space around my tent too. It's a snug fit, but with the tents close together, the four of us are as protected from the wind as possible.

Never has minestrone soup with extra noodles and rice, plus a small cheese and onion quiche tasted so decadent. It's around 10 p.m. Once tucked up in my sleeping bag, I call out "Goodnight" to Artie, Mike and Steve, in a very Waltonesque "Goodnight, John-Boy" way, and settle down to write in my logbook. Within minutes, despite us being in a remote spot and the light disappearing fast, there's a pack of loose dogs running freely around the tents. They bark loudly and playfully. These new objects must intrigue them, squished into a corner of their regular walking haunt, smelling of hot food and humans. There's a friendly "Good evening!" from their owner and with much relief from us all, the sounds drift away into the distance, as the man and his lively pack head for home.

As I teeter between sleep and consciousness, I swear I've had some of the strangest dreams – lucid dreams where you are half awake and half asleep. They appear so real. The dreams contain a colourful mixture of tents caught in a wild whirlwind and dropped into the River Erme. The four tents are eddying and thrown around with the tide. A pack of large dogs paddles out to us, each catching hold of a guy line, doggy-paddling with us all, spluttering and splashing to the far shore. Between us, we work hard to avoid sinking or getting washed out to sea. Two silent biker men in full leathers and shades point the way we should go, once at the bank on the other side of the estuary. And then there's me, looking behind in horror to see my logbook floating away.

My whole body jolts as if I had been physically dumped on that far beach. Thankful to realise my logbook is safe, I scoop it up, along with my pen, and tuck it back into its dry bag. I welcome the chance to bury myself deep into my down bag, allowing myself to fully succumb to the need for sleep.

28 My Nemesis – The Erme

Thirty-five days of walking have unfolded between leaving Minehead and the day I meet the River Erme. Thirty-five days of walking, often alone with my thoughts and my feuding left and right brain. *It'll be fine – you've come this far. You're strong, you can do it* versus *What makes you believe you can cross this? You're so accident-prone ... there won't be a helicopter to save you. Then you'll be sorry.*

After all the jokes and the what-ifs, the time has come. This is not a game any more. I'm no longer on stage weaving my scary adventure stories to students. Now it's my harsh reality and I must deal with it.

It's usual for me to wake up between 4 a.m. and 5 a.m. while out on the trail. Despite not being a morning person, the natural cycle of sunrise, birds singing and bladder activity usually prods me out of my slumber. That, and the fervent munching sounds from wildlife around the tent. It's often rabbits, but sometimes ponies or cows that I failed to spot when scouting for a suitable pitch to set up camp for the night. These are far more inquisitive beasts than rabbits so, for my peace of mind, it seems better to avoid sharing a field or common land with them, just in case.

This average August morning shows me no brightness; no glorious rays of sunshine to lift the spirits and wake me with a smile. In the gloom and with my earplugs wedged firmly in place, I discover I've slept in later than usual. It's 6 a.m.! I pull out the earplugs and watch the wind tugging at the nylon walls from multiple directions. Every so often, a gust shakes the arced pole through the middle section of my tent. End to end, the wind bursts through, leaving the unzipped air vents snapping and whipping noisily. It had been windy last night and there's not much sign of it dying down. I nip outside for my morning wee and observe the vantage point we'd selected for our camp. Not bad, I think as I hide between two large gorse bushes, heavy with seed pods ready to make their distinct click as they pop open. I make a beeline for Harry, pouring myself back into the delicious warmth of my sleeping bag just before it rains.

Artie, Mike, Steve and I pitched at Warren Point near Wembury last night, and after a chat made the obvious decision to stick together for the rest of the walk. Frustratingly, despite being a quick descent away from the next ferry, we can't leave our little camp spot until 9.45 a.m. The first ferry at the River Yealm doesn't operate until 10 a.m. I write in my journal to pass the time and with a grimace I note down "that's half the day gone". *Grrr!* It may seem like a minor irritation and hardly worth recording, but when you are accustomed to setting off around 8 a.m. at a 2.5 mph pace, this feels like serious time-wasting. With a heavyish rucksack and facing the severity of some of the terrain already dealt with on the South West Coast Path so far, any faster than this, for me, is unusual.

The ferryman welcomes us onto his vessel. He looks proud to be captaining this small white craft adorned with blue livery – I see the painted words "water taxi". With so much energy stored from my morning off and keen to move on, I skip aboard so fast I almost lose my footing. Sat in the confines of the boat, clutching my large pack, I'm quick to observe it wouldn't seat more than about eight passengers. Captain Ferryman fires life into the outboard motor to carry us across the river, barely spitting distance, to Noss Mayo. He chats heartily with us and when he hears I'm walking for charity, he gives me fifty pence. *Don't knock it; every penny helps.*

Approximately seven miles of stunning coastal landscape takes much contouring around the clifftops. At least it's straightforward walking at only one hundred metres above sea level. We can't see much today because of an unfortunate outbreak of foggy soup, but we're happy we can still see enough to graze on the plump, juicy blackberries. This is the reward for the lack of view and intermittent rain. Like clockwork, my tummy tells me it's close to lunchtime as the sea mist lifts to reveal the glory of the area. Our unit of four pad down to Mothecombe beach. It's beautiful. A wide, sandy stretch that spoons the curve of coastline lovingly as it ventures from the English Channel to be swallowed into the mouth of the Erme. Oh my god. My arch-nemesis.

Rugged, architectural cliffs dusted with trees and richly packed with vegetation, sit against a backdrop of the characteristic rolling green hills of Devon. Somehow, the jagged rocks protruding from the sand like broken dinosaur teeth offer balance to the softened, picture-postcard traits of the view. The overall visual is pleasing but, as I glimpse the vast expanse of estuary it makes my tummy kick back with a pulse of adrenalin. Like I need reminding that we are nearing the point of no return. It's the stuff of my nightmares, though I'm comforted to be in the company of new-found friends who I feel like I've known for years.

Arriving in Mothecombe a little after 2 p.m., we resign ourselves to the fact that today is going to be more a day of waiting than walking. The guidebook informs us we can cross the river by wading knee-deep an hour on either side of low tide. Consulting the local tide table tells us that 10.30 p.m. is the next expected low tide. If we are to cross at 9.30 p.m. then, we have over seven hours to kill. This beats the extra hour and a half we had to wait at Warren Point this morning by miles.

Not sure what to do with our glut of time, we wander up into Mothecombe village. A characterful man catches our attention on the way up the road. His position at a field gate is not unlike the stance of a local taking up his regular place at the local pub. As he assesses the world into the field beyond, it's hard not to notice the droopy eyelid, deep-relief features and oversized feet, more like submarines. It's as though someone had sculpted him from a bag of clay. Beside him, secured with an old piece of rope, is a coarse-haired terrier that reminds me more of a watermelon than a dog. We stop to chat to George and give his rounded companion, Trixie, a friendly stroke. George's beret perches unnaturally on the tip of his crown. His wisps of white hair float in a wayward fashion, the epitome of Einstein. He also wears a thin, long workshop coat, which leaves me wondering if he was once an engineer or carpenter.

Further up the lane, we are delighted to find a tearoom. The stone building of The Old School Rooms Tea Shop is a super little place for us to relax for a while. I enjoy at least two cups of sugary tea, even though I never take sugar in my tea. This has become a welcome naughty habit, to pick me up while on my adventure.

After an hour of charging our phones and enjoying the change of scenery, Maria, the lovely lady managing the tearoom, shows signs of clearing away and locking up. She fills up our water carriers and as we leave, she kindly offers us the last of her freshly made pasties. Of course, not wishing to see good food go to waste, we're quick to oblige. A brief chat again with George, who is now sitting in the tearoom garden, gives us the opportunity to ask him if we can take his photograph.

Sometimes a second chance arrives, but I make yet another mental note to assume that this rarely happens.

Steve and Mike construct a small fire down on the beach. We still have many hours to wait until crossing the estuary is safe. I can see a slipway across the far side, but at a diagonal to where we now sit around the fire. It's about a third of a mile away, and seems so far, with the estuarine water creating a tense divide between the two areas of land. As I tuck into my pasta Mug Shot, it doesn't occur to me that if the men are drying their socks over a makeshift twiggy washing line in front of the fire, then I should be too. With only half an hour to go before Operation Erme begins, I realise my error. I had been so engrossed in keeping my mind active, and off the topic of wading. Instead, I absorbed the view, relaxed on the beach and watched the flames flicker around the fire. It hadn't crossed my mind to get my damp socks dry for the next chapter of our walk. *Wath, you're a first-class muppet.*

Steve suggests drawing in the sand. I leave my WathWalk moniker, for those passing on the path above the beach to see before it washes away with the next high tide. At least it gives me a shallow distraction from the mission ahead of us. "What's WathWalk then, Zo?" Mike asks me.

"It's the name I gave to my blog to document this charity walk and all the training. I started a club at school and called it WathWalk too, as we raise money for the same charities. We meet every week, make stuff and sell it. The students from the club are helping me with the ball and auction in November. Thankfully, some lovely staff are going to give me a hand with it. It's a lot of work, but all good fun."

"But why the word 'Wath'? Where does that come from?" Mike asks again.

"Sorry, I didn't explain it properly. My surname is Wathen. I love to mess around with words, especially alliteration, so it became WathWalk. Our club always met on a Wednesday, so we knew it as WathWalk Wednesdays."

Mike nods. "I get it now. That sounds great."

On moving back to the fire, I am preoccupied watching the gracefully skilled sweeps of a stand-up paddleboarder. I've never witnessed this activity first-hand and had considered it to be a sport more suited to areas such as Poole Harbour, canals, or along calm rivers. I ponder this guy's bravery, to be making his way up and down the mouth of the estuary. *He must be so strong to paddle against the current.* My brain tries to make sense of it. He looks like a strapping young man, which I am not. *How the hell will I hold my own against that tide?*

By 9 p.m., although still quite light in the summer evening sky, I sense the visibility levels beginning to decrease. My awareness of the task ahead heightens, hands becoming clammy as my nerves increase. It's one thing to face your fear head-on in the daylight. But to be forced to deal with the unknown under cover of darkness feels to me, at this moment, more than I can bear. I'm aware of a tightening sensation in my tummy. It's usually the headquarters for my anxious moments. *Somebody, please remind me why I'm doing this in the dark.*

Artie, in his mid-sixties and the oldest of the four of us, paces back and forth. Since meeting him, I often refer to him as the mountain goat, but this evening, like a racehorse, champing at the bit to be released onto the chase, I can see him eyeing up his route across the water. He has more experience as a fifteen-time veteran of walking this National Trail. He knows the route inside out. Somehow, this knowledge still doesn't reassure me. If he crosses now, is that in the best interests of the rest of us? Well, me at any rate? The boys will be fine, I'm sure – but I'm not a tough cookie like them. I'm worried I can't hold my own against that current, and the estuary still looks too deep. As my anxiety rises, all the worst-case scenarios rush around my head again and again. It's like I'm stuck in a repeat of my nightmares. There's the one where I'm swept out to sea, the one where my foot gets caught under a rock and I can't move as the tide races back in, and the one where precious belongings float away. None of this is helpful, so I hum instead and try to visualise myself on the other side.

This game, this adventure, is distinctly each to their own. I started the hike solo, and although I have people around me, I am looking after myself. Therefore, I will cross solo if necessary. In a funny way, right now, I'm learning a hard lesson from Artie. We may all have opted to walk this stretch together, but we are no more responsible for one another than we were when we set off four weeks ago, alone. Yet why do I feel so concerned about Artie? My gut rolls over as high alert nerves prickle their way into my consciousness.

With the information that low tide is not until 10.30 p.m. and crossings are only possible one hour on either side of low tide, 9 p.m. feels way too early. We shouldn't be setting off until at least 9.30 p.m., but at 9.15 p.m., we watch in disbelief as Artie makes his premature move. He hoists his oversized rucksack onto his back. With socks and boots clutched in one hand, he sets foot onto the damp shore. A few more steps and he is at the water's edge, pressing forward. I hear the sloshing sounds as he paddles out into the river, slowly, instinctively finding his way. Further and further in, his body language, with arms outstretched and stilted motion, shows how much he's tackling the force of the current. His position in the river changes ever so slightly as I watch him turn towards eleven o'clock, and into the receding tide. Mike mumbles next to us, shaking his head. "He shouldn't have gone. He's struggling."

"Artie's experienced and I'm sure he knows what he's doing," I reply, hoping to convince myself too, but it feels wrong.

It's decision time. Mike feels he has to choose whether to act by wading out to assist his friend, now tackling the waters of the Erme, potentially putting them both in danger, or whether to wait until a safer, lower tide has settled in. In a split second, Mike's rucksack is on, and he looks at Steve and me. "Ready?" There's a searching in his eyes that suggests he's prepared to go out to Artie alone if we choose to stay put longer.

Shit. This is it. In the fullness of the moment, I have no time to consider my options. At this time of night, I am not about to cross solo. If I'd been on my own, I would have set up a little camp on the beach and crossed at the following morning's low tide. I secure my socks and walking boots to the side of my rucksack and double-check that Piggie has no chance of heading out for a moonlit swim. I take a deep breath and begin the sloshing. Outwards, into the water, we slowly splash towards the fading figure in the dimming light. Soon, we would have no visibility of him at all, although there's one positive – we are only two nights away from a full moon, which has been rising early evening. Even behind the cloud, it creates an ambient glow across the water that we may not have benefitted from at a different point in the month. I've noticed Mike sometimes tends to mutter under his breath. I'm sure I make out the words "silly bugger".

This is where my Keen H2 sandals perform their best. I feel vaguely smug as I consider my kit decisions. By now, I know that many of the gadgets and gizmos I'd thought necessary for this Tour de Coast Path were more of a hindrance than of use. But on this occasion, the others had to cross bare-footed. I know I have more traction on the riverbed because I'm wearing these all-terrain waterproof sandals. *Excellent move, Wath.*

Yanked sharply from my pride, quicker than a roguish gull can steal my lunch, I am forced to focus. The water level, although in theory should be receding now, seems to rise further up my legs. *Concentrate, dammit. What's happening?* The reality of the situation is that the estuary bed shelves away and in places drops considerably into dips and pools. I thrust my poles into the water. My aim is to keep at least three anchor points on the sandy bottom as I lift each leg, now like leaden weights, to force my way through the powerful ebbing flow.

The blanket of night lowers rapidly as the Erme's menacing current tugs at my body. Unable to see the water's depth, I ferret around the bottom with my poles ahead of me, checking I'm not about to stumble into a watery abyss. With my head torch on, I can just make out Mike's figure a little way over to my left, his hand now on Artie's shoulder. My progress diminishes as the depth increases and my body fights against the intense force of the rushing water. As the level creeps up my thighs, subconsciously I try to push forward on tiptoe, hoping to keep my bottom dry. It's futile and takes a nanosecond for me to realise the stupidity of this plan. The instability of my body, teetering on one set of toes and balanced only with two walking poles, renders me almost helpless to the tide.

Without a word or warning, I sense a firm grip on my arm. It's Mike. He has reassured himself that Artie is heading safely to the opposite bank. On watching my figure in the shadows, crossing with determination but labouring against the tide, he offers his support. A part of me wishes I had taken on this section of the challenge on my own, just like Jinni. She is now a day ahead of us and I marvel at her fearlessness, to have made this crossing solo, assuming that she's still walking solo. Had I failed by relying upon the support of others? Was she braver than me for taking on this river monster alone? Whatever the result of my analytical overthinking, right now, I have gratitude for walking companions at hand when I need them the most.

As we reach Wonwell Beach on the eastern bank of the River Erme, I grin at the others. We did it! Everybody is present, and the tide spared me. I have just faced my greatest anxiety of the past few months and overcome it. My smile radiates through my body, like one of those thermal kids on the old Ready Brek advert. *Yessss, I made it!* I sense a mighty inner strength rising in me I've never experienced before. I feel it pumping through my veins, filling me with an empowering energy that fuels every part of my being.

We won't camp on the beach. Despite it being past 10 p.m., we dry off our feet and, stepping back into our socks and boots, carry on up the hill towards Scobbiscombe. Despite wet knickers, there's now an extra spring in my step. As we walk, I squeal with delight at counting no less than six glow worms distributed along the side of the hill. *There's the silver lining.* For the next one and a half miles, I can't stop myself from singing "Somewhere Over the Rainbow". It may annoy the others, but I remain grateful they endure my late evening excitability, instead continuing quietly uphill to discover a *nice spaht* behind a long steel animal trough.

29

Scobbiscombe to Seaton

Some things don't change. The day after the Erme experience and we're back to the routine of rushing for ferries. The path to Bigbury gives us more steep ascents and descents again too, which, when you're pushing hard on a deadline, is a real obstacle. One other hurdle is oversleeping, which we all did this morning. We left just after 8 a.m. to catch a ferry four and a half miles away. The Bantham ferry only runs for an hour each in the morning and afternoon, so after our trail racing, we are relieved to make it with minutes to spare.

The ferry carries us for our shortest and most expensive crossing of about 200 metres, over Devon's River Avon. It's a tranquil scene. Bantham's wide sandy beach framed by dunes and grassland sits ahead of us. We're offered views of Burgh Island to our right as we leave the rocky shore of Bigbury-on-Sea and Cockleridge behind us. A tidal causeway connects Burgh Island to the mainland, and the ferryman tells us it's home to a hotel, pub and a chapel. "Agatha Christie used to come here. They say she based two of her novels on the island," Artie says. For the few minutes we're there, the place leaves a charming impression of nature, literature and artistic landscape upon me.

The ten and a half miles of walking to Salcombe is much easier, which I'm grateful for. I still end up racing to catch everyone up, though, as I keep stopping to take photos, particularly around Bolt Head, which is stunning. The eastern side of the headland is full of the striking rocks and intriguing coves I'm inspired by. Its beauty fills and fuels me.

Wild wees aren't so easy now as there are too many people around. I know the boys won't believe me, but this is another reason I keep taking so long to catch them up. I must look so conspicuous, loitering around the paths until all the holidaymakers and dog walkers have passed me by.

We walk through the crispness of Salcombe, sharp sniffs from bejewelled women here, side-eye glances from men in slacks there. It's an affluent town, it seems, and our unwashed, hobo appearances probably risk next year's title of "Tidiest Seaside Resort" or "Salcombe in Bloom". I give up on saving their neck for "Best Lavs" and head into the nearest public loo as soon as I can. Here's a great opportunity for me to do some housekeeping. My knickers, a pair of socks and a vest need rinsing out. With the breezy day we've been having, I figure I can make up a washing line on my pack to get them dry soon enough. Since leaving Lea and Steve's, I've been thinking about how to wash my smalls. Campsites made it easy, but now I'm doing more wild camping, I have to grab these moments whenever they arise. I remember the looped pegs in my rucksack given to me by Lorraine many years ago. I attach them to the back of the pack and hook up my undies. For a split second, I feel awkward as I'm walking with three men ... but the feeling instantly disappears, and I laugh at myself. *They won't give two hoots, Wath!*

Salcombe might, though ...

We escape on the last ferry from Salcombe to East Portlemouth at 5.30 p.m. Steve mutters to me that the ferryman looks like a pirate with his weathered features and faded bandana tied around his neck. Pirate or not, he didn't charge us, which saves us a whopping one pound forty each. For another forty minutes, we walk along the edge of a clifftop and around a cliff face. My tummy turns at the sheer drops. Rickham Common is full of sheep poo and open to the elements, but it's flat. It looks like an ideal spot to camp until rain and strong winds bluster their way in by 9 p.m.

The night continues to be wet and windy, but by 6 a.m. the weather clears into perfect walking conditions. It's a pity I'm so tired as I'm finding it hard getting up in the morning now. It's difficult to get going and stay enthused when your body says no. Two miles into the walking day, I can't ignore Pig's Nose rock, however. Piggie has the obligatory photo taken with his namesake in the background, although I think I spot him hiding away as we pass Gammon Head.

Bit by bit I pick up the pieces of my exhausted head and body, and by lunchtime I'm back to my bubbly self again. At just over eight miles, Start Point is the perfect location to stop and eat our lunch. The rocks are rugged with many dips and gaps, like a battlement. They make good seats for us all to spread out and the views are incredible. "There's a shadow on the horizon out there. I wonder what that is?" Artie says.

"Maybe the Isle of Wight?" suggests Steve.

"We're too far away for it to be that," I say.

"It might be Portland?" Artie says again.

"What do you think, Mike?" I ask. "You come from Weymouth."

"Nah, that's not Portland. We're too far away."

A chap sat next to Artie loans us his binoculars, and we all take turns in looking at this distant hulk on the horizon. Mike, despite disbelieving the rest of us it could be the Isle of Portland, agrees that from the shape, it most definitely is. He grew up in Weymouth so would recognise it. We calculate that as the crow flies, Portland is nearly sixty-one miles away from Start Point. It blows my mind that we can see something so far from us. "That's insane," Steve says, also finding it hard to get his head around.

South Devon offers us much history, natural beauty and interest. The tragedy of the lost village of Hallsands washed into the sea nearly a hundred years ago. The creamy beaches of Torcross and Slapton Sands dotted with buckets, spades and oily bodies. A watery nature reserve known as the Ley, a lagoon running parallel with the sands.

The landscape, including the Sherman tank at Torcross, absorbs me across the Ley to Slapton Sands. I think about the tank, amazed at how they lifted this war hulk from the sea almost twenty years ago. It remained lost on the seabed for forty years, along with a graveyard fleet of ships and other vessels. Nearly one thousand US troops lost their lives in this tragic hijacked training exercise. Now it stands in an idyllic location, and I nod to myself as I acknowledge the appropriateness of the memorial.

Despite the odd shower, the sun bounces across the landscape this morning. The clarity of the rocks makes them as clear as cut crystal. The air smells clean, too. There's a freshness that falls and sparkles with summer rain and the scent lingers for a few hours, as if with healing and purpose. I'm learning to rack up these moments of gratitude to feast upon when I'm suffering. Now is one of those times. My blisters have returned with a vengeance ... or perhaps they've never left and are simply getting worse. I find it tough getting up, packing everything away and setting my head to my walking mission for the day. Strete gave us a place to camp for the night, but as a result of my tiredness, I leave late again. It's a slow six miles to Dartmouth and I don't feel like I've done much walking. I have given my best attempt to inhale all the joy of the South West Coast Path, the sun, the palette of greens, the sounds. They all tickle my senses to help me forget about the pain in my feet. It may be working.

Quaint buildings, dramatic and almost impossible medieval first-floor overhangs, cobbled alleyways and stone fortress remnants. The ancient streets of Dartmouth distract my mind with the renewed urgency to take photos. Lots of them. We walk through the town to find a bakery. Stretched along the edge of the river, to say the character of this town is charming is an understatement.

There's a strong presence of yachties here. Unlike other seaside towns, however, from the short time I'm here it feels like Dartmouth hasn't acquired the snootiness that sometimes goes hand in hand with a waterside wallet. I'll look forward to coming back one day.

At Dartmouth harbour, we all hop aboard the car ferry as foot passengers, crossing the river to Kingswear. A traditional-looking shop fitted out with every type, look or character of teddy bear greets us on the other side. I can't resist asking the owner if I can "mingle" Piggie among the bears in the shop window for a photo shoot. "Wath, Piggie's just landed in a new style of 'Where's Wally?'!" Steve laughs. We all have a giggle at the photo, but I'm left wondering if Steve could be onto something. It's an innovative book idea and as I'm walking, the name comes to me ... *Pinpoint Piggie.* I smile at the possibility. *It's got legs (or trotters). Maybe.*

The Kingswear to Man Sands stretch is physically challenging, but there's still plenty for me to look at and keep my brain occupied. I walk with Mike for a while, chatting and simultaneously navigating the trip hazards in the woody area above Newfoundland Cove. Through a window of leaves, we spot a perfectly framed image of the sea, the rocks, distant fortifications and a flurry of small boats. We spend a few moments in appreciation and of course I take some photos before Mike makes a sudden turn on his heels. "C'mon Wathers. This won't get our miles in, will it?"

Wathers ... That's a new one.

I have this tendency to smile at people when I see others on the path. Often, it gives them the green light to stop me and ask what I'm doing. When I'm walking with Mike, I've noticed he wants to move on. Today is no different. He's polite and seems to like the social side of meeting with new people but doesn't stick around with them as long as me. A woman walking a pack of small dogs approaches us. They're darting all over the place, sniffing, cocking legs, enjoying short bursts of running, just for the sake of it. It's a bumble of legs, flappy ears and fur. Just one remains on the lead. After the usual conversation about my walk, I bend down to give some fuss to the dachshund next to her. "You're cute. What's its name?"

"Dora."

"Dora the Explorer!" I chuckle at my joke and give Dora some extra ear tickles.

"That's why she's on a lead," the woman says with an eye roll and a distinct air of resignation.

"Ohhh, I see."

I hear a "Right, gotta go then, nice to meet you" and Mike is already off down the next hill towards Scabbacombe, keen to catch up with Steve and Artie.

The chat gave me the chance for a short break, which I appreciate. My feet hurt when I'm walking, and scream at me like a banshee every night too. The pain wears me down and makes me feel like the walk isn't becoming any easier, though my legs are certainly stronger than when I first started out. I try to acknowledge this during my inner conversations and remind myself of how far I've come.

At thirteen miles, I'm pleased to be done with walking today. After the intense rollercoaster of cliffs, we decide to stop at a small beach leading onto a flat area of closely nibbled grass. It's an ideal spot to pitch our tents with an uninterrupted view of the sand, sea and sky. We're not the only ones to consider it to be perfect either, as I watch the longest and fattest rat ever scuttle past. I make a mental note not to leave anything out that would encourage more rodents ... after all, where there's one rat, there's an army nearby.

After we've all eaten, Artie busies himself with his boots. I watch, curious as he takes a small tin and pours the contents over the leather. With a cloth he rubs in a circular motion all around the tops, the ankles and down the sides in a methodical manner. "What's that then, Artie?" I ask, thinking he'd tell me it was a special leather preserver.

"Oil to keep my leather fed," he replies.

"But isn't that a tuna tin?"

"Aye, if it's tuna in oil, I might as well use it."

I hear a snort of laughter from Steve. "You'll have ratty back here overnight, looking for his dinner!" he says. We all pull a face at one another, knowing this is probably not the first time Artie has dressed his boots in tuna juice.

"I've learnt a lot from you guys on this trip, but your tuna trick has trumped all the advice put together ... I'm not sure I'll be using this one any time soon," I say, smiling at Artie. "If it's really stinky, I might have to walk a few metres behind you."

Artie grins back at me. "That's okay, then, as I work in feet and inches."

Steve and Mike make up a small fire on the beach, and as the sun sets and the night chills the air, we watch a large, bright full moon rise above the horizon. No clouds. No wind. Just a perfect beam of light reflected from the moon across the water in front of us. Within this moment, all my foot troubles melt away. I am at peace with my body and in love with the world around me.

The terrain from Man Sands continues its theme of rollercoaster, though perhaps it's not as heavy-duty as yesterday's challenge. It's not long before we hit Torbay and the coastline blends into a mix of harbour, fishing hubs and tourist magnets conducive to seaside towns like Brixham and Paignton. It's a precursor to our arrival in Torquay, now an urban sprawl of unwelcoming, littered holiday hubbub. I remember the years of visiting Torquay, the English Riviera of my childhood, yet today it seems to have disappeared behind a drape of grey. To be fair, the problem is more likely to sit with me and my memory of the area. With long-held memories come expectations ... if not met, then the sweetness of those memories is forever soured. Perhaps it's best not to revisit.

Although we finish our day in Oddicombe, we collectively decide to camp a few miles ahead at Shaldon, on the edge of the River Teign. After just over nineteen miles done, no one feels up to squeaking in another six and a half miles tonight. Artie knows Longmeadow Farm well from previous years of coastpathing, and so it comes recommended. We jump on a bus and enjoy the luxuries a campsite brings, such as hot showers and a proper loo.

I crashed out early last night, not even able to muster a vague scribble in my journal. I leave at 6.30 a.m., along with Steve and Mike, to complete the missed section of path by walking back to Oddicombe from Shaldon. Artie has done it many times before and doesn't need to reacquaint himself with the path this time.

More refreshed than usual, I find the early start has given me a brief shot of energy. We reach our destination within two and a half hours, which is pretty healthy in my book. A bus pootles into St Marychurch at just the right time for us to jump on and get back to Longmeadow. We're packed up and gone by noon. The lovely owner gives me yet another spring in my step by only charging us two pounds fifty each for our pitches.

A short walk down the hill takes us into Shaldon and across the road bridge over the Teign. We stop to chat with a guy who's just caught a sea bass in the lowering tide of the Teign estuary. His beaming grin speaks volumes. "That's my tea sorted," he says.

I can see a train on the Teignmouth side of the river and my heart skips a little. That family connection with the railways and my many years of travelling everywhere by train now flips open every chapter of my childhood all at once. It's like a flick book of images rushing through my head. The core pictures are of me and my family, sat on scratchy blue and green seats in a train compartment as it rattles along the seafront at Dawlish and Teignmouth. People regularly stopped on the promenade, just metres away from the passing loco, to wave. Toddlers jumping up and down excitedly and dogs held firmly on their leads. As a young traveller, I loved the scary excitement of the multiple tunnels, creating a dense clatter that echoed around the deep, black arches. Like we were flying on Concorde, I remember the brittle snap of sound as the train's ejection into bright sunlight flooded us with a vision of gleaming red rock, sea, sometimes with or without waves, and yet more people waiting at each of the tunnel exits to greet us.

For years, I had wanted to be one of those lucky people on the promenade. I had dreamed of being on the beach side of the glass. Perhaps I wanted to be like one of the Railway Children, waving at the driver and the passengers. The closest I ever came to it was holidaying in a static railway carriage at Dawlish with my friend Caroline and her family. We must have been thirteen. Whatever the attraction of the trains, it fills me now with the effervescent thrill of being a child again.

This time, I get to wave.

Once across the ferry at Starcross, I part company with the boys. My uncle and auntie live in Exmouth. This is Lorraine's eldest brother, John. I've arranged to spend the night at their home. I'm looking forward to Avril's wonderful food and I must admit the idea of sinking into their bathtub is a real carrot. Uncle John picks me up right on the seafront at Exmouth, and it's only a short ride back to their house. Conversation is always so easy-going with Uncle John and Auntie Avril. They are genuinely interested in my challenge, and nothing is too much trouble for them. I add a few notes to my logbook, then I'm fed, we chat, I soak, I sleep. My feet sing in appreciation of a sumptuous soak in bubbles.

The next morning, Uncle John kindly drops me back at the seafront. We hug, and he bids me farewell. There's a short walk from here up to the Geoneedle, a landmark monument that marks the start of the Jurassic Coast between here and Poole, and 180 million years of the earth's history.

I stop briefly to watch a man near the Geoneedle, lost within his morning yoga practice. Long hair tied back in a ponytail, bare chest, bare feet, tanned skin. I do my best not to leave my mouth open too long as each pose leaves him precariously close to the edge of the cliff. Desperate to ask him to move back a little, I clam my mouth shut and keep walking.

A little way on from the needle and I meet up with the boys again. "Ah you decided to join us then, Wathers?" Mike teases.

"Yep, but I could change my mind!" I grin back at him. "Where did you sleep last night?"

"Right here," he replies.

"Got some nice shots of the sunset," Steve adds. He shows me a few photos on his phone. They do look lovely, but I try not to let myself feel like I've missed out. I haven't. I caught up with family and got to soak in a bath too.

I'm amazed at the size of the gulls in Budleigh Salterton. They're virtually albatross size. We all share our experiences of how many times we've lost food to these gargantuan gull beasties. They're cleverer than we give them credit for and often work together.

For once, we all agree to stop for a beer in Beer. It has to be done really. The Anchor Inn provides a welcome break, especially as we know we're in for the long haul today. We're heading for a campsite at Axmouth – but it's just over twenty-four miles from my starting point today in Exmouth. I've never walked this kind of mileage before, so I'm not sure how I'm going to manage.

By the time we reach Axmouth Farm, I'm tired, ruffled and just want to get my head down. While I should be basking in the success of my longest day yet, I can't, though I don't show that I'm grated. Our little team has been together a lot today and I feel I'm losing sight of what started as a solo walk. Admittedly, I may not have smashed out so many miles if I'd not walked with the boys, but even so, I think I need some me time.

30

The Undercliff Storm

Often you just need to spend time with yourself and, as I quietly established yesterday, I knew today should be earmarked as one of those days. My new walking buddies mean a great deal to me, and I appreciate their company; however, that doesn't mean we have to walk with each other every step of the way, day in, day out. There are days where I need space, both personal and mental. Some things were said yesterday, and although I never reacted, inside I bubbled and hissed like a saucepan about to boil over. The rain has been torrential all morning and on waking early, I make the conscious decision to break camp as quickly as possible and head off for a solo walk today.

I leave the Axmouth campsite, right beside the River Axe, at 8.30 a.m. As I walk past the gate, I see Arthur, Mike and Steve, still packing up their belongings, desperate to keep any precious items as dry as possible. I've had company on and off for a while now, so it feels both weird and liberating to be back as a bona fide solo hiker again. No longer bound by the unspoken rule that decision-making is a group thing, I'm once again able to make my own choices and do this adventure thing my way. Head down and hood up, now tightly zipped under my chin, I walk along the road hoping the boys would understand my need for solitude.

It's clear from looking at the map and reading the description in the guidebook earlier this morning that the next few hours will not be a walk in the park. The sight of the familiar white acorn always raises my spirits during even the most despondent of days, so I'm careful to look up regularly. I don't want to miss it with my head hooded in this heavy rain. About half a mile along the road that heels the estuary, the fingerpost appears, directing me left and uphill through a local golf course. There have been a few of these now, and I've become quite accustomed to the etiquette of sharing a golf course with, well, golfers. And balls. Flying balls. I can almost guarantee that within a split second of stepping onto the edge of a green, I'll hear that telltale shallow click of metal on pitted plastic. It's the moment you know that unless you've been paying attention, you don't have a hope of knowing which direction the ball is coming from. I've learnt to treat golf courses in the same way as I would crossing a railway line or a road, using the timeless mantra of "Stop, Look and Listen". Stop at the rough. Look for the chequered slacks. Listen for the chatter or clinking of irons. It usually works.

Today is quite different, with the rain keeping even the hardiest of golfers at bay. The steep driveway up to the Axe Cliff Golf Club has become a raging torrent, and I'm shocked at how much effort it takes to walk up. Like a tsunami cascading down the hill at me, the water pours over my boots, adding even more resistance to my ascent of the slope. The back door of the clubhouse is partially open and I call in with a sing-songy "Hellooo?" The impish child in me wants to add "Is there anybody there?" but I think better of it as that's a little too Scooby Doo.

A jovial head peeks out, and a kindly looking gentleman smiles at me. "Not the day for walking really, is it?" he says.

"Not really. Perhaps a better day for swimming!" We both laugh. "Are you selling any snacks?" The man offers me a basket from the bar behind him and I pick out two Mars Bars, paying him from my scrunched-up, and now sopping, little cash bag. I continue my wet slog up the hill, having thanked him for the opportunity to purchase today's rocket fuel.

"Good luck," he calls out from the doorway. "I hope you packed your flippers!" I raise a walking pole to acknowledge his comedy and savour a bite of my dripping Mars Bar on the hoof, rapidly stuffing the rest back into my smock's kangaroo pouch.

It's not long before I reach the beginning of the long stretch known as the Undercliff. The cliffs of Dowlands, Bindon, Whitlands, Pinhay and Ware sound to me more like an upmarket partnership of solicitors than a collective of cliffs. They comprise around six or seven miles of dense wood that picks its way through an old landslip. The ground is now considered stable, not having sunk any further for many years, and the vegetation I see growing over it is evidence of how established it is. It blows my mind to think that the terrain I'm walking on now was once perhaps fifty to eighty metres above me. It's created a new, important habitat for wildlife and operates its own little microclimate.

Before entering the woods, there is a warning to walkers to be prepared for the challenge and understand there's no access by road for the next six miles. It takes a second to digest this message. It sounds scary, but I'm happy that I can move on in confidence, knowing my experiences over the last 537 miles hold me in good stead. I continue with the deeper acceptance that over the past six and a half weeks, I've developed into a long-distance walker of much hardier constitution than I'd set out with. "You're not a proper long-distance walker." Mike's teasing words echo around inside my head. "Staying at people's houses, in a bed. That's not the real deal ..." This bugs me. I know he was only jesting, but the joke had sunk deeper into my psyche, more than perhaps I was even conscious of. Mike wouldn't have been aware of this either, and he certainly wouldn't have meant to hurt my feelings. It may be more about my reactions than his words, but I also need him to know that how I choose to walk my walk is the right way. For me.

As friends for a few weeks, Mike, Artie, Steve and I have cultivated an understanding of each other, meaning a few wisecracks here and there don't feel inappropriate. We have all become firm friends and can say pretty much what we feel to one another. I am also now "one of the lads". At least, that's how I'd like them to perceive me. I don't want any of this gentlemanly business of helping me over a stile or offering to carry my rucksack when things get tough. I am in this for the challenge, to walk solo and deal with the issues I face, in my way. For the most part, that is how it's panned out too, so far. The guys are respectful of my wishes to be treated as such.

The humidity underneath the canopy of the undercliff woods is intense. With the heat of the summer still stored within the plants, trees and soil, it has created a moisture-laden, steamy atmosphere akin to walking through a jungle. Ferns sprout tall and strong in their diligence to seek the daylight. The trees are a splendid shade of green, even now in late August when many trees show signs of turning as the first calls of autumn beckon around the corner. The land here must be richly fertile, as the woods show the most abundant growth I've seen in any of the woods I've walked since the third of July. And that, if I'm honest, would be a large amount, if I ever had the time to stop and count them.

The rain hasn't let up. Even though I'm given a little extra protection under the canopy, it now intensifies into an almighty storm. Rivulets of water run down the back of my neck, despite the best intentions of my near-perfectly functioning waterproof. A tree ahead of me has fallen, maybe not in recent weeks, but it's blocking the pathway. I look at my options and decide it's too high to climb. The area around each end of the trunk seems way too dense to negotiate, so I adopt a ground-level position and proceed to commando-crawl underneath the tree. There's just enough space to squeeze me and my rucksack through, but on standing and looking down at my front, I can't help but laugh at the absurdity of the spread of mud and leaves now pasted across my chest, belly, legs and knees.

A tremendous boom resonates like a cannon, from way off in the distance. It sends a mini wave of panic through the birds sheltering from the storm in the boughs above me. They take off in a clatter of squawks and chaos, but land again a few trees away, assured they're not in any danger. If I didn't know better, I'd have said it was the army firing on the ranges the other side of Lulworth Cove, although that's thirty miles away in a straight line. However, I *do* know better ... knowing full well that the army cease firing and keep the ranges open for the six-week period of the summer holidays. Maybe I'll never find out what caused the bang, but it was powerful, whatever it was.

The magical, if sodden, undercliff keeps me within its spell for a few hours before I am released onto the warren at Ware. The rain has stopped, and the sky thankfully looks more welcoming; brighter, with far fewer dark-rimmed clouds. It's a sharp drop downhill, and I'm relieved after seven miles of hard but beautiful walking to reach Lyme Regis. I'm hungry, so I follow the prom and look for somewhere to buy grub.

The first café I reach is the Penny Black tearoom, operating out of the back of the Post Office. The ladies there ask me where I'm from and what I'm up to. When I say I'm from Poole, Ann tells me about a flash flood in Bournemouth this morning, following an almighty thunderbolt. "That's it, I heard it!" They look amazed when I tell them I heard the clap from the undercliff coast path. Ann, running the Post Office, and Hatty and her parents from Penny Black, were so interested in my adventure that they all contribute a donation towards my fundraising there and then.

With family living in Lyme Regis, it's tempting to stop here. I could head up to Jackie's to clean myself up and dry out right now. *Hmm, another hot bath.* My sensible head tells me that if I do this, I'd risk falling behind as my available days before returning to school in September are disappearing fast now that I'm drawing closer to home. On deciding to walk onwards to Charmouth from Lyme, I call Jackie to make sure she would be happy collecting me from Charmouth instead. She says it's not a problem, so I leave the Penny Black after thanking everyone for their generosity and set off for the coast path out of Lyme.

Given a choice, the countryside is always my preference, yet I observe and admire the attention given to the detail of the street furniture around Lyme Regis beachfront with the joy of visiting an art gallery. In particular, the streetlights, with their wrought-iron ammonites and conical shades, show so much effort to make it memorable and unique from every other promenade I'd walked.

"Wath!" I hear from a nearby shelter on the Marine Parade. I look back and see Steve, waving at me. Next to him sit Artie and Mike, all perched on the bench like the three wise monkeys. It's so good to see them, even though I had planned to walk solo today.

"Guys!" I bound over to them. "How's it going today?"

"That was a bloody awful walk this morning," Steve grumbles.

"Aye, it was wet," says Artie.

"Yep, yep, definitely wet, especially when I commando-crawled under that tree."

"Why did you crawl under it?" Mike looks puzzled. "We just went around."

"I didn't see a way around. The gap under the tree was just big enough for me to squeeze under with my pack on, too."

"I can see ..." Mike looks down at my mud-caked clothes and we can't help but laugh.

"It's never been that bad in all the years I've walked that undercliff," Artie says. "It makes you wonder how long it'll be before the land slips away again."

"Well, at least we're through safely and if I'm honest, I enjoyed it, despite the rain." I remember the thunderbolt. "Did you hear the loud bang earlier? About eleven-ish."

"Yeah, I heard that," Steve says. "Thought it might be the ranges over at Lulworth."

"No, they'll not be firing over summer. They always keep ranges open for the school holidays." Artie knows. He's experienced in the finer details of pretty much every part of the walk. He reels off ferry times, path closures, best campsites and is always happy to rate and recommend where we'll find the top pasty, piece of fish, bakery or curry house.

"I've just learnt from the ladies in the Post Office about a thunderbolt this morning in Bournemouth. That's almost fifty miles away as the crow flies, from where I heard it on the undercliff. There's been a flash flood in Bournemouth Gardens as a result, and it's absolute chaos down there." The three men sit on the bench, taking in my news report. There are a few raised eyebrows, but no great reaction of "Bloody hell!" or "No way!" I'm not sure what I expected. Like the three wise monkeys, they hear what they want and say little.

"Where did you get to this morning then, Wathers? You headed off pretty quickly." Mike fixes his raised eyebrows in my direction. "You gonna come and have some lunch with us?"

"Yeah, I thought it would be a good idea to have a solo day today. You made the point that I'm lucky I met up with you lot, so you could help me ..." I pause. I don't want to be all sour grapes over any help they gave me before. Equally, though, Mike has to understand that I could do this on my own if I wanted to, as I had set out to do. "I started this walk solo and just wanted some time to myself today. I guess it was my turn to head off early."

Mike nods, as if he knows more than he's letting on. I think he realises he's said more than he should have. "So, are you coming along with us for lunch?"

"No, I've just eaten, but thanks anyway. I'm being picked up in Charmouth a little later and staying with my cousin back here in Lyme." I smile at them all.

"See, I said you're not a proper long-distance walker." It's obvious Mike's teasing me, so I scowl cheerfully at him, if that's even possible.

"I'll catch up with you again on the other side of Charmouth, hopefully tomorrow!" I give them all a quick hug and then shoot off to find the path out of town.

A Second-Chance Meeting

31

It seems like I've been gone only a matter of minutes when I spy another familiar figure ahead of me. A black and green Osprey pack, hanging neatly from the shoulders. A racer-back vest with grey and black straps sitting underneath. Black cycle shorts, sturdy legs and a pair of now well-worn Inov8 boots. It's Jinni! I hurry my pace and soon catch her up. She's stationary, thankfully, otherwise I might not have reached her. Jinni walks as fast as a gazelle, graceful and agile, though right now her head faces down, studying her iPhone. As I approach even closer, I can tell she is pinching around the OS map. I've known this section would not be easy to find the way around, because of the many landslips this area has experienced over recent years. Just last year, the council closed part of the coast path at Charmouth for the same reason, so no doubt I'll be dealing with that tomorrow.

Jinni looks up and within a nanosecond, the realisation sketches a massive smile across her face, her dimples forming instantly, sinking deep into her cheeks. "Zoe!" She looks happy to see me. "Hey, how are you?"

"I'm good, thanks. Just heading for Charmouth today. I'm coming back to Lyme later to stay with my cousin. How about you? I take it you're figuring out a route for the next section?"

"Yep, it looks tricky here. We've got a couple of options – either walk up to the A35 and follow along, or head over this hill."

My eyebrows raise. "The A35? That's miles away! I'm sure that's not the official route of the South West Coast Path, is it?"

"I think it's a diversion, though I'm sure it used to go across this stretch of Timber Hill." She shows me a point on the map that's closer to the coastline. "That's the route I'm going to take. Want to come with me?"

"Definitely!" I agree without hesitation.

Jinni and I enjoy our varied conversation and time together this afternoon. The simplicity of walking and talking is like therapy. I'm certain I'm not the only person who thinks this. "You know, Jinni, the boys and me have agreed to walk together for the last few days. We're planning on arriving in Poole on the last day as a group. Would you like to join us?"

"That's kind of you, but I need to be back the day before that," Jinni says. "I had aimed to walk the coast path in thirty-nine days, so have that target to meet. I've also got masses of preparation before starting my teacher training."

I understand she needs to do this. We have a long chat about teaching, and I'm pleased to feel "qualified" to offer her my tuppence-worth of advice about her training year. It's only been five years since my initial teacher training, and in that time I have mentored a couple of new teachers coming into the profession.

The walk over Timber Hill is easy with only gradual slopes to cross. We're careful to stay well away from the cliff edges, which may or may not have been unstable. Either way, we're taking no chances. The descent into Charmouth is much steeper, however, and I'm grateful to have my walking poles. I watch in awe how nimble Jinni is on her feet, almost dancing down the hill. I remember noting this about her when we walked together earlier in the journey, but know if I tried that, without a doubt, I'd end up face-first.

The time comes for Jinni and me to part company. I wish her well on her last few days, aware she will be well ahead of us and therefore this could be the last time I see her. She wishes me luck for the final stages of my walk and promises to raise a glass in celebration to us all, the day after she arrives at South Haven Point. We'd only walked a few short miles together this afternoon, but the time spent with her passed quickly and the conversation had been full and comfortable. I'll miss her but feel honoured, once again, to have experienced this refreshing young woman, fleeting in and out of my life for such short but energising moments. We hug at the roadside, just as my cousin Jackie arrives to give me a lift back to Lyme.

It's been a few years since I've seen Jackie and her husband, Steve. It's the same old family story, no doubt; catching up only at weddings, funerals and christenings. Our last meeting could have easily been yesterday, however, as I jump into the passenger seat and we chatter endlessly for the three short miles back to Lyme Regis. I remember their family house from years ago but had forgotten how impressive it was, standing high on a bank overlooking Lyme Bay. Parts of the house, with its Georgian-style double-fronted curved bays, had been sectioned off to form a separate flat, now occupied by someone else. I'm relieved we don't enter via the huge front door of the house, as peering down at the state of my clothes and boots, I'd have made more of an entrance than anyone had bargained for.

"How are you anyway?" Jackie asks as we pull up the driveway. "Are your feet sore? You'll have to let me know what you need and we can sort it."

"All I can think about is a bath." We both laugh.

"Consider it done! Pauline, Julie and Porsche are with us too, and Hannah's contributing to the tea tonight. It's her chicken curry recipe we're using."

"Oh, that's fabulous!" I hadn't seen Auntie Pauline for ages. Julie is Jackie's older sister, and Porsche's mum. Hannah, our chef for the evening, is Jackie and Steve's daughter. I'm disappointed Adam is not around. He's Hannah's older brother and I've not seen him since he was tiny.

Once inside, the wonderful welcome from all my family who I've not seen in ages is so warming. Auntie Pauline, in her seventies now, amazes me with her ability to keep up to date and her energy and enthusiasm to want to do so. She is eager to hear all my stories of walking the South West Coast Path so far. I share a few experiences with her, and I'm encouraged by her interest.

Julie always makes me laugh with a funny story or two from our family's past and I enjoy catching up with her, reminiscing about the Sunday morning routine. Our weekly custom started with my family going to church and, on returning, everyone except Mum would walk five minutes around the corner to see my Auntie Eileen and Uncle Ken for half an hour. Dad, Ken and sometimes Uncle Malc (Julie's father) would sit there, putting the world to rights, debating the quality of coal, the state of the railways, or the attributes of our local MP. We'd then wander round to Cousin Julie's house, in the next street over, to catch up with her and the kids. Mum would stay at home to cook the Sunday dinner.

This simple routine worked well for us, and I loved the contact with the family. As we sit around the table, I realise this is probably my first genuine opportunity to chat to Porsche – I've never talked with her before this as she was born later, after our Sunday routine had passed and I was much older. It's good to hear about Porsche's future plans for college and university, and I like that I'm getting to know her better.

Hannah and Jackie serve up a delicious chicken curry, and we spend time together around the kitchen table, catching up and talking about so many things. Steve receives a call partway through the evening from the owner of a tackle shop in Abbotsbury about a shoal of tuna. He tells me this is a super rare sight to witness, recommending I keep my eyes peeled on my walk tomorrow.

The bath is as delicious as the curry, if you get my drift. With every item of my rucksack, including my tent, sleeping bag and clothing, hanging out downstairs in the utility room, which makes for a perfect drying room, I need nothing more than to soak my body in deep, hot water, full of foamy bubbles. It's another tiny moment of decadence that fills me to the brim with energy, recharge and the beauty of relaxation. Yep, the bath is delicious.

On waking the next morning in my bed of luxury, I have to pinch myself to remember where I am. I gently slide back the immense, full-length drapes that cover the equally immense bay window. Looking out over the sea ahead of me and to the coastline in the east, I can just make out the weaving up and down of the clifftop shapes, showing me a glimpse of the path I can expect to follow over the coming days. Beads of excitement scatter through my body, shimmering with the anticipation of starting the walk again today. With this flurry flickering inside me and the sudden realisation that I can even see Golden Cap from the bedroom window, I squeal quietly. In the early light, it looks more like Pastel Cap, but in its morning apparel it still looks inviting and picturesque, with a cloud inversion swathed across Lyme and the low-lying areas beyond.

Breakfasted and packed, I'm now feeling wholly refreshed. Jackie drops me back down in Charmouth at around 8.30 a.m. where we hug and I promise to stay in touch and visit again when we have the opportunity. There's a slight wrench in my stomach as I watch her car drive away. It's odd. I've been on my own for a huge portion of this walk, but staying with family before reaching the end feels like I'm starting the challenge all over again, like a new episode. It's different from all the other experiences and although not unpleasant, I know it will take my head some time to digest being alone again.

32 The Footsloggers

Here's a morning conundrum I could do without. As I stand at the roadside where my cousin left me, I look at the map, and the way I need to continue is clearly over the clifftop. A boundary tape fest means the entire area is now cordoned off. Attached to the tape at intervals are signs reading: DANGER. DO NOT ENTER. LANDSLIP. I'm mulling over what to do when a dog walker lifts the tape and wanders through, heading over the grassy cliffs. A moment later, a runner slides himself with ease under the tape.

Now I'm torn, feeling the slow drag of a hard decision. I weigh up the options: 0.9 of a mile on grass or 1.9 miles mostly on the road. I spot someone who looks local and make a beeline for them. "Excuse me, can you tell me where the path has fallen away, and is it safe to go through, please?"

"Oh yes, it's fine," the lady replies. "All the locals use it. Stay well back from the edge. There's plenty of room for you to do that."

"Okay, thank you!" I'm still not so sure. It doesn't feel right somehow, breaking the rules and stepping onto forbidden land. *But you've seen two people using it and one person says it's fine. Stop with being a goody two shoes, Wath.* Still not enough, I head to the nearby shop to ask their opinion.

"Yes, go ahead, use it," the shopkeeper says. "We all do. The cordon is being overcautious. I mean, we know it's slipped, but that was ages ago and there's no sign of it moving again. It's an extra mile to walk the road way."

Here we go then. I need no more convincing. I walk back down to the taped area, take a deep breath and clumsily clamber through, catching my rucksack underneath it. A few awkward body movements later and I'm free, heading over the cliff towards Abbotsbury, my destination for today.

My first notable feature for the day's walking is Golden Cap. Well within my sights now, it smiles at me, glowing with a friendly ombre in the warm morning sunshine. As I approach the hill, I catch up with two couples, one from Hampshire and the other from South Africa. Both are well spoken, well heeled and, well ... posh. I have no problem with answering questions from anyone interested in what I'm up to. Some people find better ways than others to make those enquiries.

"Why are you walking?"

"What made you choose this walk?"

"How many miles do you average a day?"

"What's the toughest section?"

"Who have you met?"

"What delights you the most about walking alone?"

"Are you scared?"

"What does your knapsack weigh?"

"Where do you sleep?"

"How do you go to the lavatory when there isn't one around?"

I mean, it's not a conversation of authentic questions that evolves naturally as we chat. Each question, on its own, is valid to ask someone like me. But this morning, I find myself at the end of a seriously well-loaded question-popping machine gun that just keeps firing at me. No sooner have I answered one question, another is fired, then another and another. There's no time for the normal question-and-answer progression that develops with ease.

Treated with a cold, fact-finding interest more suited for a museum piece than a long-distance walker, I realise that the prime culprit for the barrage of questions is Hampshire Man. It's now reached a point where he's almost running alongside me to keep up. *Here's your Get Out of Jail Free card, Wath. Use it.* I increase my speed a little and it sparks a new question which makes me laugh inside.

"How fast do you usually walk?"

"Oh, about this pace," I say, not fussed with the weight of a little white lie hanging around my neck. "Though often when I'm going uphill, I'll power up even faster, as it makes it easier to manage."

My plan is working. Hampshire Man's face grows ruddier by the minute and in the summer morning's warmth, beads of sweat trickle down his forehead and face. He puffs out his cheeks, pulls a large, pale blue pressed cotton hankie from his slacks pocket and mops his face and head. I glance back to see him waving it out behind him. In readiness for another precise folding, prior to restowing it in his pocket, I'd imagine.

"We'd best let you continue along your way then, young lady. It would be remiss of us to cause you any further hold-up today. Good luck for your journey!" And with that he drops back, releasing me from his attempt to keep me as a walking companion for the rest of the ascent.

"Thank you, and it was lovely to meet you!" I call back as they fade quickly into the distance. Phew! That *was* hard work. I continue powering up the hill, not wishing to be seen to slow down. There's the fear they may catch me up again, too. With a healthy mix of joy and the expenditure of energy like I've just summited Everest, I reach the trig point at the top of Golden Cap, the highest point on the southern coast section of the South West Coast Path. I smile as I remember gazing at Golden Cap from my enormous bedroom window this morning, bathed in the blue light of pre-sunrise. *Well done, you made it!*

I need to capture this moment. With many people around, I decide to select one to be my David Bailey for a few minutes. I see a gentleman in his late sixties taking a photo of the spectacular view. That's a good sign, so I ask him if he'd mind taking one of me. He kindly obliges. I hand him my camera and in a split second, like bees to honey, I blink and there's a large group of people swarming around us. They're a jolly bunch, laughing, chattering, coming up to me to ask what I'm up to. *Oh dear, I won't get anywhere today.* With four or five stood around me to hear about my walk, I ask, "Are you ramblers?"

"Haha, goodness no! We're cyclists."

Of course ...

"We call ourselves The Footsloggers. We usually do a countryside group cycle, but sometimes we choose to go on a big walk instead."

For at least fifteen or twenty minutes we stand on the summit of Golden Cap, chatting about my walk and my charities. Deep down, I know I must get moving, but I don't want to appear rude. Despite being the same questions, this is so much more enjoyable than being on the receiving end of Hampshire Man's question machine gun. The way they ask me is different. They're not trying to catch me out, and everyone appears genuinely interested.

"You know it's been wonderful meeting you all, but I should probably get going now." I motion with my arm, eastwards downhill. "Someone is picking me up in Abbotsbury today, and I don't want to be late."

"No problem!" one man says. He seems to be the "chairman" of the club. "Come on, everyone, let's see what change we have to give ..." He turns to me quickly. "What's your name?"

"Zoe." I'm grinning from ear to ear.

"... to give Zoe for her charities. I'm sure we can muster up some coins for you," he says, turning back towards me.

"Thank you. This is so kind of you all."

For another five minutes, The Footsloggers empty their pockets, bum bags, purses and wallets extracted from the bottom of rucksacks. Mister Chairman wanders around the group with an old baseball cap, collecting whatever these life-loving souls care to chuck into the hat.

Figuring I'd need something to carry all this change in, I retrieve a plastic sleeve from a dry bag used for storing sponsor forms and leaflets I'd picked up. Big Chief Slogger brings the hat and pours the change in. "There you go. I hope that helps."

"Thank you. You've all been so lovely. You've made my day!"

"Your rucksack's going to be too heavy for you to carry now!" a woman calls from the back of the throng. It sets the entire group off into peals of laughter.

"Can we have a photograph with you please, Zoe?" another asks.

"Of course, no problem." With my rucksack weighed down with coins, and like a celebrity just spotted in public, I watch as the group spends the next five minutes arranging themselves around me. One person steps out to take the photo.

"No, no, it's not right," he says. "You need the coastline in the background." We all shift ourselves a little closer to the fence nearest the sea and they rearrange themselves again. "Say cheese!" the photographer calls out, and we all fake up our best and broadest grins.

"Don't forget my camera," I quickly shout. "I can't go without a photo on mine!" I hand him my camera and we repeat our now well-rehearsed expressions.

All done with the photo shoot, I extend more thanks and say goodbye to each person individually. After at least half an hour on top of Golden Cap, I finally set off down the hill towards Seatown. The Footslogger cyclists-cum-walkers, or whatever they were, had certainly lifted my spirits, but I am now deeply concerned about how long I have left to walk the twelve miles to Abbotsbury. At the summit of Golden Cap, I was only three miles into my day's walk. Just as I reach Seatown, I'm stopped by a family on a day trip here from Broadstone, just outside of Poole. They recognise all three charity logos on my rucksack cover and want to chat, though this time, I make it brief.

About five miles in, I begin the descent off Thorncombe Beacon. There is a fire-beacon basket high on the hill, ready to light up the coastline for the Queen's Diamond Jubilee celebrations next year. As I walk down towards Bridport, I see a familiar face coming towards me. It's Lydia, an ex-student of mine, out on a clifftop walk with her family. This time, I know it's important that I stop. It's so lovely to catch up for a few minutes and connect with someone from home turf. We talk just long enough to exchange catch-ups. I share how I'm getting on with the walk, ask how she's doing, and we take a photo.

My phone buzzes, and I see a text has landed. It's Deb, and she's given me a time that she'll be at Abbotsbury this evening to pick me up. I'm to text back if I need it to be later or earlier. I reply to say no problem and I'm looking forward to seeing her and Chris again, then stow the phone back into my hip belt so I can continue. They're such kind people.

Deb and Chris turned up when I found the little bird at the side of the road. Chris had made the beautifully put point the bird wouldn't make "old bones". We'd then walked and talked together all the way to Sennen Cove, where we had said our goodbyes. Although a chance meeting, it felt like an age-old friendship. You know those people that you connect with instantly, as if you've always known them. They'd offered me accommodation for a night once I was down in West Dorset, and this is about as close as I am going to get to them.

As I pass through West Bay, where various telly shows have filmed on location, I'm not too impressed. The cliffs are spectacular, but I'm pleased to pass out of the area of shops and cafés with haste. It's way too commercialised for me. The cliffs of West Bay soon lead me to Burton Bradstock, which, along with Eype, just west of West Bay, is much quieter and nothing short of exquisite, though I hadn't expected to cross a muddy shingle river here. Perhaps I took a wrong turn, or perhaps floods took the bridge out. Whatever, I cross it and hope that my boots will dry off in time for my pickup in a few miles.

The path lowers considerably as I approach West Bexington and I think about my training walk from here, way back in the spring. I have a unique, intimate relationship with this area now that feels revealing. Though it's hard to verbalise, my best analogy is that of a dense net curtain. It's as though all these years I have only seen parts of the South West Coast Path through the curtain. With it removed, the clarity is overwhelming. Every mile of the path now holds a new connection with me. Even those stretches that didn't appeal have still made an impact in some way. The resonation leaves a lasting imprint on my body's physical memory, as well as my actual memory.

After fifteen miles of walking, I am ready to finish for the day. Abbotsbury proves to be perfect timing and Deb is waiting for me as promised. It's wonderful to see her. I bubble with the excitement of the opportunity to be with them again. She drives me back to their house, in a small village around twenty miles inland from the coast. Her husband, Chris, is a dairy farmer, although they don't live on the farm. We talk over a wonderful dinner of quiche, green beans and new potatoes, finished with a home-made Victoria plum compote. They tell me about their potential plans for retirement. We talk about the ongoing renovation work they're having done on the house, and then catch up with how the rest of their trip had panned out down in Cornwall all those weeks back. Gosh, meeting them seems like years ago! How strange the speed with which time passes, particularly while long-distance walking, yet it appears to have stood still too. How is this even possible? The brain is a funny old thing, and mine certainly enjoys messing with me.

It's been like meeting up with old friends; friends who share a long history with me. As I lie in yet another comfy bed, once again I feel incredibly lucky to have made so many wonderful friends. I've lost count of all the kind people I've met on this walk. Some pass through this open door of my world, never to return. Fleeting, but leaving an impression of love, generosity and care behind them. Others pass through and even though our meeting is brief, I know we'll be friends for life.

Welcoming the powerful weight of sleep-laden eyelids, I give myself permission to sink deeper into the pillow and into a place where walking the coast path never ends and new friends never disappear.

33

Drama in Abbotsbury

I slept well, and on waking up in a plush bed, I wonder how Artie, Mike and Steve are getting along and where they slept last night. They probably had a fabulous camp spot somewhere ... While I might be slightly jealous of their big sky, even bigger views and sensational sunset, I'm not at all regretful of staying at another house. No more Super Noodles for me yesterday. Plus, I'd connected so well with Deb and Chris.

While I tuck into an early breakfast, Deb discusses this morning's journey with me. "It'll be a forty-minute drive back to the point you finished at last night, so we should leave around 7.10 a.m.," she says. Chris surfaces through the back door, looking like he's already completed a day's work. Well, of course, he has. As a dairy farmer, he'd have been up since the crack of dawn at least.

"Straight from the cow, that is," Chris says, nodding to the milk on my cereal. "Won't get any better than that."

"Yes, Deb said it was fresh. I've not had unpasteurised milk before, but it's lovely." I pop another spoonful into my mouth. "It has a creamy taste, but with an unusual flavour."

Breakfast done, I dive off to finish off my bathroom routine of throwing a toothbrush around my mouth, before packing up the dregs of my belongings. I haul my pack to the front door. "That's it, my life's organised, and I'm ready."

Deb laughs. "Right, let's get you back on the path then!"

Another goodbye with these two feels so similar to our last one, when we'd said goodbye at Sennen Cove. Like it's only a bye for now. I have a sixth, seventh or maybe eighth sense I'll be seeing these kindred souls again. Deb waves at me once more and drives off, up the hill and away from the coast path. I look at my watch noting it's 7.50 a.m. I make my first stride out of the day, happy knowing that I've begun my day's work early.

My so-called "stride" doesn't last for long. Less than ten minutes into my walk and sudden cramping tummy pains hit me with the force of a runaway train. It doubles me over for a moment, and I hope bending might allow the pain to pass. With caution, I stand upright slowly and take a few more steps, knowing that my stomach is now feeling decidedly dodgy. This doesn't feel normal. I look around with urgency, but I don't see anywhere that looks suitable to use as an emergency loo. For a few minutes, I continue walking, though I'm unable to assume any kind of sensible walking posture as the pain persists its offensive on my belly. It's only a matter of minutes before the pain develops into strong warning signals. If I don't find a toilet soon, I'll be taking home an unexpected souvenir.

This situation I find myself in is becoming dire. As I turn a slight bend in the path, there's a wire fence around a small grove of sparsely planted trees. The pain rips through my middle before dropping, then contracting hard into my lower intestine. Oh feck, this isn't a good sign. It's no use carrying on. I simply have to go, and while this wouldn't usually be my ideal choice for an outdoor toilet, I have no option. I drop my rucksack off my shoulders and onto the path, grab some pocket tissues and some vegetable bags from one of my many supermarket shops, and awkwardly pull myself up and over the fence.

No sooner have I crouched, the deed is in full action. The diarrhoea is so instant, it's like I had drunk ten litres of vindaloo tea the night before. What on earth has caused this? Deb's gorgeous quiche and Victoria plum compote wouldn't trigger an explosion of such violent proportions. As I hurriedly try to clean myself up and scoop as much evidence away as possible, something occurs to me … oh god, the milk! Of course, it was the fresh cow I'd enjoyed on my breakfast this morning. My tummy wasn't used to unpasteurised milk. Feeling much better and relieved I'd made it in time, without ruining clothes or suffering any major embarrassment, I turn to see a man walking towards me. Oh heck! How much did he see? I hastily pull up my shorts in a panic.

Not knowing how the hell I'm going to handle this one, I hop over the fence, bend down to my rucksack and try to disguise the bag of WathWaste hanging off the side of the pack. I swing the rucksack back over my shoulder, doing my best to look nonchalant. "Morning!" I extend my greeting as cheerily as possible, despite my heart pounding inside. He's bound to say something. He must have seen.

"Good morning," he replies. "Super day for a walk, isn't it?"

"Yup, it is indeed," I say, clipping together my waist and chest straps. *Please don't say anything …*

"You look like you're in for the long haul. Going far?"

Phew, this guy's a gentleman. If he did catch me, he's too polite to say so. Hopefully, he'll be on his way soon.

"Well, I started at Minehead on the third of July and I'm heading for Poole – but not today." I grin. "It'll be Portland today."

"That's impressive. I like to travel too. I'd love to do the Coast Path one day. Right now, I just enjoy walking sections of it."

"There's no shame in that at all. Doesn't matter if you walk it one go or in sections, it's the getting out there and doing it that's important." *You certainly got out there and did it this morning, Wath.* I tell my inner voice to put a sock in it. "Where have you travelled?"

It turns out that Colin is an ex-merchant navy guy and has travelled all over the world. Five miles into us walking together, I look down in horror to realise that my shorts are still unzipped and unbuttoned. Damn that panic. I spend the next few minutes surreptitiously trying to rezip and fasten up my shorts without my new walking buddy noticing. He's a pleasant guy and probably wouldn't have batted an eyelid. This is about my embarrassment more than anything. That, and trying to keep myself walking on the side of him so my Wath Waste bag swings on the opposite side – I wouldn't want him to be too close to that. It's probably still steaming.

A little over eleven miles later, Colin and I reach Ferry Bridge, which to me always seems like the no man's land between Weymouth and the Isle of Portland. We part ways with a farewell and a generous donation of twenty pounds from Colin towards my fundraising pot. He's walking into Weymouth and I'm heading around Portland today. Time has passed quickly again having a companion, and despite my earlier fears of walking with a man who I thought had spotted me in a rather vulnerable position, I can see in hindsight it's all down to my self-consciousness and how I choose to deal with it that is the issue. Colin, as it turned out, was a jovial fellow and great walking company.

Outside The Ferry Bridge pub is a bus stop. My heart gives a little leap of joy at spotting my friends. They're sitting inside the bus stop shelter, waiting for goodness knows what. Not a bus, I hope. "Artie! Steve!" I join them to find out how they are and what they've been up to for the past couple of days. I had correctly imagined them enjoying the best of the outdoor best. They had indeed witnessed some superb wild camps with big skies and cracking views.

"Mike's gone to his sister's," Steve says. "He'll be staying there a couple of nights, but he's going to catch us up."

"Okay." I pause for a moment. "Is there a plan, then?"

"We thought we might stop in the pub for a pint before heading off again." This is unusual, as apart from our beer in Beer, we try to avoid pubs during the day, saving drinks for after our walking day is done. I look at Artie and he's sat there looking at the sky with a wistful half-smile resting on his face.

"No problem," I agree. I guess it'll only be half an hour, anyway. In a blink, I realise it's still mid-morning, and the bar isn't even open yet. Haha, that's why they're sitting in the bus shelter. Steve and Artie are waiting for the pub doors to open, and then they'll be in there like the first day of the sale at Harrods.

We find a table, with a view that's not too shabby. From one side, I can see the start of Chesil Beach and from another window out along Ferry Road, the causeway that leads to Portland. The pub itself is large, dank and dingy. It swallows us up, with no other bodies inside, except the barman, to give it life. As I sip on my half a pint, I look up in astonishment to see a slim, long-legged figure carrying a rucksack over one shoulder and a large camera in his hand. His grey, branded walking trousers are instantly recognisable to me, as is his green T-shirt, bold glasses and a head of slightly receding, short and spiky dark hair with the distinguished smattering of grey flecks that so many men gain in their forties.

Dumping my glass on the table, I jump up to greet Ross with the longest hug that still doesn't feel long enough after I step back. How I have missed these arms. A little tear falls and runs down my cheek. It is, of course, a tear of sheer happiness.

"Hello," Ross says quietly, looking down at me, a silent message of love sitting gently over his lips.

"Hello you." I brush my forearm across my eyes to make sure they are dry. "How did this all come about, then?"

"I found Steve on Facebook and messaged him to let him know I was planning to come down to Weymouth to walk with you."

That's why the boys were so keen to come into the pub during the day ... Ross had been scheming to surprise me and they were both in on the secret. This is just so sweet.

We stay at the pub long enough for Ross to enjoy a pint and then set off. This time, in a different direction. It would feel weird as we'd be walking south and covering the full perimeter of the Isle of Portland. We'll reach this same spot, either later tonight or tomorrow.

The weather is another hottie. Not so ideal for the rest of the walk we'll be doing today. Portland comprises a handful of villages, various quarries and a great deal of wide-open space. If it's shade we're looking for, we are most certainly in the wrong place. Although I've walked the Portland circuit before, once again I see it with a fresh pair of eyes now that I'm on the South West Coast Path, with a rucksack and walking it as a long-distance walker. I seem to take even more notice of the rocks, their patterns, their position, their cunning ability to balance with such skilful precariousness. One balances against another, looking like it's trying to push the other over the cliff at least 150 feet down to the sea below.

Stone around here is well regarded and shipped to countries all over the world. Portland stone has become iconic over the years for building and flooring and is recognisable with its uniform, pale-grey hue. Sometimes you'll see the odd shell, shrimp or shark's tooth shape set permanently into the cut of bedrock. If I remember rightly, there are many examples of Portland stone in use in London, hence its popularity. St Paul's Cathedral, the Palace of Westminster, and Buckingham Palace were all built from this plain, clean-looking stone. Odd, then, to consider that sitting within the walls of those historic buildings are millions of years of data, recording our world's history through every age known to man. Triassic, Jurassic and Cretaceous, et cetera. I don't profess to know anything about these eras or any part of geological studies, but it still fascinates me. The childlike excitement when discovering a fossil stays with me even now as an adult.

As we walk, it becomes like a treasure hunt, looking for ammonites in the rocks that surround us. Some are large enough to see from a distance, others more discreetly hidden. We'd need to look closely to find them, but we have such little time now. Occasionally we'll spot an enormous shell or ammonite and realise a sculptor has carved the shape into the rock, as there's an art trail around here too. Stone carving and sculpture are a popular artists' medium on the Isle of Portland; after all, the environment is perfect for it. I enjoy walking hand in hand with Ross for a while, savouring the preciousness of being close to him again.

The Pulpit Inn at Portland Bill is our destination to enjoy beer and food, sharing stories of our walking, and life at home for Ross, with Laura and Lorraine. He tells me more about his journey to London to see Iron Maiden a couple of weeks ago. I thought I'd feel like I'd missed out, but I don't. I'm just pleased Ross was able to go.

Two guys walk in wearing matching T-shirts. They're out on a charity bike ride for Alzheimer's UK, which involves them cycling to the extremes of all the pubs in the country. They had been making "Inn-Roads" to the pubs in the furthest west, north, south and east, to the highest, the smallest, the oldest and so on. What a great way to do a pub crawl, we joke with them. I have my photo taken with the lads and as we all put on our best, cheesiest grins, we promise one another to share the photos to give a bit of social media exposure for each other.

News coming in from earlier in the day stuns our enjoyment of the evening for a while. The beloved Bournemouth Air Festival that each year, living locally, we had either heard or watched from a distance, had suffered a significant loss. This afternoon, we read on Ross's phone, one of the Red Arrows planes crashed near Bournemouth Airport, killing the pilot. Such a sad piece of news. We share our thoughts about the accident, about air festivals and of the mammoth safety plans that must have to be followed to keep the public safe. It's not long before another round of drinks is required, bringing the spirit of the evening back to its usual level as I drink a silent toast to a lost young life.

It's clearly too late to continue any further walking tonight, so Danny, the landlord of The Pulpit, gives us permission to pitch our tents on the open grass to the rear of the pub. I only have my one-man Harry Hilleberg, but Ross and I squeeze into it perfectly, with a few giggles and a little rearrangement of belongings to fit everything in. The night, while balmy as a summer night should be, is hot under the canopy of the tent. Particularly with two of us in there. But I have missed him so much and am not about to make any complaints. I have all six feet two of Ross in my tent, and that's where I will relish him being for the next few hours. I know how hard I'll find saying goodbye again tomorrow, so every moment with him right now is precious. The look in his eyes tells me he feels the same.

34

Weymouth

The new team, now made up of Artie, Steve, Ross and me, break camp behind the pub. I pack up my belongings without my usual chatter. The night had been tropical, and although I'd enjoyed having Ross with me, I hadn't slept well. I'm not feeling fully rested. The morning starts off bright when I hop out of the tent for an early wee, hoping there won't be any dog walkers around at this hour. As I look across the water and beyond, the sky tells me it has other plans.

We take a while to organise ourselves and it whizzes me right back to the beginning of the walk, when I relied on staying in the Bongo van with Ross. Those days where I could never get away on time because everything felt in disarray. We are finally up and away by 9 a.m., so I guess that's not too bad, by some day's standards at least.

The gathering storm clouds spur on our team's departure, though the air still feels sticky. With the atmosphere closing in, it sits heavy, awaiting the explosive release it needs to cool everything down. It comes within minutes of us leaving the rough land behind The Pulpit Inn. There's a mild rumble across the sky and then, without warning, an almighty crack of thunder breaks above us. Instantly, the heavens open. Cats-and-dogs rain of epic proportions. Rucksacks off again, we scrabble for our waterproofs and trudge along, soggy and clammy. With my shorts on, the waterproof trousers stick to my bare legs, yet I don't care. I may be tired, but I'm happy to have my man with me. I push aside the thought that he's leaving again today.

After paying our respects to Pulpit Rock, so-called for its stark resemblance to a lectern or pulpit, and a magnet for climbers and thrill seekers alike, we make our way past the recognisable red and white stripes of Portland Bill lighthouse. As we embark on the second half of Portland, heading north, I'm reminded of turning the corner at Land's End and walking in the opposite direction. I know this route well, and the views out to Poole, Bournemouth and beyond never disappoint. In particular, the high and turbulent landscape of the last section of the Jurassic Coast is now within sight, the cliffs looking as magnificent as they are daunting.

The storm lasts no more than an hour, having rocked our world with gallons of heavy rain, thunder, and lightning, fizzling and flashing across the sky. At last it clears, leaving no trace it had ever showed up. The sun is hot, the sky is blue, and our waterproofs dry within minutes, as does the path. We descend into Fortuneswell at 11 a.m., just as a little clifftop café is opening up. A lad of about fifteen is setting up chairs and tables outside. It's a Sunday, so many people will head out for a traditional roast dinner at the local pubs and restaurants within the hour, but the pull of tea and cake is too much for us to resist. We have, after all, just battled through, and survived, the worst storm in the history of Dorset. Or perhaps only the history of Portland – sitting beyond the causeway, into the English Channel, it operates its own microclimate. It wouldn't surprise me in the least if there had been no storm at all a couple of miles away in Weymouth.

Ensconcing ourselves at a table with a super view down to the sea, the boys elect me to place the order. Two coffees, two teas, a slice of chocolate cake for Steve, and Victoria sponge for me, Ross and Artie. The glass domes in the café display a wide variety of freshly baked cakes, none of which has seen a knife yet.

I place the order with the young lad and watch as he considers the cakes. His brain is clearly spinning as he struggles with the knife in mid-air, wondering which way to cut the first cake. He gestures his arm animatedly a few times along the direction in which he should cut. Just as he's about to slice, a woman's face appears over a high counter at the back of the shop.

"That's got to serve twelve," she says bluntly, throwing her young weekend worker into a fluster.

"I'm not much good at maths." He looks up at me sheepishly. "Fractions hate me."

"Don't worry," I say, smiling. "Fractions were never my strong point either." He looks like he wants to sort this out on his own, so I avoid interfering.

As he contemplates, the lad's spare hand frequently passes up to his spotty face, scattered with a hundred or more yellow-filled pustules. After touching his face several times in great thought, he runs his hand back and forth through his hair while concentrating on his dilemma.

"I've got it, I've got it!" he says at last and hovers over the cake, about to cut. I can't stay silent.

"You might need to try it here." With my finger, I show him the invisible markings. Then I step back to allow him to try again and feel less panicked without a customer watching.

"Okay, yes, yes, I really have it this time." He sounds confident, and I relax a little, knowing that our cake is finally on its way. Ross pokes his head through the door to check everything is alright, as time is ticking on and I've been gone for ages. I nod and give him a little thumbs up to let him know me and the cakes will be there soon.

It's the weirdest twenty minutes of five-star faffing, visible thinking, gesticulating, and me cringing inwardly with Weekender's insistence to keep touching his sebum-filled face and hair, but at last, we're there. He serves me the tray, and he seems more or less happy with his grand accomplishment. I pay the bill and carry everything back out to the table, trying not to look disappointed until I'm sat down, with my back to the café. The men look at the cake on each of the plates, and then look back up at me, wide-eyed. Not one slice shows any semblance to the next. One portion of Victoria sponge is at least double the size of another. The portion I opt to give myself is so tiny it's more of a mouthful than a portion.

"What happened here?" Ross's face is disapproving as a frown ripens across his brow. He is a top-notch connoisseur in the tea and cake department.

"Don't ask," I say hurriedly. "The weekend lad didn't have a bloody clue, bless him. I don't want to complain as it'll get him into trouble."

Ross replies with a nod and a mild laugh under his breath. Steve chuckles. "No way. I think we need to have a photograph of this ... it's unbelievable!" He reaches down for his camera.

"Good idea." I grab my camera to take a photo too. "Nobody would believe it, would they?"

Artie sits back, taking it all in. Smiling in disbelief but appreciating the entertainment unfolding in front of him.

It's been a relaxed hour of sitting at that outside café table, but we're ready to move on. We have to reach Osmington Mills today as Ross is being picked up there by his parents to go back home. He has work tomorrow and needs to get himself organised. I think he's been happy to have a break with some male company, too, as our household back in Poole is high in the female camp with Laura and Lorraine. Even her dog is female. The only male in the house is the cat. And once I'm home, we can add yet another female to the team.

Our circuit of Portland is complete, and we walk back along the causeway towards The Ferry Bridge pub. It's hotter still by now, and my cheeks are feeling increasingly rosy. We stop at a car park with public toilets, and I dive in to splash my face with cold water.

There's a footpath, an old railway line, that follows from Ferry Bridge towards Weymouth. They are easy miles as the path funnels us towards the town, with no possibility of veering off in the wrong direction. I see a couple walking towards us. One is a male figure I recognise, with a female figure I don't. It's Mike! What a chance meeting. He introduces us all to Flo, who I assume is a girlfriend, as I know from our conversations his sister is called Joan. While he talks of staying at Joan's, my thoughts wander. *Who's not a proper camper now?* I keep my thoughts to myself. "Mike, this is Ross, my partner," I say after we've all greeted Flo. "Ross, meet Mike, our other walking bud."

Ross offers his hand to Mike, who beams his big smile of white teeth. I notice a leather plaited friendship bracelet on Ross's wrist that I'd not spotted last night. *He's gone all hippy ... is this a midlife crisis?*

"So you're the one who has to put up with this one" – Mike motions his head towards me – "every day?"

"Hehe." Ross chuckles under his breath. "Yep, I guess I am."

Mike and Flo continue their walk and we head off in the opposite direction, towards Weymouth. At a viewpoint near Nothe Fort, we meet up with the Australian hiker, Bob, who I'd chatted with a few weeks ago.

"G'day, guys!"

"Hey, Bob!" He has a healthy head of wayward grey curls and a much longer grey beard than when I'd last seen him. Looks good for his age. He must be at least seventy. We spend a few minutes catching up on his news, hearing about his own adventure along the South West Coast Path and how he's experienced it coming from another country to walk this well-known trail.

"I'll tell you, it's been an utter beaut. Tough but a beaut. Mind you, I nearly carked it not long after I'd met you at those mines. Can't quite believe I made it here, to be honest."

"God, no! Whatever happened?" It's not hard to sense a dramatic story is brewing.

"I was just walking along the path, nothing too difficult, and yeah I slipped. Reckon I tripped over my own darn feet. Couldn't stop myself, especially with the weight of this thing on my back, and I fell over the cliff." My heart's in my mouth. I can't believe what I'm hearing. Even Artie and Steve have stopped to listen to Aussie Bob's tale of misadventure.

"No way! So what next? How did you get back up?"

"I'll tell you, Zoe, I lay there for a moment and thought, *Bob, this is it.* And then, once I'd got my wits about me and my breath back, I put my old boy-scout skills into operation."

Still open-mouthed in shock, we all stand in front of Aussie Bob, listening intently like a bunch of schoolkids.

"I looked up and was probably only about twelve or fifteen feet down. Luckily, I'd landed on a ledge that had a few bushes on the end, so it stopped my fall down to the rocks below. I'll tell you, I'd have been a goner if I'd fallen the whole way." He brushes his mane of grey curls back a bit, as if to take in once again the magnitude of how fortunate he was to survive. "I knew I had it in me to climb back up the cliff, but I didn't know how I was going to get my backpack up with me. There was no way I could manage carrying that as well as climbing." Aussie Bob pauses. "I'm not as young and nimble as I used to be."

"What did you do?" I ask.

He grins at us. "Well, that's where the boy-scout skills came in. I took the laces outta my boots, tied them together and then tied one end onto the top handle of my pack. Then, I tied the other end to my wrist. I climbed up to another ledge partway up, and once I felt safe on the next ledge, I hauled the pack up behind me. I climbed the last stretch and then did the same. It worked a treat."

"Genius," Steve says. "Anything broken? Hurt?"

"No, not really. I scored a few deep scratches from those bloody blackberry bushes and a bruised elbow."

Absorbed by the story, Artie nods. "You were lucky."

"Too right," Aussie Bob agrees.

"What did your family say about it?" I ask.

"Didn't dare tell them. They won't let me out on my own again if I admit to this!" We all laugh with him, nodding in a shared recognition of his predicament.

"Fair point," Ross says.

We say a last goodbye and, still walking towards Weymouth, we watch as the coastguard helicopter comes in and embarks on a rescue. This time, it doesn't look like a training exercise as I'd witnessed at Porthcurno. It hovers high above the water, creating huge, frothy ripples in the sea below. It lowers a man down to a boat, and a few minutes later, it lifts a body strapped to a stretcher. The rope lowers again, and the team winches up the crew officer into the belly of the chopper. It turns and takes off towards Southampton. "The bends, I'll bet," Steve says. His girlfriend, Liz, is a diver, so he hears about this sort of stuff a lot, I'd imagine.

"Sad if it is," I reply. "I hope they make it."

At last, making it through Weymouth and out the other side, we arrive at Osmington Mills, tired, hot and hungry. Ross and I meet with his parents at the Smuggler's Inn, where they treat us to a meal. It's good to see them again too. It feels like I am being gently reintroduced and reintegrated into my Dorset friends, family and acquaintances, both with the chance meetings and the arranged stops. Ross and I share a farewell hug at the clifftop car park, and I wave as his parents taxi him away. The tears aren't there this time as I know it will only be a matter of three days before I'm home for good.

Steve and Artie have set up home for the night in the campsite at Osmington. The kind owners give us the pitches for a fiver each, but in less than an hour I regret agreeing to stay here. It's so noisy, especially with the large number of families on site tonight. There are a lot of LOUD people, many drunk and in the mood to party. I prep myself with earplugs and a strong inner guard, as I've experienced campsites like this before, and it's never pleasant.

Brace yourself, Wath. This could be a loooong night.

35

Tears on White Nothe

A quick unzip of Harry and I'm on a beeline for the campsite toilet block. The early morning sea mist hangs as heavy around my head this morning as it does over the trees and, no doubt, the water, half a mile away. It's atmospheric, but I'm not appreciating anything at the moment, apart from the joy of making it to the loo block in time. On returning to the tent, I make the mistake of tucking myself back into my sleeping bag. Getting up and out can sometimes be *so* hard to do; however, this morning my motivation has gone, gone, gone. I am so dog-tired as I'd not fallen asleep until late because of the party campers. A pesky blister on my right foot and agonising heel pain meant I'd managed only fitful sleeping throughout the rest of the night. Then the babes and toddlers around us woke me at the crack of dawn. The blister is sore, but the heels throb and radiate pain like a double of dose of toothache in my feet. I'll need time to muster up my usual spring and positivity today.

My mobile phone buzzes:

HOPE U HAVE A GOOD DAY 2DAY. WHERE R U?

It's a text from my sister, Sara. She's my biological father's daughter, so officially, we're half-sisters. In my book, she's very much my sister and since I was eighteen, which is the length of time we've known one another, we've always viewed one another as such. I tap out a reply:

CAMPED AT OSMINGTON. STRUGGLING 2DAY

We don't see one another very often, but when we do, it's another opportunity to catch up on those early years we missed together.

At last, Artie and I make tracks eastwards, leaving Osmington Mills campsite at 10 a.m. I know I'll be slower today because of my feet and I don't want to have the added pressure of trying to keep up with Steve Long Legs. Mike is planning to leave Weymouth and catch up with us again later today. Steve hangs around for a while in Osmington, knowing his stride is long. He makes quick work of the miles. Artie and I reach Ringstead, only a mile and a half away, and we decide to stay put for a while, to let Steve catch up. It'll be good to reach Lulworth Cove together, even though they all know I've made plans to stay with someone at West Lulworth tonight. No doubt I'll be the topic of teasing again for not camping.

Artie and I wait for a long time, wondering where Steve had got to. We chat about all sorts as we linger near the kiosk at Ringstead. Artie tells me about some of the rarer species of plant he'd spotted this year. "What's that plant called again? The one you showed me that creeps over everything – it looks a bit like it's from a sci-fi story. Red ...?"

"That's dodder," Artie says. My inner smile inches outwards as I appreciate the way he says "dodder" in his strong North Yorkshire accent. "I've heard you can get something on your phone that tells you what a plant is," he adds. "I'd like to get that."

"I'm not that up to speed with phone technology, but I'll bet Steve knows how to find it," I say. Artie's phone is probably too old to accept apps, although it did have an annoying key noise that sounded every time he pressed a button. So glad we sorted that out.

"Forgot to put money on lottery," Artie says suddenly. "Not sure I'll be able do it now until Swanage. Reckon I can get into Wednesday's draw if I find a shop in town when we arrive."

The mention of Swanage jolts me. It's the reality that we are in fact so incredibly close to Poole, and for me, to home, that it has entered normal conversation. I'll see more people I know, familiar places, and now the pull of walking on home soil fills my soul with an indescribable energy. It had already started way back at Lyme Regis when I crossed the last county border, from Devon into Dorset. While pain and exhaustion batter my body, this homeward energy fuels my inner drive.

"What would you do with the money if you won the lottery, Artie?"

"I'd buy myself a cottage down this way, in Cornwall. I do like Cornwall. Then I'd get a big van I can sleep in. You know, one of those plush, top-notch motorhomes."

"Could you drive one of those?" I ask him this with sincerity, not wishing to sound like I'm poking fun.

"Ah, gee whizz, I don't rightly know that ... hehehe." I assume Artie is chuckling at the thought of himself driving a huge vehicle. "I'm sure I'd be fine. There are many gadgets and gizmos to help you park them things these days."

A buzz from my phone shows another text has landed. It's Sara again:

HIYA, WHERE R U NOW?

That's nice. She must have been following my updates online and is interested in my progress.

OK THX, BIT SLO THO. ONLY AT RINGSTEAD XX

I've had a few texts from friends and family, and colleagues at school. They're a real boost, often turning up at just the right moment when my morale is low.

Out of the blue, Aussie Bob sails around the corner, stops for a quick chat and, in a flash, is off again. It's good to have seen him for a third time. This may be the last time, it may not. It's funny how people keep bumping into one another on a long-distance trail, the way we have done. In particular, the way Artie, Mike, Steve and I kept meeting, a day here and a day there. There are powerful elements of coincidence and fate in our encounters, almost as though a stage show or movie is being played out, with me as protagonist, and all these other characters fleeting in and out of the storyline. I wonder where the tale will end. For most, those I've met on the path will simply remain in my memory as people I've chatted with. I may keep in touch, perhaps on social media if they've given me their details. But for others, I have a sense that we've built the foundations of a solid friendship and I can't imagine never seeing them again.

There's a cheer from me and Artie as Steve strides around the corner. We set off together and chat for a while, but it's not too long before we assume our natural walking pace and positions in the pack. Steve, way ahead at the front, Artie in the middle, and me, hanging back to walk on my own, still desperately tired and needing some solitary headspace.

A break where I can lose myself in my own thoughts and connect with the environment surrounding me. It's hard to believe that with all the artistry of the landscape, much of this morning's walk has faded into a chatter stream and washed out to sea. I think of it like driving, listening to the radio or away in thought, and then arriving at the destination with no recollection of the actual journey. It's a how-did-I-get-here moment and I'm desperate to reconnect with this landscape and my experience.

Walking on my own up to White Nothe coastguard cottages over the last mile and a half from Ringstead has been utter medicine. The wander above Burning Cliff and onwards, through a small group of three or four individual-looking homes, envelops me in a cloak of reverie and imagination. I remember the time I walked across the top of Burning Cliff with Ross and the girls. The news that Burning Cliff had spontaneously combusted, before its demise into the state of landslipship, had astounded Laura and Lara. A few of the cottages at Holworth that I walk past give me food for thought. I'd love to live in something like this one day. Close to the coast ... although I'm not so sure I'd be that happy about living so close to a cliff that had a history of bursting into flames, or falling away, umpteen feet down.

Reaching the old cottages on the headland of White Nothe, I see Artie and Steve sitting on the grassy cliff, watching the dots of distant container ships while basking in the sunshine, and waiting for me. They suggest we break for lunch here. Seems like a good idea, so I park my rucksack on the ground and join them, cutting open a pack of cheese I bought in Weymouth the previous day. I hear voices heading our way. It feels like a delightful welcome, listening to the chatter as I recognise the familiar Dorset accent with fondness. A moment later, I realise it's not just the accent but the voices that I recognise. With my hand resting behind me for stability, I turn my head, but it's not enough to get a full view. I shift my bottom and swing my body to see a young stocky lad walking towards us, arms swinging deliberately, striding wide, and a cheesy grin plastered across his face.

The approaching lad looks like Jack, my thirteen-year-old nephew, but it can't possibly be, because he doesn't come to places like this. *How funny, he must have a double.* I spot a female striding not too far behind him. She looks rosy and carries a bottle of water. There's a man, about the same height as her, looking hot and trudging wearily beside her. "What the—?" *That is Jack!* "Jack, oh my goodness, what are you—" I spot Sara and Lyndon, my biological father.

Up here, high on a Dorset clifftop, the sky is blue and the sun is strong. I have two of my new friends sitting beside me, eating their lunch, and my family has come all this way. *To see me. They've made such an effort. For me. To surprise me!* Suddenly, the power of emotion is overwhelming. I scrabble to my feet, dumping my hunk of cheese on the rucksack, and throw my arms around each of them, sobbing with joy. The tears keep falling and Jack just keeps grinning like a Cheshire cat. What a picture this would make. It's an ambush reunion at its absolute finest.

In a joking way, Sara scolds me. "I kept texting you to find out where you were and you weren't giving anything away, were you? You do like to make things hard for us!"

"Sorry, I had no idea at all that's what you were fishing for." In between snotty sniffs, I laugh along with her.

"I know, and I'm glad – that was the plan. We didn't want you to know, otherwise it wouldn't have been a surprise!" We all laugh again. Lyndon is carrying a walking pole but looks less than fit and fresh. The furrow in his brow tells me he is concerned.

"Everything alright, Lyn?" I wipe my eyes and tear-stained face. "You're not looking so good."

"I'm better now than I was," he replies, with a puff out of his cheeks for added effect. "Those hills are an absolute killer. I honestly didn't think I was going to make it, especially when I got chest pains."

"Oh god, no!" I clap my hand to my mouth in horror. I know Lyn's been having some heart issues over recent years. I didn't want to be the reason for another scary heart episode. "That's awful. How are you feeling now?"

"Wondering how the hell I'm going to get back again!" He follows this with his reassuring signature roar of laughter, promptly causing him to bend over to catch his breath.

We all laugh along with him. "Going back, Lyn, we can go as slow as you need to. Don't you worry about that. I hope you've got your spray?" I have so much admiration for Lyndon, Sara and Jack for coming out to find me and making it this far. The severity of those hills between Lulworth Cove and White Nothe is not for the faint-hearted ... or the dodgy-hearted, for that matter. When I first started walking the hills of the Purbecks and the Jurassic Coast, as it's now known, a few years ago, I froze at the crest of a hill as I stood in disbelief, looking down. How on earth would I walk down that and remain upright, or in one piece? Of course, it was my fear talking. Again. That's happened a lot over the years, and it's taken me a long time to realise how much it has held me back and prevented me from having a go. As I stand there, absorbing this precious moment with my family, who have not been regular walkers, or at least not regular walkers of any great distance or ascent, I sense a warm ball of pride growing inside me. And the understanding that these hills really *are* for the faint-hearted. Because if you don't push yourself to try, one can never move forward out of that place of feeling unable.

I make introductions between my family and walking buddies, and after a suitable rest for Lyndon, we head off again, towards Lulworth Cove. My rucksack fascinates Jack and he gallantly suggests he should carry it for a while. I let him until he realises that it's way too heavy to carry and especially not on these steep descents. He soon offers it back again. Besides, it's strange walking with no weight on my back when I've carried it for so many weeks. I almost feel unsteady on my feet. There's a grounding that happens within me when my shoulders feel the connection of the rucksack. It's as though the bag is hugging me from behind, filling me with just the right amount of positivity and energy for the next stage, regardless of how much my feet might hurt.

At Bat's Head, Steve takes a wander out onto the thin strip of headland to appreciate the view and to share a little male courage with Jack, who is open-mouthed at his bravery. I snap a quick picture for posterity and then realise that I don't have any pictures of Lyn, Sara or Jack with me. This is such a monumental moment of the trip that I need to make sure I have a visual record of it. Sara and Lyn stop at the top of the hill and Steve returns the favour of taking a few photos of us together. The absurd cliffs shelve steeply towards the sea, weaving their mighty outlines away into the distance behind us.

Despite the slow walk, Lyndon makes it back with fewer stops than I had expected. At Lulworth Cove car park, I wrap my arms around them all and say goodbye once again. I know Sara would never let me forget this moment, in a humorous you-made-us-walk-three-miles-more-than-we-needed-to kind of way. She had devised and executed their plan to perfection, however, as not once throughout her string of texts had I suspected any funny business. I'll bet they'd not thought they would finish up today's adventure having walked six and a half miles over the most challenging terrain. They did so well.

Lyndon, Sara and Jack drive away and now it's time to say goodbye to Artie and Steve for a while. They're off to find something to eat in a local pub, wait for Mike to catch up and then head back up onto Hambury Tout, the hill we had just descended, to sleep for the night. I plan to walk half a mile up the road to the village I'd spent a few years calling home.

Destination West Lulworth, to the house of a gorgeous couple who I'd become friendly with over my time here. Phil and Marion had invited me to share dinner with them and stay the night in their chocolate-box, sixteenth-century cottage. I also had plans to visit my old neighbours. Without a doubt, they'd never believe how far I'd walked to see them. Forty-six days, to be exact. But they'd always thought I was bonkers, and here was the confirmation.

Lulworth Locals

36

What a magnificent evening I've spent with Phil and Marion. They are truly looking after me, as all my hosts have. Prior to arriving, I stopped at Finley's Café down at Lulworth Cove for an ice cream. Ann and Doris, who I'd never met before, were so taken with my walk that they donated a generous twenty pounds to my ever-growing charity pot. I met up with Adrian, another old neighbour. He still lives about eight doors down from my old house here, with his mother, Cissie, now eighty-five. My heart ballooned with joy, reconnecting with these people, some of whom I hadn't seen since leaving the village seven years ago.

I wandered up the hill out of Lulworth Cove and into the village of West Lulworth, first to see Terry and Myrna, my old neighbours. Terry had been ill, so perfect timing for me to pop in. I loved catching up with them, despite feeling a tinge of sadness that Terry could no longer manage the garden in the way he had used to when we lived next door. It was a sizeable garden, as ours had been. He and Myrna kept it beautifully. Set on the side of a hill, overlooking the valley that wound down to Lulworth Cove, with the view beyond to Bindon Hill. *Stunning.* Bindon Hill often disappeared and reappeared from the contrary curtain of sea mist. As I sat in their living room, looking out across that valley, I remembered how, on the days the hill was invisible, we used to tell Laura and Lara that Bindon Hill had gone on holiday. Lara used to visit with us for one weekend a fortnight, and she was still quite young then. I wondered what memories they have of that now, if any.

I needed this. Revisiting with these delightful friends from those fond days I spent living here. I headed down to Phil and Marion's cottage. I used to pass it every day when taking Laura to school – that's partly how I came to know them. That, and being involved in community events at the village hall, like Artsreach that Deb in Abbotsbury is involved with too.

Phil and Marion greeted me with such warmth and friendship and found pleasure in showing me around their cottage. After all these years of knowing them, I'd never been inside. Phil proudly shared that although it dates to around 1587, they have records that suggest it could be even earlier. I'm guessing there was once a thatched roof. West Lulworth is well blessed with many thatched cottages. This one is now protected with a slate roof. Its clean lines, inviting pitched storm porch and beautiful garden have always attracted me. The typical cottage garden flowers, a lush carpet of grass and, I imagined, many outdoor nooks and crannies to explore. Behind the low wall, next to the lane I walked daily, stood an off-white statuette of a half-naked woman, partially draped with a sash of sorts. She clutched a pitcher or basket and I admired this moss maiden every day for years. There's a welcoming aura that pulls me every time I see the house ... and of course, Phil and Marion. They are the heart, creating the warmth that invites a chat over the wall or, as in my case this time, a visit.

As I lay in the bath, the cerise glow of light emanates through the windows and into every corner of the room. It's 9 p.m. and the sun is just beginning to set. Wrapping a huge fluffy towel about me, I poke my head out of the bathroom door and into the long narrow corridor at the front of the house. The sunset's firelight hits me. The sky, in full theatrical performance of ever-changing hues of pink, red and orange, touched with a taste of pale blue around the lower edges. The cottage's location, set in a small valley that runs down to the cove, means I can't see the full extent of the sky drama. From the little I can see, however, I know it's spectacular.

For a nanosecond I envy Artie, Mike and Steve. Tonight, their camp atop Hambury Tout will have served them the very best sky Mother Nature had to share. This is what it's all about for me. Those skies, the connectedness, the experience of falling asleep as the light fades and waking as dawn breaks. Just as nature and our human cycles had intended. This visit to my old village of friends and familiarity holds much importance, and I wouldn't have missed it for anything. But, combined with the many other missed opportunities of sunrises and wild camps, I realise there may be some truth in the jesting and teasing from Mike about me not being a real hiker. *Not a proper camper ...* Those words tumble around my head, and I see it. There's a great deal more for me to learn from the path. I just need to allow it to show me. At some point, I'll have to trust in myself more and know with confidence that the path will always provide.

I clamber into a bed dressed with crisp white sheets and a pillow that supports and puffs around my head with delicious comfort, and drift into a state of exhausted dreamery.

With all those sky colours last night, it surprises me then to wake up this morning to a sky of attitude. Whatever happened to "red sky at night"? It's heavy, grey and dank. Rain had fallen already overnight, and more is due. After thanking and hugging my hosts, promising I'll be back to visit again, I leave the cottage just before 8 a.m. garbed in full waterproofed armour, ready for whatever the weather throws at me today.

The boys are waiting for me at the turning circle in Lulworth Cove. This would be the first time I'd walked with Mike in a few days as there have been walking guests with us, or one or both of us has been elsewhere. They are equally ready for the rain as I am, having packed up their tents in wet weather this morning. "Despite the rain, it was totally worth it," they tell me, "for the fireball sky we witnessed last night." *Yep, thought so. Would have loved that, but I loved my bath too. And my comfy bed ...*

The narrow path that leads out of the village and above Lulworth Cove is a rude awakening for our early start to the day, though my body is much more finely tuned to this type of terrain now. Low cloud obscures the view down to the "dragon" in patches. To locals, the dragon is the shape of the cove, with the head being the chunky eastern side of Peplar's Point, and the western, thinner stretch of headland swinging back in to form the curvaceous tail of the beast.

We leave behind Fossil Forest, the fossilised remains of a prehistoric woodland, and continue upwards out of Mupe Bay, where the way is steep and muddy. The memories land thick and fast now. I used to walk with the family down to Mupe on a hot summer's day to reach a secluded beach. Back then, with half a million visitors expected most years in Lulworth Cove alone, it was never worth trying to enjoy our doorstep beach. We preferred to walk just over a mile and a half to Mupe, benefitting from the exercise, the beauty, the excitement of the Fossil Forest, and the tranquillity of the quiet sands.

I had forgotten the severity of the Mupe Bay climb, back up to the ridge walk that would take us down to Arish Mell. To be honest, I'm not sure if I am hesitant because of my fear of heights, or fitness; even after forty-six days of building up my strength on this walking malarkey, I still sweat at any ascent. My muscles quiver and ripple a few times on reaching the top, and just like that, we've entered military land. None of this is accessible during the week, but today, despite being a Tuesday, the range footpaths are open to the public for the summer holidays. Although the footpath through the army ranges opens at weekends and holiday time, the army keeps the rest of the land well and truly secure. We're reminded by regular signs that it's an offence to trespass across this area. The flat lands way below us, littered with the remnants of warfare, spent cartridges, tanks perforated into bits and firing dugouts, also serve as a prompt to "Keep Out". Dotted around the hills are enormous numbers. Targets. Around these, the hills look shredded, although I have been told the ranges truly sustain the habitat and that wildlife flourishes here.

Arish Mell is no different. The fenced hillside forms part of the private ownership of the army. After we pick our way carefully down the steep, mud-packed hill, we stop at the chained gates of the beach and stand for a moment in the rain. What it would be like to set foot on this small waterside haven within a land of guns, decaying tanks, jeeps and holes blasted into the side of every surrounding hill? The beach has always tempted me, but Arish Mell sits so close to the firing ranges that the likelihood of unexploded ammunition is too great a risk for the public to be allowed access.

The foul weather is relentless, and as we recommence our slog up and out of Arish Mell, towards the Iron Age hill fort of Flowers Barrow, I feel a wave of sadness. Not just for the last hours of the walk as it closes around me, but for the lack of visibility and views all round for my friends. Artie has seen it before, having walked the path so many times, and therefore wouldn't be too concerned, but for Mike and Steve, who have never walked this stretch of the Jurassic Coast, I'm sorry they'll miss it.

On our descent into Worbarrow Bay from Flowers Barrow, the visibility reduces to zero and the mud is dire. It weighs my boots down, like carrying two five-kilogram bags of sugar, one strapped to each foot as a punishment. It makes for a near-impossible walk. At once, being held back with every step, my eyes open to the saying "it's like wading through mud". With only another day and a half left to go before reaching our destination, I can say in truthfulness that this is probably *the* most challenging and brutal stretch of the whole South West Coast Path. Is that a weather-related decision? Probably, although this is a super steep part of the route too.

Our perception of how challenging a walk is can be so subjective. Right now, I would undeniably state this is the hardest walking I've ever encountered. On another day, it might be different. Today, the terrain and weather skew my perspective. Mood and physical sensation add to this too. The niggling blister on my right heel is still giving me grief and I have to compensate by walking with a slight tiptoe effort to avoid unnecessary pressure. It's not a blister that I can pop, as it's underneath a mile thickness of hard skin. Combined with heel pain from the repeated pounding both my feet have endured, I'm not as on top of my game as I could be.

We heave a sigh of relief when the rain that has been so ruthless all morning subsides. Now, at 1.30 p.m., the weather and our clothes dry off a little. This said, I'm still struggling to walk the terrain. The mud is persistent, clagging to my boots. No matter how rugged the soles are, two inches of sticky clay slapped to the underside turns regular walking boots into a pair of ice skates. On steep inclines, the only way I can manage the terrain is to cling to the fences and hedges. I'm careful to avoid the savage barbs that sit at intervals along the wire by only pinching the gaps in between.

Chapman's Pool. Wow! More memories come pouring back. The sharp gradient of these steps is so pronounced that my fear of heights corners me once again. The boys seem to have skipped down. Artie, the mountain goat, Mike with his military efficiency, and Steve, whose long legs carry him at double everyone else's pace. Yet here I am, taking each step individually. I'm painfully slow. I ensure I have landed both my feet on the tread before starting the descent to the next one.

My friends are patient with me, however, and once in a while, even through the thick of the rain cloud, I glance up to see one or all of them looking back to check on my whereabouts. Honestly, I don't want that. It sounds weird and ungrateful, but I came on this path to walk it solo, and I'm not seeking support from anyone to guide or help me through each day. It's supposed to be my grind, my problems and my own solutions. The stars have simply connected in a way I could never have imagined, gifting me with some amazing walking friends and offers of dinner or a bed for the night from kind souls I've met along the way.

The path beyond Chapman's Pool is clear to see. Like the track of a runaway train, it dips and rises into the distance towards a headland faced with vertical rock shapes, sculpted into a row of teeth, and topped with a little square stone building that has a cross adorning its roof. A short row of cottages to the left and a coastguard lookout to the right, St Aldhelm's Head is going to be one for us to do tomorrow. Today, after nearly twelve miles that have felt like twenty, and despite normally making it our business to stay on the path instead of stray from it, as a group we decide to walk inland a short distance, to the village of Worth Matravers. It has, after all, been a rough-tough day. Both the path and the weather have put us through our paces, testing us to our limits. Between them, they have whipped, drenched, pushed and tormented us to the point of needing a more social stop. Something to lighten our day. The Square and Compass pub will bless us with that well-earned liquid welcome, not to mention their heavenly pasties, which are a meal in themselves.

With the rain now subsided, the beer garden is as I expected it be; busy. There's no bar at the Square and Compass, only a beer hatch, for which the queue is seven or eight people deep. It winds its way along a narrow, stone-flagged hallway and out onto the pub frontage. We're lucky to find a free table right at the front of the building, comprising a large slab of stone set atop four stone piers. The history of quarrying and, more important to this pub, stonemasonry is evident, with a few sculptures dotted around the garden. There's an enormous stone carving in the shape of a pine cone marking the front drive of the pub, besides the many carved seats and table slabs.

As I queue for the hatch, I turn to see a man of about five-feet-three-inches tall. I note his mop of wavy hair, a certain glowy-looking tan to his face, and he wears a chunky white puffer jacket that almost encloses him entirely. He catches my glance and smiles, a friendly, gleaming and well-rehearsed grin. He looks familiar but at that moment, I can't place him. Steve stands with me, also recognising him, and we both decide he must be a celebrity. As I wrack my brain inside-out, trying to think about where I've seen him, at last I make the connection.

"It's Mike Bushell," I say in a whisper. "You know, that guy who presents the sport on BBC at the back end of the week. He has a little slot where he goes off and tries out unusual sports on the Saturday morning Breakfast Show."

"That's it. Yep, I see it now," Steve says. "You should get a photo with him."

Weird as it is, my tummy rolls a little, but I take a deep breath and go over to introduce myself. What a charming man! He tells me he's visiting the area with his family, including his parents. They had heard about the legendary Square and Compass, so thought they would drop by for a drink. He kindly obliges with a photograph, first with me and my rucksack and the charity sign visible. Then another one with Piggie. Poor bloke. I can't quite believe he agrees to hold my little mascot for a photo, but then superstar Piggie has become quite the conversation starter!

A brief chat together and an introduction to his parents brings some normality to an otherwise potentially awkward meeting-a-man-off-the-telly scenario. I'm thankful the conversation flows, and he's a real down-to-earth, friendly guy. Just as we are saying goodbye and thanks, he empties his pocket of small change to give me for the charities. He apologises profusely that there's nothing more, but otherwise, he only has a bank card with him. I am touched that he donates every coin. "Email me the photo and I'll tweet it," he says. "I'll look at doing something from Saturday onwards, if possible, on TV." Both my heart and my spirit jump for joy.

"Thanks, this is really kind of you! I massively appreciate anything you can do." I shake his hand. "It's been lovely meeting you. I'm so glad I said hello now."

Our evening at the pub lasts much longer than planned, but that's usually how a visit to any pub goes. It's not surprising when you've just walked 615 miles ... and you're almost done. I recognise a young lady serving at the beer hatch as Katie. She's an ex-student from a school I used to work in and although it has been many years since seeing her last, I remember one of her works of art – an ammonite. Funny how some things plant themselves in your memory more than others. Having reacquainted myself with her earlier in the evening, as the sun sets I pop back inside to have a quiet chat.

"Do you think the landlord would let us pitch our tents in the beer garden out the back? I'm on a charity walk and although we're heading off again in the morning, I can't see any of us wanting to walk far tonight to find a camp spot."

"Let me talk to Kevin," Katie says. "I'm sure it won't be a problem."

And so here we are. Kindly Kevin agrees to us camping at the Square and lets us into a private area of garden beyond the pub's beer garden. He's even left the outside toilet unlocked for us to use. What a top guy.

A Walker's Nightmare

37

When beginning a trail of such magnitude, it's hard to imagine what it will feel like finishing. In fact, it's hard to even imagine being at the end, full stop. Your entire world is so absorbed with the planning, preparation and logistics of the whole adventure, it can seem like that last day will never come. It's probably best if the focus remains in the present because a fixation on the end, for me, would be unsettling. I like to organise and plan, but I also appreciate living in the moment. It's better for me to take stock of each few days with their challenges, opportunities and any adjustments needed as they arise.

Today is a fine day, and I am relieved that the forecast says it will continue. I've woken up with a mash of excitement brewing inside my belly. At least, I think that's what it is. With arrangements to make, it's keeping my mind off becoming too overwhelmed, overexcited or tearful. There are several students, parents, charity representatives, friends and family coming to walk with me for the last seven miles of the trail. If the weather is kind, it will make it way more pleasant and easy to manage. After yesterday's horrific levels of rain, rivalled only by the infamous rains from the Book of Genesis, it's such a welcome change to just walk, talk and appreciate the landscape. I want no more of this struggling to stay upright in claggy mud more at home on a potter's wheel.

As the four of us pack up our tents for the last time, we're in no hurry to get moving this morning. This time, there is none of

Mike's regimented "Let's get some action on this contract" demands, although I suspect he might throw a couple of random quips into the day to chivvy us along in his teasing manner. There is none of my aiming-to-be-the-first-to-leave-to-prove-Mike-wrong style of dashing around. It doesn't matter that Steve is happy to kick back with a coffee and a smoke, or that Artie sits with his current paperback of choice, losing himself in another world for an extra half an hour. This morning is ours. It's divine and we are going to take the time to enjoy it for this one last opportunity.

Over a small dry-stone wall, I watch a flurry of white with black flecks and creamy-gold feathers to pass the time. They have styled themselves into a collective of attractive chickens within the Square and Compass garden. Enchanting, their pert little tail feathers swoop curvaceously around their bottoms and up over their backs like a troupe of cancan dancers, vivid red combs sitting like tiaras atop their heads. They parade and peck, clucking and sashaying around the garden in full view of their highly strung and super-feisty guardian, Mr Cockerel. He's been up and about since around 4 a.m., which, although early, didn't bother me. I'd slept well overnight and it's all part and parcel of country life, after all. I regard Mr C's mood and movements carefully and conclude that he's just strutting his stuff and showing off in front of his ladies. I'm not prepared to take any chances, however, and am quite thankful the private section of the garden is his territory. His vocal performance alongside his dominant attitude is enough proof for me of his no-messing, unforgiving approach.

I turn from the wall. "I can't believe it's almost over, guys."

"Well, we'll just have to do it again next year, then," Steve replies. "Think about what I said the other day. The Wales Coast Path opens in May. We could all do that."

"What's this?" asks Mike.

"Oh, you were on ahead. It was when we were walking through Mount Edgcumbe," I tell him. "Steve suggested walking this brand-new path that's opening up next year, the Wales Coast Path. It's 870 miles. You'd have time to do it, but I don't think I'd be able to walk it in the six weeks of my summer holiday."

"That sounds great. I'm up for that," Mike replies. "What about you, Artie? You fancy walking Wales?"

"I might, though I know it would clash with me doing the South West Way again. It'll be hard to change my dates next year as there's a hundred-miler I'm planning to do with the Long Distance Walker's Association. It's an organised thing."

"Why don't we all meet up in Cardiff next May for the opening? We could camp and make plans for the summer then," Steve says.

"That's a good idea. I can do that. Let's meet in Wales next spring and figure it out." The pangs of finality are lessening with the buzzy anticipation of another long-distance walk growing on the sidelines.

"Anyway, Wathers, you're almost an experienced coastal walker now ... If you've got six weeks of holiday, my calculations tell me you could just about squeeze that path in." Mike looks at me and nods, with a there-you-go-get-out-of-that expression. I grin back at him.

Artie, Mike and I decide to head off and walk the Worth Matravers to Winspit stretch, leaving Steve back at the Square and Compass to chill and do his own thang. He's not bothered about missing this stretch as, starting from the halfway point, he never came to do the full coast path. We walk westwards again, along the road towards the village centre. There are many quaint, stone-tiled cottages built in the traditional Purbeck stone of the area, decorated with heavily scented climbing roses. The duck pond to the east side of the village green creates a central meeting area, adding even more calm and beauty to this already picturesque Dorset village. Latently guarding, holding the community together with its steadfast sanctuary, is the church of St Nicholas, tucked into a little corner, yet bidding passers-by to take a moment to stop and visit. *One day, I will.*

Beyond the farms on the way to Renscombe, we take a northward route along a track that drops into the valley of West Hill. The rough, scrubby nature of the valley sides breathes out an ancient air – it's not smelly, just olde worlde. There's a tiny brook bubbling along on its way down to find the sea. Faint evidence of strip lynchets, a farming system of using terracing around the contours of the hills, adds to the history of the area. Looking at the map, I can see there will be more of these in their full glory around the eastern side of the hill.

Lulled into believing that the steep steps were now behind us, and the last fourteen miles of coast path would be a breeze, I'm soon brought back into our brutal reality. We face the steep descent from Emmetts Hill, down a flight of around 220 steps to a valley known as Pier Bottom. As soon as we reach this verdant stretch of pasture and level ground, in an instant we're catapulted upward again onto the headland of St Aldhelm's. The spectacular views and the knowledge that it's not the easiest flight of steps on which to pass other people propel my motivation.

With all the activity and talk about next year's potential walk, my mind has stayed busy. If I'm focused on what I'm doing, I tend not to get too hung up about what's happening next. The awareness that I'm finishing soon is sliding into the forefront of my mind. That well of emotion I felt in my belly earlier now sits somewhere in my chest. Excitement, uncertainty, delight and disappointment ... I'm not sure which I'll end up with when I complete this walk. It feels like a roulette wheel, where a ball will land on an emotion and that'll be the one.

Right now, I'm too preoccupied soaking up every last clifftop, stack, wave and step, so I'm cool with going with the flow.

This stretch of coastline is a popular setting for stone seats and benches, and I'm interested to read the inscriptions as we pass. Some commemorate young men, pitifully snatched away in the prime of their lives while enjoying and succumbing to the results of a misadventure. Others mark those who have experienced many years of enjoying the view from the clifftops over the breathtaking landscape of the Jurassic Coast. They may have expressed their wishes to be memorialised here on a bench on which others can rest awhile, appreciating the same view.

It's hard to fathom how yesterday was so grotty. Today, as I look across the water, I can see Weymouth and Portland in the west. In the south-east, the Isle of Wight is visible with such clarity. It's like I have a new lens over my eyes, sharpening and bringing the view into focus. As we pop up from the last of the few hundred steps, a small square block of stone chapel sits in front of us on St Aldhelm's Head. To the right is a coastguard lookout building, and to our far left I see a row of cottages. Judging by the location and their proximity to the lookout, I'm guessing these must be old coastguard cottages.

Mike, Artie and I wander into the chapel, after which the headland is named: St Aldhelm's Chapel. The stone floors and walls draw me in. The transition from the wildness outside is stark as I experience a dark, womb-like envelopment on entering the building. It feels reassuring in here. The single, narrow slit window, located just behind the altar and the doorway, provides the only source of light. There are a handful of old pews which look a touch on the damp side, and I wonder for a moment who even attends services here, way out in the middle of nowhere on the edge of a clifftop. A baptismal font near to the large oak door looks new, carved from the recognisable creamy Purbeck stone. The arch above the doorway into the chapel remains open to the elements, even when the door is closed.

As I look around, transfixed by the atmosphere, I have a sense that this place, though stripped bare of decoration and pomp, has many stories to tell. Its very presence in this remote, clifftop location, in full acceptance of the openness to the elements, is testament to its longevity, strength and history. I trace the engravings of multiple lovers and graffiti artists with my finger, leaving their moniker or initials for future visitors on the central stone pillar. Eight hundred years old. This place is truly ancient, and I make a note to add St Aldhelm's Chapel to the list of places that will absolutely require a revisit and more reading about once I have returned home.

We have a date with Swanage, however, so the troupe rallies and we reluctantly leave the calm shade of St Aldhelm's Chapel. It's time to return to Worth, collect our bags, and Steve. Beyond the coastguard lookout is a modern metal sculpture that twists and turns with static energy. After a brief acknowledgement of admiration for its position on the cliff and the artistic efforts realised in creating it, we move on towards Winspit.

The entire area, apart from the odd farm here and there, owes its history to stone. Quarrying is still alive in the region. Only the transportation of it has changed from bygone years. The Square and Compass pub is just a mile or so inland from the old Winspit Quarry which we now wander through. This isn't the first time I've visited here; twelve or thirteen years back, I took a trip down here on my own to use a home-made pinhole camera around the hewn stone and inside the quarry caves. There's something quite disconcerting about the caves in that they are manmade, held up with irregularly stacked lumps of stone. I pass through them, remembering the level of bravery I'd had to muster all those years ago to step foot inside the blackness, on my own. *Hmm. So you weren't such a coward back then, after all, Wath.* It's bizarre how I have perceived myself over the years and the moments of courage that I've forgotten at the times I've needed them the most.

After a quick reminisce and a wander below the sheer faces of rock, patterned with angular lines and ledges fashioned in the manner of a Cubist painting, we move on. The invisible clock ticks away and I know we must reach Swanage in time to meet whoever comes to walk with us on this last day.

There, outside the pub at the large stone table, is Steve, waiting for us. I'm grateful for Steve's backpack babysitting service, as it served the purpose of allowing a speedier circuit of an arduous section of the path, giving my shoulders and knees a brief respite from the weight of the pack.

We're not due to meet up with the welcoming party until around 3 p.m., so although I know we need to push on, I'm not too concerned about the time, yet. The walk to Swanage should be fairly easy, with a few climbs but nothing compared to the previous days.

About two and a half miles from Worth Matravers, we reach yet another stunning section of the path that descends into a plateau of green fields, with an extension of the hills and clifftops stretching up to our right. On looking at the map, I can see there is an alternative footpath on the ridge above us. Below us, looking down over the cliff edge, is a rough path leading to a flat rock. Its superpower is a large cavity blasted out in the early twentieth century, creating an open-air swimming pool for a local prep school. It's known as Dancing Ledge, and famous to all who live in the local vicinity and beyond.

The boys and I decide to take a quick break for chocolate above Dancing Ledge. Maybe we're stalling to prolong the last few miles of our adventure for as long as we can. We all know that once today is over, we will never recreate the magic of this journey. The making of new friends, the experience, the memories. The magic may be gone once the adventure is done, but those memories and the friendships, if we want them to, will always be there.

We sit at the bottom of the large sweep of a hill that swings up and away behind us, tucking into our snacks and enthusing about some of our great camp spots. The lads continue to tease me about the number of proper beds I've accepted. I am permanently dubbed as "not a real camper". I'll have to change this at some point, though I'm not sure why it bothers me so much. After all, it's *my* walk. If I've chosen to meet people and accept their hospitality, why is this an issue? What started as a tease has mutated, but it still prompts me I could have experienced the walk in other ways, too. That doesn't make it right or wrong. Just different.

As we rest and talk, I'm distracted by a lone cow in the field to our left. We're taking our break on the slopes of the hill, overlooking the sea. The cow is beyond the wall, mooing incessantly. What's the issue? I wonder. Its herd, I now notice, is behind us, further up the hill. In the same field as us. Before we have time to think, one cow begins to run at full pelt down the hill towards the only open gateway leading to the field on our left – and the vocal, lonely cow that occupies it. As happens with cows, when one runs, all the others run too. Lonely cow, still noisily mooing its sombre notes, and herd, stampeding towards the cliff edge, open gateway ... and us! "Move, quick!" I shout.

"Shiiiit!" The cool, collected demeanour of Steve suddenly launches into action. I've not known him long and had only ever seen him stride in the way only long-legged gents can. I'd not seen him move so quickly! Mike swiftly scoops up his rucksack and Artie scrabbles with his bootlaces while simultaneously hauling his oversized pack onto his shoulder. We all dash for the gateway, which we are closer to than the cows. Fear and thoughts flood through me. We've got to be quick if we're going to make it to Swanage alive. The cows build up momentum and speed with an eerie look of hysteria in their eyes. The deep rumbling and movement of the ground increases with every step, and all the while I feel like I'm running through quicksand.

Steve, with his mile-high legs, is first through the gateway, with me close behind, working my short little pins as hard as they can manage. I drop my rucksack on the other side of the wall, spurting out a nervous laugh. Mike bursts through the gateway next, his little cycle shorts rambling around his buttocks, and I chuckle to myself, knowing full well that they weren't actually shorts at all. Underwear. Of course, I wouldn't get away with it, but somehow, Mike has done and continues to. Or he simply doesn't care. Artie, with his trailing bootlaces, open rucksack, scrunched-up carrier bag clamped tightly in his clenched fist, scoots his way through and to the safety of the wall just a split second before the earth rumbling takes on a crescendo of immense proportions. The ground sounds hollow as the cloven hooves bluster and roar through the gateway. It's a wonder that the cliff doesn't collapse below us with the vibrations of such intense thundering of bovine bodies over the land. Over a matter of seconds, and yet for what seemed like long minutes, we have somehow successfully dodged a tragedy.

With our backs now resting against a skilfully constructed dry-stone wall, indicative of the area, the lone mooster seems to be satisfied with the outcome of being reunited with its herd, totally oblivious to the terror it had inflicted upon its human visitors. We all look at one another. There are a few huffs, puffs and nervous sniggers of relief. Mike readjusts his "shorts" and hoists his rucksack onto his back. "Right, let's get some action on this contract then." He smiles at us wryly.

The next stretch to Swanage is only four and a half miles, and far from demanding. It proves to be of great interest as we walk past the old Tilly Whim caves, a lighthouse and through Durlston Country Park. It features an unusual stone globe and a nineteenth-century castle, recently renovated. We can't resist stopping for a pasty at the takeaway kiosk in the country park, though I'm starting to wonder if we'll ever make it if we keep having tea breaks.

38

Swanage Welcoming Party

With our loop of St Aldhelm's Head this morning, we've managed to crack out twelve miles by the time we reach Swanage, and still have two hours to kill. We pitch ourselves at a café in the High Street, ordering tea, coffee and hot chocolate to see us through. We reminisce over the highlights of the past weeks and can laugh now at some of the crazy lows through which we've all struggled. It's pretty incredible that even if you think you're unable to achieve something, you can still fight through and succeed, regardless. And, embedded in those moments are the best stories. There's a lesson in that somewhere.

A text from Doog, Ross's friend, confirms he's on his way. He soon arrives at the café, joining us for our extended tea break. There are people in this world who can light up a room the moment they walk in. Doog is one of those people and his jolliness had already lifted me when I joined the happy campers way back at Padstow. When Doog smiles, his eyes and whole being radiate the warmth, energy and enthusiasm of a giant puppy. It's such a delight to see him again, and one of my first familiar faces in a long time – aside from when Lyndon, Sara and Jack surprised me on White Nothe a few days ago, of course.

Conversation is easy, laughing and joking about the final stage of the walk and how it's going to pan out – particularly with the expected students coming from school to walk with me. The boys discuss tactics about how they'll manage to walk past a pub without going in. I've realised I'll probably switch into teacher mode for these last few miles.

There's a slight air of awkwardness about having a group of students walk with us, so the lads decide to keep a low profile and stick together, leaving me to stay ahead with the girls.

At around 3 p.m., our expanded group wanders down to an area on Swanage promenade, close to the Mowlem Theatre. Andy Clarke and his daughter, Sarah, a student at the grammar school, are there to greet us with two of the older Woofability assistance dogs. Soon after, students Hannah and Kelly arrive with Hannah's mum and younger sister, Emily. Evie is not long behind, brought to Swanage by her father and with her younger sister, Lily, in tow. How honoured I feel at this moment. These people hold value in my challenge. So much so, they've put themselves out to travel to Swanage and walk with me – or at least to drop their daughters off so they can do the walking. Someone, after all, needs to be at the other end, seven miles eastwards, to pick them up.

Our growing posse sets off along the promenade towards Ballard Down. I've walked this area many times before and am fully aware of the steep hill that some students might struggle with. If they succeed, they'll be in for a glorious reward walking along the prominent ridge towards Old Harry Rocks at Studland. From this point, they will see for miles. My teacher's head is excited to share this moment with them, knowing that potentially, they may never have walked up here before. I'm impressed as they conquer the hill with an admirable show of determination. The views out over Wareham, Poole Harbour and across to Bournemouth, Hengistbury Head and even as far as the Isle of Wight are not unusual to witness up here, as long as the clouds are high and the lowland clear of mist.

It can be a poignant and affirming moment for those who have never experienced a walk with a view like this. While I can't quite tell at this stage, I think the students are enjoying themselves. Hannah, who is about fifteen, asks if she can carry my rucksack for a while. I ease it off and onto her shoulders, reminding her it'll feel heavy and she can pass it back to me whenever she needs to. I hope it inspires her to go for a long-distance walk one day.

After a quick pit stop at the loos at the foot of the track near Old Harry Rocks, our group moves on again. This time we turn down onto the long expanse of sand that reaches from Middle Beach, onto Knoll Beach and through the naturist section of Studland, prior to Shell Bay and the end marker at South Haven Point. Of course, I have the obligatory photo next to the naturist beach sign! For some time, I've considered how to manage students walking along a beach potentially dotted with nudists. One option is to walk them through the sand dunes. As I scan the beach, despite the beautiful weather, I'm thankful it's clear of bodies, except my own colourful walking caravan of supporters.

By the time we reach Knoll Beach, like a snowball, the group doubles in size as more family, friends, colleagues and parents of the students join us. Ross is among them, with his parents, while his daughter, Lara, is also here with her mother and stepsister. Laura and Lara wear their broadest grins. They may be teenagers, but they look so proud, and I wrap my arms around them both. Lorraine is beside them, with her dog, Rosie, and gets a longer hug from me, as I know life is upside-down for her right now until she finds somewhere to call home. Things will be very different for a while, at this end.

So many people have walked along from the start of the beach to meet us. I'm lifted with endless hugs, smiles and uncontrollable tears of joy. The overwhelm fills me with honour that these wonderful souls gave up their afternoon to welcome me home and I'm pleased to share this moment with my new friends, Artie, Mike and Steve, though I'm aware they are keeping themselves to the back of the pack. For once, I experience the buoyancy of pride and achievement, and hope this will be a significant memory for Laura and Lara when they're older.

With just the last couple of metres to go before we reach the end sculpture, I spontaneously drop onto my knees. After walking 630 miles, I dramatise the "crawling" over the finish line bit. Inside, my eyes are rolling at me, but a few crawling photos later and that joke's all done and dusted. I'm touched by the balloons that I'm told Lorraine has taken the time to hang from the end marker, which is an impressive sculpture, considering there is only a limited area in which it to site it.

With the expanse of sand, sea and harbour entrance on one side, and the road that carries the many cars waiting for the chain ferry to Poole on the other, the sculpture needed to stand out. The artist achieved this, creating a work of art that seems instinctively at home in its environment, too. Tall, at maybe twelve or fourteen feet, the blue steel post holds two sails on either side – at least, that's what they look like. Within the frame of the sails, depicted cutaway features of the South West Coast Path, such as a lighthouse, a tin mine chimney, and dolphins, silhouette beautifully against the wild backdrop.

By coincidence, while I was working as an art technician at the Purbeck School in Wareham back in the early 2000s, students worked alongside the artist commissioned to create this commemorative marker. They made designs that were cast in bronze and set into the star-shaped floor plaque around the base of the sculpture. I'd never imagined, despite wanting to walk the path for years, that I would reach the end with such layered sentiment surrounding the structure and the experiences that connect it with me. This public work of art means so much more to me now than it had ever done previously.

What a team. Piggie and I made it. We achieved the impossible – or rather, we walked what I had thought impossible for my capabilities. The world around me is still the same, the people are the same and the expectations of me remain the same. And yet, I am different. I know this now. I am changed and I am going to need some time to compose a plan and consider my navigation of this new me. Until then, I must continue as if nothing has changed and return to school next week with the excitement and enthusiasm of being able to share my adventure stories. Forty-eight days' worth, to be precise.

Glancing over at Ross, looking like a pro as he busily captures the event on his camera, my heart skips. Ten years we have been together as a couple, and never in those years have I loved him more than I do today. His long legs move him gracefully from each photographer's vantage point. His poise is strong, keeping his photographs steady and focused, despite his tall, lean frame. I have missed his company and missed sharing and comparing notes for composition and detail with our artistic eyes.

Without doubt, I'll grieve my relationship with this path, living a life of daily survival and simplicity, meeting like-minded people and making new friends. But I'm relieved to have finally arrived home, to be with Ross, Laura and Lara. To be within familiar territory. To experience recognisable sounds and smells around me.

To hold my man. I catch my breath at the thought.

The sadness of ending the journey balances with the delight of accomplishment, the gratefulness to those who have supported me, and the pleasure of being close to my love, once again.

Ross lowers his camera to his chest and looks over towards me, sensing that I'm watching him. Our eyes meet and he glows with the cheeky upturn of his lips that engages his signature smile. He rarely shows his teeth – he doesn't like his teeth. The creases around his mouth further show his acknowledgement of the indulgence of our extended gaze and where it might lead. *Later* ... In this moment, I could almost read his thoughts.

My heart skips again. *Yes, later,* I silently reply with a twitch of my eyebrow and a returned smile.

39

A Full House

Knowing that Artie, Mike and Steve would all still have to travel long distances to get home made our decision super simple. I'd taken a moment to discuss it with Ross as we walked along the beach towards South Haven Point, and he agreed that although we already had a houseful with no spare rooms, the boys should indeed stay over. It would allow us time for a celebration of sorts and for them to eat, shower, have a few beers and head off refreshed in the morning.

I had accomplished my challenge. As our gathering bustles around the end sculpture, we entertain the queue of traffic waiting to board the chain ferry on its next arrival at Studland for at least twenty minutes, with multiple combinations of photographs, as if it were a wedding day shoot. Me with Laura. Me with Laura and Lara. Ross with me. Me at the wooden signpost that points to Minehead, 630 miles away, and me at the official South West Coast Path sculpture. Then it's Artie, Mike and Steve and me. Artie on his own, then Mike and just Steve, plus a whole ton of other combinations. It's a feat of utter disorganisation in itself, but it gives us an opportunity to loiter at the end of the path for longer than we might otherwise have done. A chance to savour the moment. It's a moment where I feel a little like a celebrity, with everyone wanting to take photos, walk with me at some point, ask me questions and tell me how brave I'd been. It's a boost to my confidence, and for once, I'm not feeling like an imposter.

It's time for us to walk away from the trail sculpture. With cheeks aching from grinning so much, I say goodbye and thanks to all the friends, family, colleagues and parents who had taken time out of their summer holiday Wednesday afternoon to welcome me home. It had been the right decision too, to agree to walking much of the last two weeks with my new friends. We hadn't stuck side by side – it simply doesn't work like that. But we had, mostly, met up in the evenings or at lunchtimes to camp or take a break together. In doing so, it had enriched the experience for us all.

Ross parked the Bongo van a short walk away in the National Trust car park. Like a line of ducks, our single-file group must have looked amusing, wandering along the side of Ferry Road. We dump our rucksacks into the back, then pour ourselves into the van. It's a squeeze, but fortunately Lorraine had brought her own car to accommodate her dog, so Laura travelled back home with her. Artie's in first and onto the back seat, with his rucksack beside him. Steve and Mike take the middle seat, and Ross and I are up front.

The vehicle is an eight-seater, but for eight adults it honestly would be too intimate. Here, back in my van, with my man next to me, driving, and my friends from another world, another life, feels weird. But I sense a warmth that feeds and raises my soul, too. This is the "line in the sand" that I'm guessing many walkers who meet other walkers never cross. It's that boundary between adventure and home, and it slides easily into the saying of "What goes on tour, stays on tour".

My friends, who had shared so many days of walking, wild camping and weather-related experiences with me, had somehow passed the test, found the magic word, or stumbled across the portal back into the real world. Here they are, having stepped over that line and now live in my world. It's not spoken about, but as I listen to them chattering in the back of the van to one another, I know this will not be the last time I see them. I suspect, or at least hope, we'll always remain good friends and walking buddies.

How disorientated I am as we drive up the street, approaching our house. I haven't seen the road, the house or the neighbours in weeks, yet nothing seems to have changed. I'm not sure what I'm expecting, but when something so huge in my life has taken place, I guess I'm supposing that everyone and everything else has grown, altered or developed too.

We unload, bodies and bags piling out onto the driveway and chaos ensues. One by one our house fills with people, sounds, and the curiosity of Lorraine's dog, Rosie, and her three-legged cat, Rudy, towards all these new humans.

There's a slight awkwardness that I sense from Lorraine around the subject of food. She has sweetly prepped tea for us – but only enough to serve four people. Naturally, she wasn't expecting such a houseful on my return, so had only made enough for a welcome-home dinner for Ross, Laura, herself and me. I reassure her it doesn't matter and that the boys would be happy with a takeaway. We order curries to be delivered.

Our lounge fills with us sitting around in any available space with our trays of food, talking about our funny experiences. We're still all trapped in the disbelief that the adventure has come to a close. It's a great way to debrief, reminiscing over the antics of the trip, the highlights, the low points and the dark days. I'm not sure how much Ross, Lorraine and Laura appreciate the chaos that's landed in their home. Ross perhaps is enjoying the male company for a change and the chance for alternative conversation over a few beers. Laura does her best to chat to everyone, but soon, as any sixteen-year-old would, she retreats to the sanctuary of her bedroom. Lorraine is amazing, keeping everyone in conversational flow and retrieving all the eating irons, trays and dirty plates once we've had our fill.

To me, this is pure gold. It's precious and I cannot think of a better way to have closed the book on the final unforgettable chapter of this, my fortieth-birthday South West Coast Path adventure. I'd spent a beautiful few hours walking back to South Haven Point with so many people who put themselves out to be there. No one would have realised, me included, that the story, the adventure, simply doesn't just end when you reach the last mile of the walk. How deflated I would have felt if my friends had left to go their separate ways at Studland. This time spent with them in gentle decompression and reflection is like transitioning from one world to another in the most compassionate and fitting way possible.

While we sit around chatting, one by one we take it in turns to leave the social gathering in the lounge to make the most of the bathroom. The act of standing underneath the steady tumble of raindrops feels as though I'm making peace with myself, washing away the dirt of the trip. It's like another step towards finally accepting that I have arrived home. This is going to take time – a fact that I am only just beginning to realise. I'm not sure that Ross, Laura or Lorraine are aware of my post-walk feelings. Who would understand that I feel like a fish out of water, even in *my* home?

As I return from the bathroom, fresh and with a little more clarity, I know that something has to go. Artie's boots! They're in the hallway and on opening the bathroom door, the pungent aroma of stale cheese, sweat, years of trodden farmland, and another smell which I can't quite place hits me. I sniff again. *Tuna!* I'm surprised the cats of the street haven't taken up residence outside our front door. Well, they are welcome to them. Picking the boots up with the tiniest tips of my fingers and holding them at arm's reach, I dump Artie's pong-ridden footwear outside for the local feline community to discuss. No doubt they'd reach the decision that, despite the smell of tuna, the standard of scent was way too low for the likes of a cool Poole cat.

Body Shock

40

It's been a couple of days since returning home. As my life marbles fall back into some kind of expected routine, I'm not sure whether I fit into that life fully as yet. It's a start, and what other options do I have? I can hardly pick up my rucksack and say "See ya!", leaving my bemused family behind as I waltz back off into the world for another adventure into the unknown.

There is little over a week left before the schools reopen, so I've taken an afternoon to reacquaint myself with the shopping centre in Poole. It's been over two months since I was last here and as I walk in with Ross, I have that awkwardness sometimes experienced on entering a locals' pub for the first time; you know, that feeling of all heads turning to stare at the stranger swaggering up to the bar? I don't swagger, but I appear to have gained a renewed confidence since returning from the walk. This doesn't change my heightened awareness of the difference about this shopping centre, however. Or perhaps it's not the place. Perhaps it's me.

The thing with being a teacher, a local teacher at that, is that everywhere I go, someone recognises me. It's not always the students either; sometimes it's parents, keen to make a good impression on their daughter's teacher. The student sightings are often comical. It might be a younger student excited at seeing me. She's nudging her mother's arm and whispering to her siblings, all the while beaming incessantly to avoid missing any sign of a glance or acknowledgement from me.

Then there are the older students, the too-cool-for-school types. I might spot a covert side-eye glance, but the poise, the chin in the air, the headphones and the stride tell me this one's not interested in making any kind of contact outside of school. Not even eye contact.

The friendship groups who come into town together are another beast entirely, and while there are many, the two main types I notice are the "style-shoppers" and the "hang-outs". The style-shoppers may go round in small groups eager to "look the part", wearing the fashion of the moment, hoping to strike up a conversation with a boy or two. They sashay down the aisles of the shops to shrieks of shared delight and overexcited laughter.

The hang-outs, I notice, often dress in black with accents of red or purple, full-length coats, buckled boots or DMs, even in the height of summer. There is an emphasis on black eye make-up, dyed hair and multiple piercings. They're not here to shop. As their nickname suggests, they're here to hang out, in larger groups. They feel the safety in numbers and in the routine of meeting in the same place each week. It's their spot, and although they have a visual air of vampire-meets-thrash-metal-god, they're harmless. They know how to have sensible conversations and are deep thinkers, even if one or two have slipped off the rails recently by starting up experimental use of addictive substances or smokes.

As I wander past Dorothy Perkins, two Year Ten students are sitting on a bench, surrounded by a collection of carrier bags that shows me they've had a spree today at Primark. I recognise these girls instantly as the friendlier branch of the kool kids. I smile and give them a little wave but choose not to embarrass them further by going over to chat. They know I've walked 630 miles. The entire school knows. I did enough assemblies and fundraising in recent months to ensure that no one missed this. It was the big news of the school year ... well, it was for me anyway. These girls surprise me with their reaction of nothing more than a vague cursory smile. Hardly what I'd expected, seeing as I know them both and I'd attempted to acknowledge them. Seconds later, the veil of recognition lifts and I see broad smiles creeping across their faces.

"Oh, my god!! Miss Wathen?" one girl exclaims. I nod and grin.

"Hello." I wander over to them. "How's your holiday been?"

"Yeah, it's been great," the other confirms. "What happened to you? You look ... so different! Haven't you been on your walk?"

"Um, yes, I may have lost a bit of weight." Outwardly, I am laughing, but inside I am still in shock. Not only have I returned a different person mentally, but physically I have returned as a different person too. And I hadn't noticed it until yesterday.

The recall of the events of my discovery to these two students is cathartic. Not the usual conversation I might share with my students in school, but it seems appropriate and I have a willing audience to lend an ear. I share how I'd been so keen to get my clothes from the trip into the washing machine for a super double-length wash. Apart from staying at Lea and Steve's, I'd only been able to rough hand-wash my clothing here and there.

I had bagged a few sale bargains in an online shop back in June, from one of my favourite stores, Joe Browns. In readiness for the new school year, I'd ordered a bunch of clothes so that I knew I'd be in something fresh once returning from my walk. When looking for something to wear the morning after my arrival home, I was dismayed to find that nothing fitted me. I mean *nothing*. I whisked item after item off the hanger, throwing it over my head, scrambling my arms into the sleeves. Top after top tried on resulted in the same outcome. What used to be my old faves had now become nothing more than old sacks. Jeans, trousers and skirts would not stay up. As I held out the waistband of my brand-new, still-tagged white Joe Browns jeans, I could see a gap of at least fifteen centimetres. All I needed was some face paint, a pair of oversized colourful shoes, and a flower on my lapel that squirted water, and I'd have been a dead ringer for Krusty the Clown.

The students listen in amazement as I finish my short story by saying the only item I had of my own to wear was a summer dress with a tie-back. Today, I had come into town in my sixteen-year-old daughter's clothes, who stepped up to help me. I'm grateful Laura gave me the nod to raid her wardrobe as much as I needed to. The girls laugh, saying it's a great way to get a new wardrobe. We finish up our conversation, and Ross and I move on. I turn back to give them a little wave with a "See you next week!" to catch them still sat there with shock written right across their faces.

Those girls reeled at my transformation. With positive reactions from everyone, it's hard to imagine how I felt initially inside this new body of mine. Laura had giggled in surprised amusement when she realised my dilemma. Lorraine had commented, "Wow, look at you!" Ross, as you may have realised, a man of few words, didn't need to speak. But my body mesmerised him and his hands kept dropping to squeeze my waist and lovingly stroke my well-tanned and super-strong-looking legs. Something had ignited in him and in those first few weeks of being back at home, our intimate moments were some of the most passionate. "I hope you stay this size," Ross had whispered quietly to me, in one of those loving moments. Caressing the curves and toned muscles, he seemed in a faraway place. Dreamily, he took me back into his arms and I smiled contentedly as the night seemed to last longer with every movement and touch. I couldn't help but wonder why my size was so important, though, as I had only been a size twelve or occasionally a fourteen previously.

The pressure of expectations about how we *should* look is deeply ingrained in our culture. As women, if we are not thin, we're not fit. If we carry extra curves, we're not healthy. The Special K advert from the 1980s has always stuck with me, bearing in mind that was during my teenage years. "Can *you* pinch more than an inch?" it asked. It is evidence of how damaging advertising can be, and testament to the responsibility of companies to ensure they don't feed impressionable minds with such messages. At a UK size twelve, I had a healthy figure, so Ross's comment makes me consider, is it a cultural fashion for thinness that feeds his desire, or something else? Oh my god – did he think I was fat?

Over the following days, the ebb and flow of my emotional state mirrors the terrain I'd walked over the past seven weeks. One minute I'm basking in the glow of success, as others would predict. The next, I feel teary and confused. Up and down. I have heard of the adventure blues and although I think this may be a mild dose of it, I have little time to dwell on my low mood. I am due back to school in a matter of days, so must screw my head back on tight and reawaken my teacher self, as opposed to my new, long-distance walker self. More than the transition of coming home is the issue of my clothing and my new body. Everyone seems to love it, but something isn't right.

On spending time with my thoughts, I get it. The reason for my unsettled head is about losing me. My identity has vanished almost overnight. My favourite clothes, the colours, the styles. Everything in my wardrobe that I've spent years building up reflected the true Zoe. Everything that Zoe loved and how Zoe had wanted to turn up and to be seen by the world. It's a very personal thing, and to have that unexpectedly taken away is an indescribable wrench. Now I'm stripped back to nothing, bare. I'm feeling more exposed than I'd ever expected. I hadn't been planning to diet. If I had, I might regard my situation differently, pleased at the reactions of others. But the more people who express their delight at my new look, the "new me", the harder I find it to adapt. Why *is* the way I look so important to them? *Why am I suddenly so ... sexy?*

Aside from the clothing predicament, I walk back into the rest of my routine well. I drive to North Somerset to visit with Mum and Dad and tell them about my adventure. Just being behind a steering wheel again after nearly two months without driving takes some mental adjustment in itself. At seventy-seven, Dad's reaction to my tales of camping and walking solo shows me how impressive he thought it was. He kept laughing, raising his eyebrows and shaking his head, saying, "I can't believe you did that. How far? 630 miles? How far?" As for most people, multi-day distances like that are beyond comprehension.

I rapidly step back into planning for the new school year as a teacher and think hard about the responses I would give to people's questions – students and staff. There would be no more hiding in the corner, hoping to have some introvert quiet time alone in the staffroom, in the corridors, or even in the toilets. Everyone would want to hear more, and I would have to learn how to share these moments succinctly and effectively, without wearing myself down.

Laura prepares for the return to her school, as a sixth-former. She did well in most of her GCSEs and needs support to consider her chosen subjects for A levels. I want to give her my time again, too. Although most sixteen-year-olds think they've grown up, they still need Mum ... and I haven't been around for a few weeks, so Laura and I need to catch up.

I switch into food-shop mode, cooking, and now dog walks, too. With no dog of our own, it's novel having Rosie around and I like it. It's a blessing having Lorraine here, as she helps out with fixing meals for us and inviting me out to walk Rosie with her. It's made for a softer transition to coming home, instead of going from walking every day to hardly walking at all. I hope it's helping Lorraine too, having company, as Nan's death has been hard on her. Maybe there is a transition period here for her as well.

A reporter from the *Daily Echo*, our local newspaper, arrives at the house to take a photo of me in the back garden with my rucksack. An article appears the following week, just in time for our first day back at school in September. Dad is the first to ask me for a clipping and he makes sure it gets published in the following month's parish news magazine, back in the village where I grew up.

I plan my assemblies for a couple of weeks later, delivering three talks to the lower, middle and upper years of the girls' grammar school. Something about sharing my thoughts out loud in these talks cements the new aspects of me into my persona and everyday life. It's as if first announcing the walk, and now the highs, the lows and everything in between, gels the adventure aspect of my life alongside the work and real side of my life. They're no longer separate, often blending well.

The overanalytical brain and doubt-ridden imposter syndrome haven't left me completely, but the adventure I've been on seems to have constructed a new backbone for me. I am definitely stronger and feel like I have more of a voice now. A voice that might be heard. I have no idea where this will lead, yet I know I have returned with a new, deeper understanding of myself. But those I've come back to haven't been on this journey with me. They remain as they were.

I'm changed, inside and out. It's not all about physical strength and appearance. I can tell I've returned with a mental resilience I never knew I had, although that still doesn't make me fearless. Thinking this walk would be a one-off adventure to mark my rite of passage into middle age, I have indeed travelled through that rite of passage and experienced unexpected transformations. I carry myself with pride. I have more belief in myself. The respect I hold for my body and what it's capable of has grown.

While I can't quite believe that I might head off again, I'm excited beyond words that I can now look forward to another challenge next year. The seeds of walking another path have been sown and I'm going to do everything possible to ensure I make it. I pinch myself, realising that I can at last call myself a "long-distance walker", and when I'm asked the most popular of questions, "What's next, then?", instead of saying, I haven't a clue, I can tell them I'm planning to take on a brand-new trail. It's not just walking around a county or three. It's walking the coastline of a whole country!

The Wales Coast Path.

Wow.

Now I have to figure out how I'm going to squeeze 870 miles into my summer holiday ...

Epilogue

If you've got this far, then you've finished the book. Thank you! Unless, of course, you cheated and flicked to the back first, to read my closing thoughts, in which case you'll have missed so many gems. There were countless teachings I garnered as a midlife woman walking the South West Coast Path. I'll do my best to summarise these as my nuggets of wisdom below, and give you, my lovely reader, an insight into how this trail changed my life for the better. Since undertaking this path in 2011, I've walked many more trails. Each has been amazing in its own way, but none as life-changing and poignant as the South West Coast Path. This one will forever remain as my most epic overture to long-distance walking, and the walk that taught me more about myself than any other outdoor challenge.

There's no question that having Ross around at the end of each day was a blessing to begin with. I had the reassurance of someone familiar to talk to, to share the pains and the positives of my day, especially on receiving the news of Nan's death. It also meant I had one less thing to think about in finding my next sleeping spot. It became a time for discovering a routine, of sorts. Some people may argue that I should have dived headfirst into the walk and mustered the courage to explore and find my way, fully solo. I, for one, am guilty of believing this. I know I *could* have created my own routines from the start, being independent from Day One. However, as one of my beta readers pointed out to me, it's important to remember that I did the best with the little knowledge I had and then learnt "on the hoof".

I'm often messaged or emailed by women who are considering a similar adventure. I recognise their questions as my same fears and anxieties about the unknown. Appreciative of the enormous help I gained from others, I pledge to pay it forward by continuing to share my knowledge of the reality of the walk, answering questions with honesty, and offering advice and top tips to those who ask for help. You will find the details of my website and how to contact me at the end of the book.

My first nugget of coast path wisdom is that there's no such thing as a proper camper! Your way is the right way, even if you deviate from any original plans you may have made. I've laid Mike's teasing about my camping choices to rest ... and that's just as well, because he still teases me about it to this day. I remind myself that any challenge I choose to do will be *my* challenge and therefore undertaken in any way I think is appropriate. If I opt to face the path on my own but then decide to accept support, there's no rule-breaking, because *I* made the rules. I also discovered that walking alone opens up more opportunities to connect with others, as solitude invites interactions along the way. It may sound odd, but being on a solo walk doesn't mean total isolation or rejecting the company of fellow walkers. In fact, I've realised that I'm *more* likely to meet people when I embark on a solo adventure. But while I enjoy the camaraderie of walking alongside others, allowing myself the freedom to walk alone provides much-needed space to learn, adapt, and make choices that suit me at the time. It's a delicate balance between my need for solitude and occasional companionship.

My second coast path nugget of wisdom refers to the delight of accepting hospitality and the kindness of strangers in general (or, as in my case, sometimes people you know). This closely connects to the first because it relates to taking on an adventure to be independent and to choose your own experience. I have so much gratitude for the kindness shown to me by my hosts and I'm utterly grateful for the incredible support they all gave me. It eased me into my new role as a long-distance walker. I would have loved more sunrises and sunsets and the beauty of mindfulness me time, but this new thing I was learning about meant I've also had to learn to be kinder to myself. I have not failed by accepting help, and I am no less of a long-distance walker or proper backpacker than the next person. It has taken me thirteen years and the writing of this book to reach such levels of surrender. Again, I have my super beta readers to thank for this, as I've spent years giving myself a hard time for not wild camping sooner and accepting so much support. There is no failure in receiving help, and often in doing so, magical connections and lifelong friendships happen as a result.

The third nugget to share is about the acceptance that physical pain is part of the experience. I'd done nothing like this before, and will admit I often doubted my sanity while out on the coast path. When things were tough, like with my blisters, I questioned why the hell I was there. My scepticism about my physical ability and my mental toughness hung around for quite some time, and I wondered how on earth I'd cope when the weather, life, or unsatisfactory gear threw a curveball at me. Accepting all this from the start and understanding that you can and will get through it, returning as a stronger and more wildly interesting person than when you left, will help you no end. Whatever I went through was usually temporary and is part of the challenge. I tell myself now, if it's not a challenge, how can I expect to grow and develop my physical, emotional and mental skills? They *do* need continual work, however. I've discovered I can't just go on an adventure and expect my gained resilience to remain with me as a permanent fixture.

My fourth nugget of coast path wisdom lies within the planning of the challenge. Even now, fourteen years on, I'd still have the tendency to plan my trips to within an inch of their existence if I allowed myself to. But for it to be an adventure, I know I need to allow some room for flexibility and gorgeous opportunities to blossom. Plan by all means to give yourself the safety net of knowledge, but I've learnt that I may not follow this to the letter. This is part of the reason I actively choose to wild camp now. It means I don't have to be in a set place at a specific time. I can walk until I feel the day is done and then pitch my tent quietly out of the way. The sun sets over the horizon. I sleep, and hear the birds awaken. Then I watch the sun rise. It's a simple existence. When I pack the tent up, I'll leave no evidence that I've camped there, except an imprint in the grass. It's pure outdoor medicine for the heart, mind and soul. As a side point, I'm less likely to overplan things in my day-to-day life now, too. I think that's a direct learning from the coast path and understanding the importance of allowing room for opening doors to new possibilities.

South West Coast Path Nugget Number Five is about finding a community. With all the best intentions, family members and close friends are not always best placed to support us in making a dream adventure become a reality. I know those looks of horror from some people when I shared about my plan to walk solo for seven weeks. I've found groups and individuals, mostly online, where I can voice my ideas, giving them a chance to grow before being trampled on by doubters and those with my "best interests" at heart. Some of those people I connected with online have become friends and I've met them in person, walked with them or we've met up at events. I've also created my own online group, where we share our outdoor wins through stretching our comfort zone.

My sixth nugget is about realising how much more I am capable of than the diatribe I tell myself. Granted, it's easier to talk myself out of doing something than it is to challenge myself – but the benefits of the challenge are greater and far outweigh the reasons for avoidance. Even now, I *still* have to remind myself of this, but having a significant walk such as this under my belt means I now can't forget how much I achieved.

Nugget Number Seven is about mental resilience, and probably could have been at the top, alongside number three, physical pain. I've deliberately placed it underneath Nugget Six, where I learnt about my capabilities and nurturing a belief in myself. Although mental resilience is different to capability belief, consider this: it's *because* I stretched my comfort zone beyond what I perceived my capabilities to be that my mental resilience grew. Please, think on that. It's gold. It's about not breaking at the first hurdle, not giving up. Physical pain can put us in a position where we want to give up, but the mental game that we face on long-distance walks can be so much harder to block out and manage, day after day after day. This is a big part of who I am, and I know I have so much resilience now to handle the personal challenges life throws my way. Adventures like this teach us skills that transfer into regular daily life.

Nugget Number Eight is about healing and the outdoors. Nan's death hit me like a freight train, but I honestly felt like I grieved more quickly because I was outside so much. The space, the greenery, the sound of the sea, the wind, the rain – oh god, the rain! – the wildlife. Plus the physicality of the walking. I had time to be with myself and my thoughts and battle through them while exercising. That creates endorphins, which help to relieve stress. I cried intensely during those first couple of days, but I don't believe I would have met such deep peace so soon if I had not been outdoors. That doesn't mean to say I wasn't sad. Of course I felt sadness. But moving through the grief cycle came differently with what I now call my "outdoor medicine". This time spent outdoors also has a way of helping me find solutions. I love to walk if I need to solve a problem, to find the words to put to an article, or if I'm looking for a fresh idea. Creativity comes to me in droves while I'm on my feet in nature.

The ninth nugget is about facing fear. At least three of the nuggets above could include fear, but I decided it's a solid take-home that warrants its own paragraph. I faced fear in bucketloads while on the South West Coast Path. I'll admit here, I didn't realise I had so many fears either. They all came together like a perfect storm, but other than nearly peeing myself with fright a few times, I have walked away stronger. Heights, deep water, cows, wind, walking solo, wild camping solo, spiders ... there are probably more. In some ways, imposter syndrome could fit in here too, as that creates a fear within me. I feel so much more comfortable with many of these now because I spent time with myself, face to face with the fears. In one school assembly I often deliver nowadays, I talk about how fear is primal and instinctive but how we can retrain the brain to think about the object or the act in another way instead. We need to take risks in order to develop the brain and further our chances for success. It takes time, patience, kindness to ourselves, and practice, but my time outdoors has had a positive impact on reducing my fears.

Just as I thought I'd filled my basket brimful of these little nuggets of wisdom, another popped up. It's too good not to include it. My last Nugget de Coast Path, number ten, is learning that I'm never too old for an adventure. I turned forty when I walked these 630 miles. How do you perceive age and what you *could* do or what you *did* at that age? Does age play a part in what you allow yourself to do? Is that because of health, disability or self-imposed limitations? At fifty-three I hope more challenges are waiting in the wings for me. I certainly long to be like Nan, thrilled by the wonders of the Great Wall of China, aged seventy-five. When I think about it, Lorraine set off on her own adventure to drive herself and her animals across the United States and then, after a relatively short time, she repatriated back to the UK at sixty. Perhaps there's an adventurous gene in there somewhere.

A definition of adventure shouldn't be specified by anyone other than yourself. My expectations of an adventure is likely to be different to yours, and my neighbour's expectations would be different again. As long as we're pushing ourselves a *little* more than what we're used to, in an environment beyond the four walls of our home, then I see that as an adventure. So whether you're eight or eighty, there's no excuse – because you can make it work for your circumstances, age, body, ability, health, interests and in the time you have available.

If this has inspired you to try your own adventure, I'll leave you with these thoughts.

Enjoy all the demands your adventure promises to deliver and aim to appreciate them for what they are, without expecting it to be a walk in the park. That way, you're set up to experience your best and most memorable trip yet. For me and for many others like me, as a newbie long-distance walker, we would describe the first multiday walk as life-changing. I'm sure it would be the same with any other type of adventure, too.

Resilience I had never dreamed of developed because of my walk, yet it still needs nurturing. I know I need to walk, be outside, or at least maintain the ideas and planning and challenge myself in other ways. My motto is about finding ways to encourage myself to keep putting one foot in front of the other, taking every opportunity to head out of my comfort zone, however insignificant it seems. Like me, this could be your chance to discover who you are *now* and who you might want to *become* if you can allow yourself to let your guard down and face those darned fears.

We all have a future adventure in us. It doesn't have to be climbing Everest or even walking the South West Coast Path. But it should be a challenge. Something that pushes you out of your comfort zone; not so uncomfortable that it causes trauma – just enough to stretch you beyond your familiarity, but without breaking your spirit.

And there it is. I leave you with my first long-distance love ... the South West Coast Path. The path that birthed a thousand others. At least, I hope it'll lead me to walk a thousand paths across the rest of my lifetime. And who knows, you and I may even meet out there, on one of those thousand trails some day! Wouldn't that be amazing?

Acknowledgements

I couldn't have brought this book to life without some truly amazing people in my corner. At the top of my gratitude list is my brilliant editor, Nicky Taylor of Nicky Taylor Editorial, who just gets me in a way that still makes me smile. Those laughs we shared over many Track Changes comments! Her intuitive understanding of my voice has been invaluable, and she has this magical way of making me see my writing in a whole new light; never criticising, always supporting. Nicky, I can't believe I found treasure the first time round and I look forward to working with you again.

Thanks to my incredible beta readers and friends – Jude Caton, Ursula Martin, Professor Celia Wells, Frankie Dewar, and Rhiannon Moore. Thank you for giving your precious time and candid feedback. It shaped the manuscript so well before it reached the editor's desk. You're absolute stars.

Jane Simmonds of Jane Simmonds Editorial for her lightning speed proofread. Jane, you made a potentially stressful time an utter breeze for which I'm grateful. I hope I might stumble into your neck of the woods while on a walk one of these days!

To the amazing members of my HeadRightOut Hub Facebook group – your enthusiastic first-view feedback on drawings, styles and features has been invaluable. Thank you for being my sounding board for helping shape the visual and creative elements of this book with such generosity and encouragement.

The writing community – wow, where do I start? Jon Doolan and the Adventure Writers Club, you've been waving my flag since day one, pushing me along in the early days with your Lockdown Write-ins. My wonderful Somerset crew at The Cursive Appreciation Society – Sarah, Ken, Valda, Jonathan and Elizabeth – while I've not known you long, you've been my local anchors through the latter part of this journey. The London Writers' Salon kept me going through those endless lockdowns, and NaNoWriMo gave me the nudge I needed to achieve what felt impossible. The fantastic Orna Ross and everyone at the Alliance of Independent Authors (ALLi), you've been there with encouragement exactly when I needed it. And Joanna Penn – your *Creative Penn Podcast* has been my constant companion for five years, reshaping how I think about the whole creative author-life potential. Our walks and talks have been pure gold, helping me trust my gut about where I'm heading.

Chief Tough, adventurer Sarah Williams of Tough Girl Challenges and the *Tough Girl Podcast*, thank you for your friendship, mentoring, and consistently believing in me, championing me as a speaker and storyteller. We made great walking buddies, as well as a lifetime of memorable experiences just from a few days walking together!

Jo Moseley, paddleboarder, podcaster, speaker, award-winning filmmaker, author and friend – thank you for your gentle presence, unwavering support in lifting me up and helping my profile to be seen. Your motto "we rise by lifting others" truly embodies how you've shown up for me, and I'm deeply grateful for the connection we've built and the way you consistently live those words.

Huge thanks to my daughter Laura; you're genuinely the best for understanding when memoir-writing had to trump nanny duties. To all my friends and cheerleaders – but especially Jacquie Bolash, Kate Hunt and Keith Hunt – thanks for always asking "how's the book going?" in a way that kept me honest. My Happy Mondays ladies. Gosh, we've known one another since our first day at infant school in 1975, but you help me keep it real. Family talk, body talk, head talk, work talk. Nothing is off limits. Thank you for listening. Grateful thanks go to Alison Menzies – we met at a local literary festival and now you're not just a friend but my go-to guru for all things publicity.

Belinda Kirk, author, expedition leader, friend and founder of Explorers Connect and AdventureMind has been a huge inspiration. Her book *Adventure Revolution* is a transformative read, illuminating exactly what I'd experienced first-hand about adventure's profound impact on resilience and mental health. It's funny to think I've attended as many AdventureMind Conferences as I have spent years writing this memoir. The benefits explored in *Adventure Revolution* mirror those I experienced on my South West Coast Path adventure, and they are interwoven throughout these pages. I'm now honoured to be part of an exciting AdventureMind Ambassador team and thrilled to carry this message forward on our upcoming long-distance walk.

A special thank you to Judith Scarfe for bringing me *The Salt Path* back in 2019 during my skiing accident recovery (sorry, I still have it and yes, one day, I'd love to return it!). And to Raynor Winn – your book landed in my hands at exactly the right moment. Your evocative words resonated far deeper than a heartbreaking and heartwarming tale of personal adversity via a coast path, though I admit to shedding tears. Your courage in sharing painful truths helped me realise I wasn't alone in how I experience walking, giving me the confidence to tell my story. Thank you for your inspiration and your humble welcome each time we meet. May the world hold you and nature continue to guide your life and words. I hope we can walk together one day.

And finally, my immense love and appreciation to Mike my "can-do" husband extraordinaire. You make the best long-distance walking partner-in-crime. Thank you for your unwavering belief in me even when I was running on empty. You've picked me up, dusted me off, and kept me going. Our thousands of adventurous miles together have given me the strength and perspective to bring this book to life. Without doubt, it is your love and support that has made the conclusion of this journey possible.

About the Author

Zoe Langley-Wathen's life transformed at forty when she walked the South West Coast Path – a catalyst for her mission to encourage midlife women to "HeadRightOut" of their comfort zones into a more adventurous lifestyle.

Since then, Zoe has walked thousands of miles, including becoming the first woman to walk the Wales Coast Path. She has created many resilience-building challenges through her HeadRightOut initiative.

A Fellow of the Royal Geographical Society and award-winning teacher, Zoe hosts *HeadRightOut,* a podcast featuring conversations with adventurous midlife women. Her story has appeared in national women's magazines and broadcast across UK media.

When not exploring or inspiring others through her talks, Zoe teaches in South Somerset, practices daily yoga, enjoys the delights of grandmotherhood, and finds walking to be her "outdoor medicine". She performs in a local ukulele club while her lifelong passion for the arts extend to drawing, photography, and writing poetry too. Zoe lives her AdventureMind Ambassador philosophy that a true adventure begins where comfort ends.

To connect with Zoe or follow along with her future adventures: www.headrightout.com @HeadRightOut

Inspiration spreads through the stories we share. If this has sparked something in you, please pay it forward – leave a review on Amazon, Goodreads or Bookshop.org, or with your favourite reader community. While adventure is for everyone, Zoe writes from the perspective of a midlife woman because that's the experience she knows. When you share your interest in her work, your words might be just the encouragement someone else needs to take the first step into their own adventure.

SD - #0008 - 120325 - C0 - 203/127/19 - PB - 9781068411113 - Matt Lamination